INDEX FUNDS

Index Funds

The 12-Step Recovery Program for Active Investors

by Mark T. Hebner

IFA Publishing
Irvine, California

ISBN: 978-0-9768023-1-0

This book is dedicated to: Beth, Brie, Kory, Ian, and Tyler.

Acknowledgements

I would like to extend my gratitude to the many people who have assisted in the creation of this book. They include: Mary Brunson, Melissa Johnson, David Bennett, Jackson Lin, Jay Franklin, Robert Bray, Kris Cooper, Michael Auchterlonie, Cindy Mason, John Resurreccion, Michael Baker, Roger Trinwith, Tyler Collins, Erik Halvorsen, and Harry Markowitz. Many original works of art by Lala Ragimov and Aftab Alam bring color and life to the science of investing. A picture is worth a thousand words.

Thank you also to the many IFA team members, clients and friends who have assisted and encouraged me on my mission to change the way the world invests.

Table of Contents

Foreword

"It will fluctuate."[1]
– J.P. Morgan's reply when asked what the stock market will do.

In this volume Mark Hebner meticulously refutes the idea that individual investors can beat the market by stock selection or market timing. Some readers may react with the thought that "perhaps most investors cannot beat the market, but some can. I merely have to emulate those with superior performance." Examples of investors with sustained superior performance include the legendary Warren Buffett and David Swensen, Yale University's Chief Investment Officer, whose performance over decades has been widely admired and imitated by endowment and retirement plan managers, but with rare success.

If you examine the words and practices of these distinguished investors, you will find their above-market performance is not due to a set of rules which can be followed by individual investors. Rather, it is due to resources and opportunities which individual investors and most institutional investors do not have. Mr. Swensen tells how he does it in his book, "*Pioneering Portfolio Management: An Unconventional Approach to Institutional Investment.*" As noted in the title, Swensen's book explains how an institutional investor (as distinguished from an individual investor) might achieve above-market returns. He observes there is little chance for beating the market with well-followed securities such as large cap and small cap stocks. As to opportunities available to the institutional investor from less conventional sources, Swensen writes: *"Populated by unusually gifted, extremely driven individuals, the institutional funds management industry provides a nearly limitless supply of products, a few of which actually serve fiduciary aims. Identifying the handful of gems in the tons of quarry rock provides intellectually stimulating employment for the managers of endowment portfolios."*[2]

Few, if any, individual investors have the time and skill to separate the "gems" from the "quarry rock," even if they were presented with similar opportunities. Any individual investor who believes he or she can achieve above-market performance is almost sure to underperform the market substantially, as Mark Hebner documents.

Hardly any institutional investors are able to outperform their proper benchmarks. Among those who do accomplish this feat, their ranks largely change from year to year, making their discovery a moving target, as Mark Hebner shows in this volume. Swensen affirms the difficulty of identifying skilled fund managers. He states, "*I erred in describing my target audiences. In fact, I have come to believe that the most important distinction does not separate individuals and institutions… few institutions and even fewer individuals exhibit the ability and commit the resources to produce risk-adjusted excess returns.*"[3]

Indeed, the challenge of ferreting out the gems from among

the "tons of quarry rock" is more challenging than it might first appear.

While Warren Buffett has not written a text on the subject, his actions show his success—like Swensen's—is in part due to his being offered opportunities not available to the individual investor. Specifically, he is offered the opportunity to take large positions in established companies at favorable prices. At such times, company information is made available to Mr. Buffett and his staff which is not routinely available to the public. Ultimately, however, it is his and his staff's ability to evaluate such positions—to separate the gems from the quarry rock—that explains their long-run success. As in the case of Swensen's outperformance, few individual investors have the time and skill to evaluate such opportunities, even if they were presented to them.

As to market timing, I know of no one who has consistently outperformed the market by market timing. Since there are always countless "authorities" who say to buy, and countless others who say to sell, there will always be many instances in which someone called correctly the last turn of the market, and even the last two or three turns. As Hebner documents, it is a foolish hope to try to emulate such market timers. It is better to go with J.P. Morgan's advice—that all one knows about the market is that it will fluctuate.

J.P. Morgan's observation has at least three implications. The obvious one is: Don't try to time the market. You will make your broker rich, not yourself. Another implication is you should choose a portfolio you can live with despite market fluctuations. For example, the year 2008 was not an "outlier," nor was it even the worst year on record. Rather it was tied for the second worst year. It was a one-in-forty year event, not a one-in-a-thousand year event. The frightened investor who decided to get out of the market in March of 2009 locked in his or her losses for good. The chief problem with small investors is they buy when the market has gone up and believe it will rise further, and they sell when the market has fallen and believe it will fall more. One of the principal functions of the right financial advisor is to make sure the investor understands the volatility of his or her specific portfolio and is willing to stick with it for the long run.

As Mark Hebner explains, a third implication of the fact that markets fluctuate is the need to rebalance. Suppose an investor is comfortable with a 60-40 mix of stocks versus bonds. If the market rises substantially, the portfolio's equity exposure will greatly exceed sixty percent. The rebalancing process sells off the excess, bringing the portfolio back to a 60-40 mix. If the market falls, then the portfolio will have less invested in stocks than the target 60 percent. The rebalancing process then buys. This process of rebalancing—which sells when the market is up and buys when the market is down—is sometimes referred to as "volatility capture" and leads to what Fernholz and Shay (1979) refer to as "excess growth."[4] The rebalanced portfolio will grow faster than the average growth of its individual constituents. It may even grow faster than any one of its constituents due to the rebalancing process. Thus, if handled knowledgeably, market volatility can be the investor's friend.

"Money in the bank" sounds safe, but will do little to outpace inflation. On the average, over the long run, a well-diversified portfolio that includes stocks and bonds will almost surely continue to outpace both inflation and money in the bank. However, as this book documents so well, a foolish attempt to beat the market and get rich quickly will make one's broker rich and oneself much less so.

– HARRY MARKOWITZ, PH.D.
1990 Nobel Prize Recipient

Harry Markowitz, Ph.D. is best known for his pioneering work in Modern Portfolio Theory, for which he was awarded the 1990 Nobel Prize in Economics. In 1952, he developed the simple, yet profound notion that investors must consider the risk associated with their investments, not solely the return. This groundbreaking discovery sparked a financial revolution pertaining to the relationship between risk and return. He is widely known as the father of Modern Portfolio Theory. Dr. Markowitz is also the recipient of the 1989 John von Neumann Prize in Operations Research Theory for his work in the areas of sparse matrix techniques and the SIMSCRIPT programming language, in addition to portfolio theory. He currently serves as an Adjunct Professor of Finance at the Rady School of Management at the University of California, San Diego and an Advisor to Index Funds Advisors, Inc.

About the Author

Mark T. Hebner is the Founder and President of Index Funds Advisors, Inc., author of ifa.com and the book, *Index Funds: The 12-Step Program for Active Investors*. That original book received praise from the financial industry and academic legends, including John Bogle, David Booth, Harry Markowitz, Burton Malkiel, and Paul Samuelson. This is a condensed and updated version of that book.

Mark is considered a leading author, speaker and internet provider of investing education. He is especially knowledgeable about the superiority of index mutual funds, as well as the research indexes designed by financial economists. He earned an MBA at the University of California, Irvine.

Index Funds Advisors, Inc.
19200 Von Karman Avenue, Suite 150
Irvine, California 92612
www.ifa.com
888-643-3133
mark@ifa.com

INTRODUCTION

Americans work hard. On average we log 8.5 hours each working day, with many of us amassing far more hours to secure success. We are dedicated, and we are driven to working and saving for our nest eggs—that little slice of financial security that is our reward for a job well done.

Unfortunately, rarely in the course of this frenetic pace do we stop to learn how to properly invest our earnings so they can best work for us.

I was one of those people. I was fortunate enough to start a successful company right after I graduated from college. I was thirty-two years old when I sold that company, and I walked away with a nice sum of money. Without giving it a second thought, I deposited that money with a big-name brokerage firm. They seemed competent to properly grow my wealth. They had offices in high-rise towers. They had well-dressed analysts and impressive looking reports. Indeed, I was confident they would effectively put my money to work for me.

Twelve years later, I woke up to the ugly truth that my confidence in that brokerage firm was unfounded, and my earnings opportunities up to that point had been largely wasted.

Until that time, I believed the financial success of Wall Street brokerage firms was the result of jobs well done in creating wealth for their clients. Too late, I learned that big brokerages did not get rich by enhancing their clients' wealth, but rather (and ironically) by depleting it, transferring it slowly in the form of commissions and margin interest that were in no way justified by the lackluster returns accompanying them. This steady transfer buys plenty of full-page ads in the *Wall Street Journal* and ample commercial time on CNBC to lure in even more clients, thus perpetuating the slow and sure transfer of wealth that comes with each buy and sell.

Prior to my revelation, I lived with a nagging suspicion that my investments could do better. I knew there was a better way to invest, but I never really had the motivation to find it. I was busy with my family and my work, and I could never put a finger on what I should have had or could have had relative to what I did have.

My revelation about the investment world came to me through a tragedy. A friend of mine was killed in a car crash. I told his widow I would help her in any way I could. Shortly thereafter, she said what she really needed was help with her investments. I knew she was relying on me to provide some good, solid help, and I also knew I was ill-equipped to give it.

"What do I know about investing?" I asked her. "My portfolio hasn't done well." I knew I had to do some research. I knew I needed to find a better way to invest, and I needed to share it with her. I went to the library and the bookstore. I bought countless books on investing, and I read them all. I dug into Burton Malkiel's *Random Walk Down Wall Street* and John Bogle's *Common Sense on Mutual Funds*, among many others. What I discovered in the pages of those books was nothing short of stunning: managers don't beat markets.

At first I asked, "How could this be? We have all these

managers in the world who are in business to beat the market, and yet, they're not beating the market. The market is beating them."

It struck me like a bolt of lightning: I didn't just have the wrong advisors, I had the wrong strategy altogether. With all of the time, effort and money spent trying to find the next hot stock or mutual fund manager, I would have been far better off had I simply bought, held and rebalanced a portfolio of index funds. How much better off? When I compared my own actively managed portfolio's performance against the value of a risk-appropriate passively managed portfolio, I was struck with the harsh reality of the price I paid for my lack of investing knowledge. I call this my $30 million lesson.

I paid a very steep price for relying on an industry that profits handsomely when investors are kept in the dark. I wondered just how many others had paid the price for too little knowledge and too much trust. I questioned how many more would suffer before the investment industry would awaken to its very own Howard Beale who would finally muster the courage to step before the CNBC cameras to declare, "I'm mad as hell, and I'm not going to take it anymore."

Awestruck by the glut of misinformation that served as the basis for poor investment decisions, I could not remain silent. I knew I had found my mission in my lesson, and I was determined to change the way the world invests.

Just as in the movie "Network," in which Beale used the airwaves to deliver his message, I leveraged the Internet to deliver mine. In 1999, I launched ifa.com, a free and comprehensive site that contains hundreds of charts, graphs, articles, podcasts, and videocasts to help investors learn about investments that can better enhance their own wealth, rather than the wealth of their brokers. At the same time, I launched Index Funds Advisors, Inc. (IFA), a fee-only financial advisory firm that works with individuals and institutions to invest in risk-appropriate portfolios properly benchmarked for each investor's specific situation and risk capacity. Today, nearly 40 employees and $1.5 billion strong, IFA's mission has taken hold.

This book incorporates the quality research and data that IFA uses to advance the financial futures of its roughly 1,800 clients. It is precisely the information that I incorporate daily to change the way the world invests by replacing speculation with science. Step by step, this book will lead you away from the pitfalls of active investing that threaten your long-term financial success and lead you instead toward a strategy that will efficiently put your money to work for a better financial future.

You work hard enough. You don't need to log any more hours or commissions to fund your broker's retirement instead of your own. Read the following pages well, as they hold the key to your ability to optimally reap the fruits of your labor. Yes, you can finally invest and relax.

– Mark T. Hebner

Step 1: Active Investors

"The investor's chief problem, and even his worst enemy, is likely to be himself."

– Benjamin Graham, *The Intelligent Investor; A Book of Practical Counsel*, 1949

"The neural activity of someone whose investments are making money is indistinguishable from that of someone who is high on cocaine or morphine."

– Jason Zweig, *Your Money & Your Brain*, 2007

"There is something in people; you might even call it a little bit of a gambling instinct… I tell people investing should be dull. It shouldn't be exciting. Investing should be more like watching paint dry or watching grass grow. If you want excitement, take $800 and go to Las Vegas."

– Paul Samuelson, Ph.D., Nobel Laureate, "Ultimate Guide to Indexing," 1999

"The road to financial perdition begins with a call to your broker who claims to be able to beat the markets."

– Daniel Solin, *The Smartest Investment Book You'll Ever Read*, 2006

The lure of fast money makes you think active,
but the record proves you're better off passive.
– The Speculation Blues[5]

WHAT WOULD YOU DO IF YOU NEVER listened to another financial media pundit, watched another financial news show or spent another hour in front of your computer feverishly tracking the stock market? How would that make you feel? Anxious and nervous that you were missing out on something? Or relieved that you could spend your time doing what you really enjoy? More investors are discovering the solution to anxiety-free investing, learning the strategies that enable them to shift their focus away from the frenzy of Wall Street and put their attention on what they value most.

That's what this book is about—to show you, the investor, that you no longer have to lose any sleep worrying about your investments. It's actually possible to invest and truly relax. What is this groundbreaking way to invest? The truth is that it's not groundbreaking at all. Like most "secrets" or solutions, the answer has been around for a long time. It's not riveting or thrill-inducing and provides no emotional rush. It's not a quick fix. On the contrary, it's sound and prudent and offers a wise alternative to what is termed "active investing" in the financial investment world. What is it? It's *passive investing with index funds.*

This *12-Step Recovery Program for Active Investors* will walk you through the land mines and pitfalls of active investing and show you a better way to invest. When you complete this

12-Step Program, you will understand the differences between active and passive investing and be fully aware of the emotional triggers that impact investment decisions. You will also obtain an enlightening education on science-based investing that may forever change the way you perceive how the stock market works. You will learn the hazards of speculation and the rewards of discipline. The best part is that you can learn to change your own investment behavior, which can lead to a more profitable and enjoyable life.

As you embark upon the 12 Steps, an important concept to understand is that most people tend to make investment decisions based on emotions. The challenge for all investors is to ignore emotional triggers that impede rational decisions. Emotions often override reason when it comes to investment decisions, leading to irrational and destructive behavior. The financial news media and Wall Street feed the fear, anxiety and other stressful emotions experienced by investors, resulting in less than favorable investment outcomes. This book will teach you how to hang on in the midst of turmoil and show you the destructive nature of active investing.

As you climb the 12 Steps illustrated in the following painting, you will abandon the gambling and speculative behaviors of the active investors located in the bottom right corner, ascend the stairs to claim your risk-appropriate portfolio (symbolized by the woman handing out colorful balls), and continue up to the balcony where individuals who have successfully completed their 12-Step Journey enjoy the tranquility of an investing state of mind I call, "Tradeless Nirvana."

SILE
STYLE DRIFTE
MANAGER PICKERS
TIME PICKERS
STOCK PICKERS
NOBEL LAUREATES
ACTIVE INVESTORS

INVEST AND RELAX
RISK EXPOSURE
SK CAPACITY
HISTORY
RISKESE
RTNERS

Active Versus Passive Investing

Active investing is a strategy investors use when trying to beat a market or appropriate benchmark. Active investors rely on speculation about short-term future market movements and ignore vast amounts of historical data. They commonly engage in picking stocks, times, managers, or investment styles. As later steps demonstrate, active investors who claim to outperform a market are in essence claiming to divine the future. When accurately measured, this is simply not possible. Surprisingly, the analytical techniques that active investors use are best described as qualitative or speculative, largely including predictions of future movements of the stock market based on too little information. Bottom line, these methods prove self-defeating for active investors and actually lead them to underperform the very markets they seek to beat.

The first step in any 12-Step Program focuses on recognizing and admitting a problem exists. In this case, this means identifying the behaviors that define an active investor.

These include:

- Owning actively managed mutual funds
- Picking individual stocks
- Picking times to be in and out of the market
- Picking a fund manager based on recent performance
- Picking the next hot investment style
- Disregarding high taxes, fees and commissions
- Investing without considering risk
- Investing without a clear understanding of the value of long-term historical data

There are sharp contrasts between the behaviors of passive investors and active investors. Passive investors don't try to pick stocks, times, managers, or styles. Instead, they buy and hold globally diversified portfolios of passively managed funds. The term "passive" translates into less trading of the fund's portfolio, more favorable tax consequences, and lower fees and expenses than actively managed funds.

A passively managed fund or index fund can be defined as a mutual or exchange traded fund with specific rules of ownership that are adhered to regardless of market conditions. An index fund's rules of construction clearly identify the type of companies suitable for its investment. Equity index funds would include groups of stocks with similar characteristics such as size, value and geographic location of company. This group of stocks may include companies from the United States, foreign countries or emerging markets. Additional indexes within these markets may include segments such as small value, large value, small growth, large growth, real estate, and fixed-income. Companies are purchased and held within the index fund when they meet the specific index parameters and are sold when they move outside of those parameters.

Figure 1-1 illustrates the differences between active and passive investing. Introduced in the early 1970's, index funds now account for about 25% of all individual investment assets and about 40% of all institutional investments, by my estimates. Index funds investing has caught on, and for good reason. As the chart shows, index investors fair far better in returns, incur lower taxes and turnover, and enjoy a relaxed state of mind.

Figure 1-1

Active Versus Passive Investing

Subject	Active Investing	Passive Investing
Return Objective	Beat a market	Obtain the return of a market, index or asset class
Style Definition	40% drift from classification	Pure and consistent classification
Average Equity Fund Investor Return Over 20 Years	3.83% per year according to Dalbar for 20-year period ending 2010	S&P 500 = 9.14% Annlzd Return Global Equity Index Portfolio 100 = 11.70% Annlzd Return for 20-year period ending 2010
Approach	Stock Picking, Time Picking, Manager Picking, or Style Drifting	Buy, hold and rebalance a globally diversified portfolio of index funds
Taxes	High Taxes (about 20-40% of return over 10 years)	Low Taxes (about 10% of the return over 10 years)
Portfolio Turnover	Turnover of about 80% in 2010	Turnover of about 10% in 2010
Net Performance	Well below the index by the amount of fees, expenses, taxes, and mistakes	The index return minus low fees, low taxes, and tracking error
Individual Investors	Currently about 75% of equity funds	Currently about 25% and growing
Institutional Investors	Currently about 60% of domestic stock assets	Currently about 40% and growing
Proponents	Virtually all Brokerage Firms, Mutual Fund Companies, Market Timing Services, Investment Press and Brokerage Training Programs	The Univ. of Chicago, Nobel Prize Recipients, Vanguard Group, Dimensional Fund Advisors, Barclays Global Investors, Warren Buffett, and Charles Schwab & Company
Analytical Techniques	Art - Qualitative, Disregard for Risk, Forecasting, Predicting the Future, Feelings, Intuition, Luck, Betting, Gambling, and Speculation	Science - Quantitative, Risk Management, Long-Term Statistical Analysis, Accurate Performance Measurements, Evidence Based
State of Mind	Stressed	Relaxed

Sources: Dalbar, Greenwich Research Assoc., John Bogle, ifabt.com, Author's Estimate

Problems

Emotions-Based Investing

The emotions of investors tend to match the wild gyrations of the market itself. Investors might feel euphoric when the market hits a new high and panic-stricken when the market has dropped like a rock. Who can blame these investors? The stock market can be a scary place when gut instinct overrides knowledge of the specific market dynamics at play, including fair prices, randomness, efficiency, and the benefits of diversification.

Behavioral Finance is a field that studies the connection between investors' emotions and their financial decisions. In *The Little Book of Behavioral Investing: How Not to be Your Own Worst Enemy*,[6] author James Montier talks about the importance of planning ahead to protect us from the "behavioral biases that drag down investment returns." He highlights the need for investors to pre-commit to an investment strategy in order to avoid the pitfalls of emotional decisions.

In *Your Money & Your Brain*,[7] financial writer Jason Zweig details evidence of the release of addiction related dopamine in our brains when we anticipate big wins. "The dopamine rush we get from long shots is why we play lotto, invest in IPOs, keep too much money in too few stocks, and invest with active portfolio managers instead of index funds," Zweig states. "Our brains are wired to force us into forecasting; it is a biological imperative. In fact, humans are born with what I've come to call 'the prediction addiction.'" Several researchers working in neuroeconomics, including Harvard's Hans Breiter have identified a striking similarity between the brain's reaction to cocaine, morphine and the prediction of financial rewards.

Even wealthy individuals struggle with emotions management and investing discipline. A 2011 Barclay's study[8] found that 41% of high net worth investors wished they had more self-control over their investing decisions. The study concluded that emotional trading can cost an investor about 20% in returns over a 10-year period. Investors who prevent themselves from over-trading through specific strategies are on average 12% wealthier than those who don't use self-control mechanisms. These self-control strategies include minimizing time spent checking on a portfolio or talking to someone prior to making a buy or sell decision.

Several behavioral biases that tend to affect investor decisions include the following:

- Overconfidence: People mistakenly believe they can outperform the market.
- Hindsight bias: Investors think past events were predictable and obvious and believe they should have known better. The truth is that news moves the markets, and past events could not have been predicted in advance.
- Familiarity bias: Investors invest only in stocks they know, which provides a false sense of security. An example may be a "legacy" stock that's been passed down in a family through many generations. Regional or geographical bias also comes into play when investors choose stocks of companies headquartered in their state or region of

residence, which can lead to undiversified investments.

- Regret avoidance: Investors vow to never repeat the same decision if it resulted in a previous loss or missed gain, not understanding that the future cannot be predicted.
- Self attribution bias: Investors tend to take full credit for investment gains and blame outside factors for losses, wrongly attributing success to personal skill or ability.
- Extrapolation: Investors base decisions on recent events, assuming past market trends will repeat themselves.

These behavioral biases cause investors to believe they have control in areas where they actually have none. A disciplined investing approach involves the understanding of the factors we can and cannot control, planning ahead and not giving into emotions when making investment decisions.

Figure 1-2 depicts the roller coaster of emotions active investors experience. In the emotional cycle, they wait until they feel confident their selected investments are on a perceived upward trend; then they place their orders. But once prices fall, doubt sets in. When that turns to fear, they often sell the investment, resulting in a loss.

In contrast, Figure 1-3 shows the constant relaxed emotions that indexers enjoy by accepting market randomness and relying on investing science instead of making decisions based on emotions. Passive investors invest regardless of market conditions, because they understand short-term volatility is unpredictable. They know succumbing to gut instincts and emotions undermines long-term wealth accumulation. They also know that news about capitalism is positive on average—but involves some stomach-churning volatility, as many experienced in the downturn of 2008 through March 2009, and again in 2011.

Figure 1-2

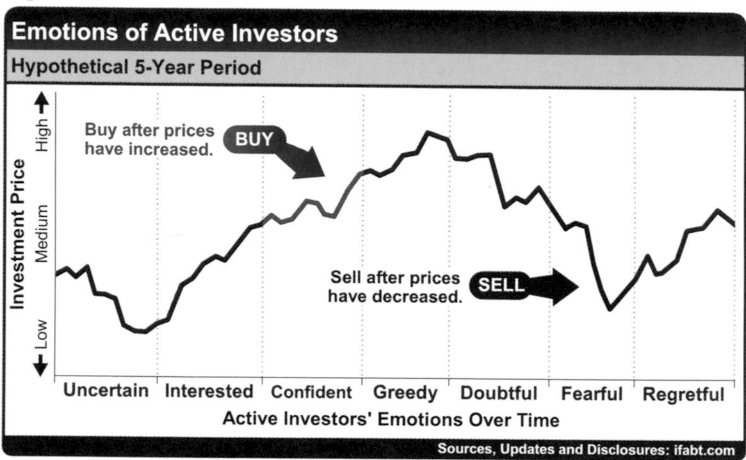

Figure 1-3

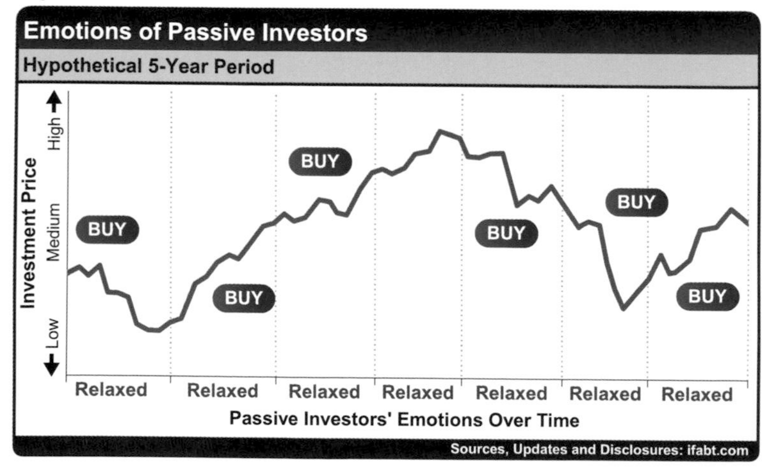

Passive investors also engage in periodic rebalancing and are rewarded in the long term for their discipline. Figure 1-4 depicts the disciplined emotions and approach of "Rebalancers" who sell a portion of their indexes that have grown beyond their target allocation and buy more of other indexes to restore their target allocation. This is actually the opposite behavior of active investors, because rebalancers will sell a portion of their portfolio after it has gone up and buy more of those investments that have declined in order to maintain a specific asset allocation. This strategy seems counterintuitive and can be emotionally difficult to implement. Annual rebalancing requires discipline and ensures that a portfolio will remain diversified in volatile markets. This discipline also enables passive investors to better fulfill the age-old investing axiom: "buy low, sell high."

Figure 1-4

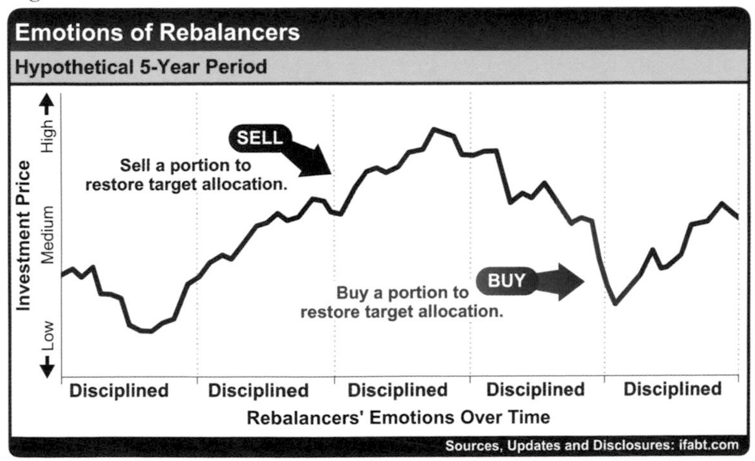

The impact of emotions on investor performance is a subject of much analysis. An annual study called the Quantitative Analysis of Investor Behavior (QAIB),[9] which has been conducted by Dalbar since 1994, measures the impact of investor decisions to buy, sell and switch into and out of mutual funds. Each year, the study has shown the average mutual fund investor earns significantly less than the mutual funds over the same time period. In fact, the report issued in March 2011 carried this headline: "Investor Behaviors Continue to Fall Prey to Market Forces." The study further concluded, "As this report has shown for the 17th time in as many years, mutual fund investors consistently underperform the relevant index. The report also shows that most of this loss in performance is due to psychological factors that translate into poor timing of their buys and sells (investor behavior)."

The 2011 Dalbar study further addresses the problems with investor behavior by stating, "While this contradiction between the psychological drivers of investor behavior and prudent investing continues to create enormous lost opportunities, some investors and some advisors have been able to avoid the returns-robbing behavior. This has been achieved by a better understanding and management of the psychological factors coupled with the understanding of the investments being used."[10]

Figure 1-5 illustrates the results of the Dalbar study, a comparison of the returns of an average equity fund investor to the returns of the market from 1991 to 2010. Permitting their decisions to be driven by short-term volatility, the average equity fund investor earned returns of only 3.83%, while the

Figure 1-5

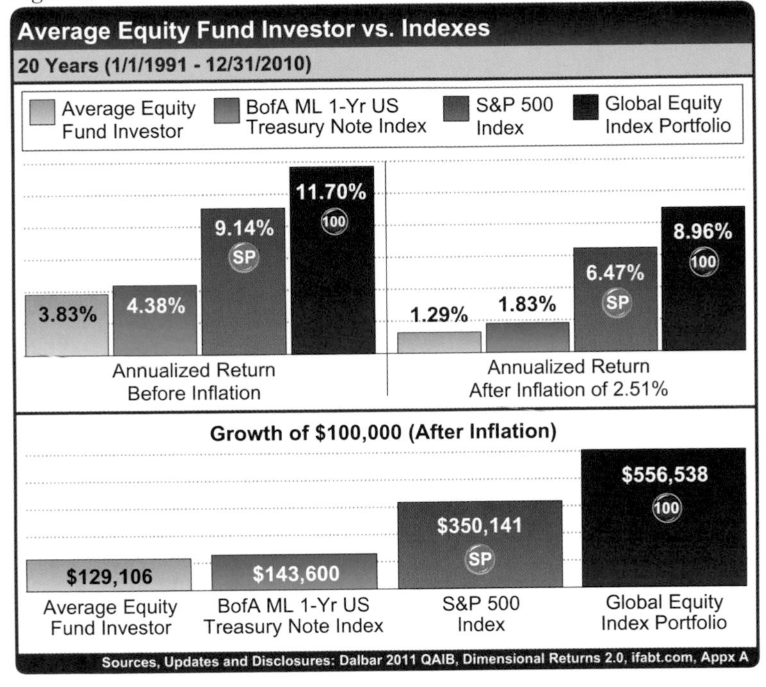

S&P 500 returned 9.14%. An investment of $100,000 made in 1991 grew to an inflation adjusted amount of $129,106 over the 20-year period for an average equity fund investor, while the same amount invested in the S&P 500 grew to an inflation adjusted amount of $350,141. Even better, an investor who owned an all-equity, small value tilted, globally diversified index portfolio would have grown a $100,000 investment to an inflation adjusted amount of $556,538. Clearly, investor behavior can have a far more negative impact on investments than investors realize.

Active Investors Lose

In the June 2002 issue of *Money* Magazine,[11] Jason Zweig described a study conducted by Indiana University Professor of Finance Charles Trzcinka, illustrated in Figure 1-6. The study used a similar technique to Dalbar by showing the difference between the annualized returns of the average mutual fund (time-weighted returns) and those of the average mutual fund investor (dollar-weighted returns). As the chart indicates, the average active fund advertised a 5.7% time-weighted annualized return from 1998 to 2001. The average fund investor, however, only earned a 1.0% annualized return. This discrepancy in returns arises because funds often obtain large returns when there are fewer dollars and shareholders invested in the fund, and fund declines often occur after a large inflow of investors chase those large returns. Once word of a fund's success spreads,

Figure 1-6

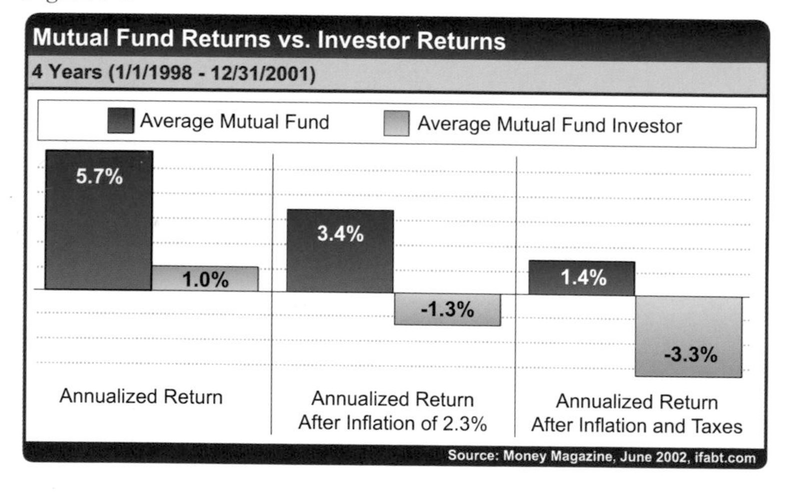

investors swarm to the fund. When it inevitably declines, the fund is much larger than when it began, and it loses far more wealth for investors than it had previously gained.

Active investors also pay higher expenses, taxes and fees. When taxes and inflation are considered, I estimate that the average mutual fund investor lost a 3.3% annualized return over the 4-year period. This outcome is despite the fact that the average mutual fund reported annualized returns of 1.4%, a 4.7% gap between the return reported by the mutual fund and the return to the investor after inflation and taxes. The disparity between the fund returns and those that are actually earned by average active investors confirms the benefits of passive investing and emotions management.

Solutions

Index Funds Investing

While active investors seek to outperform the markets, buyers and rebalancers of index funds seek to capture the returns of the entire market in a low-cost and tax-efficient manner. Index funds investors select passive funds that track defined asset class indexes. Regardless of market conditions, they stay the course and do not make investment decisions based on emotions. Since the global markets have delivered the returns of capitalism at a generous 9.5% annualized return over the last 83 years, a wise investment strategy is to hold and rebalance a portfolio that is globally diversified across many asset classes or indexes.

Matching Risk Capacity With Risk Exposure

Stock market returns are compensation for bearing risk. Higher expected returns require higher risk. Therefore, investors should take on as much risk as they have the capacity to hold—their risk capacity. One of the most effective ways to determine risk capacity is to examine five distinct dimensions: an investor's time horizon and liquidity needs, investment knowledge, attitude toward risk, net income, and net worth. This is explained more fully in Steps 10 and 11.

Value Of A Passive Advisor

Passive advisors play an integral role in emotions management. Knowledgeable, passive advisors help maximize investor success because they provide the critical discipline needed to combat emotional, reflex reactions like pulling out of the market the way so many did in late 2008 and early 2009 or in 2011. Passive advisors not only help to manage an investor's emotions, they serve as fiduciary stewards of their clients' wealth.

Figure 1-7 is a compilation of 12 studies which depict varying levels of investor success with or without passive advisors. It shows that the average fund investor without a passive advisor (blue bars) captured only an average of 36.75% of fund returns. Indexers without passive advisors (purple bars) were more successful at capturing fund returns than average fund investors, due to a less active approach. However, they also failed to capture the full returns of the index funds they owned. The average passive investor captured only an average

Figure 1-7

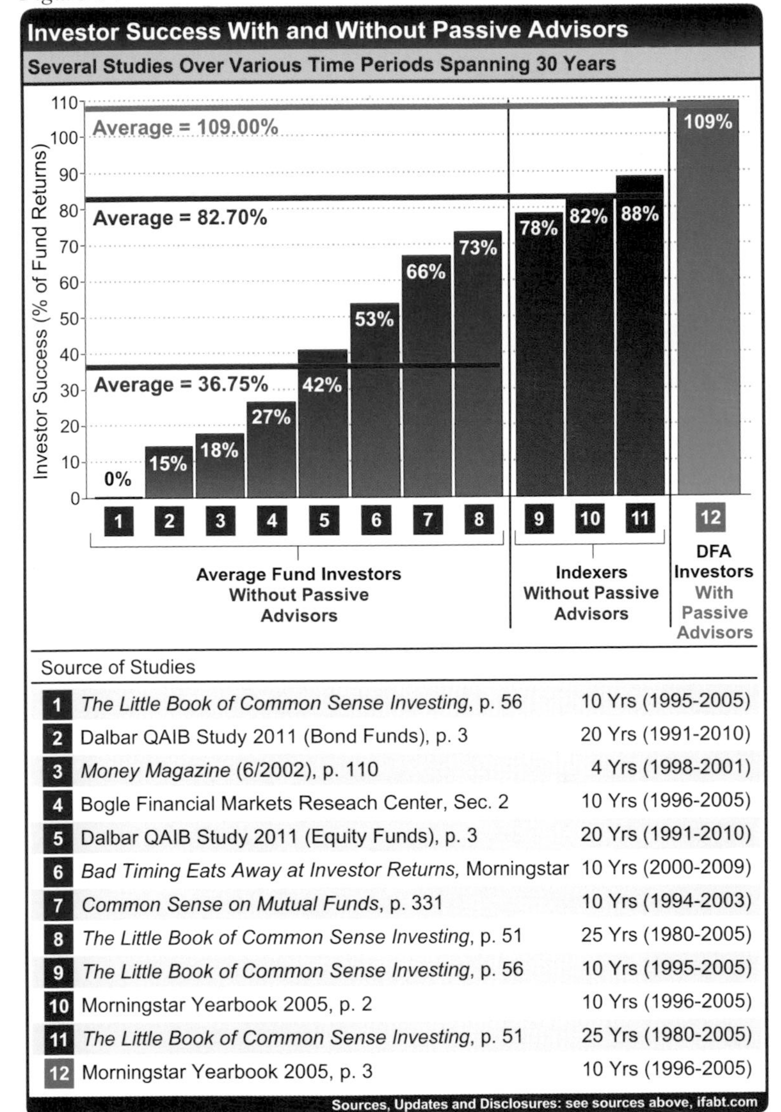
Investor Success With and Without Passive Advisors
Several Studies Over Various Time Periods Spanning 30 Years
Investor Success (% of Fund Returns)
110
100
90
80
70
60
50
40
30
20
10
0
Average = 109.00%
Average = 82.70%
Average = 36.75%
0%
15%
18%
27%
42%
53%
66%
73%
78%
82%
88%
109%
1
2
3
4
5
6
7
8
9
10
11
12
Average Fund Investors Without Passive Advisors
Indexers Without Passive Advisors
DFA Investors With Passive Advisors
Source of Studies
1 The Little Book of Common Sense Investing, p. 56 10 Yrs (1995-2005)
2 Dalbar QAIB Study 2011 (Bond Funds), p. 3 20 Yrs (1991-2010)
3 Money Magazine (6/2002), p. 110 4 Yrs (1998-2001)
4 Bogle Financial Markets Reseach Center, Sec. 2 10 Yrs (1996-2005)
5 Dalbar QAIB Study 2011 (Equity Funds), p. 3 20 Yrs (1991-2010)
6 Bad Timing Eats Away at Investor Returns, Morningstar 10 Yrs (2000-2009)
7 Common Sense on Mutual Funds, p. 331 10 Yrs (1994-2003)
8 The Little Book of Common Sense Investing, p. 51 25 Yrs (1980-2005)
9 The Little Book of Common Sense Investing, p. 56 10 Yrs (1995-2005)
10 Morningstar Yearbook 2005, p. 2 10 Yrs (1996-2005)
11 The Little Book of Common Sense Investing, p. 51 25 Yrs (1980-2005)
12 Morningstar Yearbook 2005, p. 3 10 Yrs (1996-2005)
Sources, Updates and Disclosures: see sources above, ifabt.com

of 82.7% of a fund's return, according to the studies. This is likely explained by a failure to rebalance asset allocations during market turbulence, a delay of investing when cash is available, or even the inability to stay invested during rocky markets.

In sharp contrast, the Morningstar Indexes Yearbook states individuals who invested in Dimensional Fund Advisors (DFA) funds and used passive advisors (green bar) captured all of the fund returns and then some—109% of the fund returns.

A 2005 Morningstar report says, "Consider the success Dimensional Fund Advisors (DFA) has had in selling its funds through advisors who undergo training on the merits of passive investing and in portfolio construction theory. Consider that over the past decade the dollar-weighted return of all index funds was just 82% of the time-weighted return investors could have gotten with those funds. Yet, the figures for DFA are much better. In fact, the dollar-weighted returns of DFA funds over the past 10 years are actually higher than their time-weighted returns, suggesting advisors who use DFA encourage very smart behavior among their clients, even buying more out-of-favor segments of the market and riding them up, rather than buying at the peak and riding the trend down, which is usually the case with fund investors."[12] The findings of this Morningstar report are shown in Figure 1-8.

Knowledgeable passive advisors encourage their clients to stay invested and rebalance through market turbulence. Such behavior enables these investors to maximize their ability to capture returns and provides justification for the right passive advisor. Many investors are lured into do-it-yourself indexing

Figure 1-8

DFA Passive Funds with an Advisor vs. All No-Load Index Funds

10 Years (1/1/1996 - 12/31/2005)

	10-yr Dollar Weighted Return	10-yr Time Weighted Return	+/- Difference	Success
DFA Funds	10.81%	9.90%	+0.91	109%
All No-Load Index Funds	7.07%	8.65%	-1.58	82%
The DFA Advantage	**3.74%**	**1.25%**	**2.49**	**27%**

Source: Morningstar Indexes Yearbook, 2005

through exchange traded funds (ETFs). That is a step in the right direction, but without a passive advisor, these investors have not experienced the full value of advised indexing. Quality passive advisors offer valuable services, such as rebalancing, tax loss harvesting, a glide path strategy, and other wealth management tools that are rarely properly applied by do-it-yourself investors. Step 12 provides more information on these topics.

The Ulysses Pact

Homer's legendary story about Ulysses (Greek name Odysseus) tying himself to the mast to avoid destruction can be aptly applied to investing. Ulysses was able to hear the beautiful siren songs without being led to his destruction, because he made an agreement with his seafaring crew as they approached the sirens. He ordered them to plug their ears with wax and keep him tied to the mast despite his protests and cries. Under no circumstance were they to untie him. Ulysses desperately tried to break free upon hearing the sirens, but the men kept their promise, and the entire crew sailed safely through danger. They all worked together to strategically prevent their own demise.

$
GE
AAPL
AMZN
GOOG
PG
GM

DOW
YUM
CSCO

The lure and noise of financial media often drive the behaviors and decisions of investors. A Ulysses Pact is like an investment policy statement, a proactive and strategic agreement that is made between a client and advisor in advance of any market turmoil or uncertainty. An advisor can guide clients through the murky or turbulent waters and ensure they don't jump ship in response to the noise by signing a Ulysses Pact. This pact allows an investor to agree up front that under no circumstance will he act on emotions that can lead to irrational and wealth destroying decisions. It can serve as a promise to one's self to follow a passive advisor's counsel to hold on and not buy or sell as a reflexive reaction to the short-term movements of the market. This encourages a client to hold on and understand that the free market will set prices for a positive expected return, so that the storm will pass.

Legendary Investors Agree On Index Funds

Renowned investor Warren Buffett is an advocate of index investing and has recommended it to his shareholders in three annual reports. "Over [the past] 35 years, American business has delivered terrific results. It should therefore have been easy for investors to earn juicy returns: All they had to do was piggyback corporate America in a diversified, low-expense way. An index fund they never touched would have done the job. Instead, many investors have had experiences ranging from mediocre to disastrous," Buffett said in his 2004 letter to shareholders. Buffett not only advocates index funds, he's betting on them.

The June 2008 issue of *Fortune*[13] Magazine reported that

Buffett wagered a million dollars that an S&P 500 index fund's ensuing 10-year returns would beat those of five actively managed funds or hedge funds chosen by a prominent New York-based asset management firm.

Many highly respected financial experts affirm Buffett's high regard for index funds. For its "Core and Explore" program, Charles Schwab and Company recommended investors put a large portion of their large-cap assets in index funds. In his book, *Charles Schwab's Guide to Financial Independence*, Schwab revealed, "Most of the mutual fund investments I have are index funds, approximately 75%."[14]

Benjamin Graham

Benjamin Graham, influential economist and mentor to Warren Buffett, spent most of his professional life analyzing companies for stock market bargains. However, shortly before his death, Graham rejected his long-held belief that investors could expect to beat the market through individual stock analysis. Graham was forward thinking in his early description of what is now known as a value index fund when he stated, "The thing that I have been emphasizing in my own work for the last few years has been the group approach. To try to buy groups of stocks [index funds] that meet some simple criterion for being undervalued—regardless of the industry and with very little attention to the individual company."[15]

Noteworthy institutional investors also advocate index funds investing. David Swensen, Chief Financial Officer of the highly successful Yale Endowment Fund and author

of *Unconventional Success: A Fundamental Approach to Personal Investment*[16] and *Pioneering Portfolio Management: An Unconventional Approach to Institutional Investment,*[17] has been particularly outspoken about the downfalls of active investing and the merits of index investing for individual and institutional investors alike. In an August 2011 opinion piece which appeared in the *New York Times,* Swensen blasted active investing and its facilitators, including mutual fund companies, retail brokers and advisors, citing that market volatility causes ill-advised investors to behave "in a perverse fashion, selling low after having bought high." He asks, "What should be done? First, individual investors should take control of their financial destinies, educate themselves, avoid sales pitches, and invest in a well-diversified portfolio of low-cost index funds."[18]

So what is the lesson here? In a nutshell, when you fully embrace a new way of investing, you can substantially reduce the stress and anxiety commonly experienced by active investors. You will be calmer, relaxed and more centered in the midst of the noise and frenzy of media pundits and Wall Street. Your unwavering commitment to your investment plan will allow you to let go of unnecessary worry and enable you to focus on what truly matters to you most. You will not only be rewarded emotionally, you will also improve your probability of investment success. Why would you want to do anything else?

Step 2: Nobel Laureates

"We next consider the rule that the investor does [or should] consider expected return a desirable thing and variance of return an undesirable thing."

– Harry Markowitz, Ph.D.,
Nobel Laureate in Economics, 1990,
"Portfolio Selection," 1952

"Properly measured, the average actively managed dollar must underperform the average passively managed dollar, net of costs. Empirical analyses that appear to refute this principle are guilty of improper measurement."

– William F. Sharpe, Ph.D.,
Nobel Laureate in Economics, 1990,
"The Arithmetic of Active Management," 1991

"... *Any pension fund manager who doesn't have the vast majority—and I mean 70% or 80% of his or her portfolio—in passive investments is guilty of malfeasance, nonfeasance or some other kind of bad feasance!"*

– Merton Miller, Ph.D.,
Nobel Laureate in Economics, 1990,
"Investment Gurus," Peter Tanous, February 1997

"Question: So investors shouldn't delude themselves about beating the market? Answer: They're just not going to do it. It's just not going to happen."

– Daniel Kahneman, Ph.D., Nobel Laureate in Economics, 2002, quoted in the *Orange County Register*, "Investors Can't Beat the Market," 2002

Professors came to a shocking conclusion,
the active advantage was just an illusion.
– The Speculation Blues

IN 1709, ENGLISH POET ALEXANDER POPE WARNED "a little knowledge is a dangerous thing." This observation describes the plight of the active investor. Armed with advice from media pundits, many active investors discover too late how much they really do not know. They think active investing is the only way to make serious money. However, that conclusion is debunked by the wealth of knowledge produced by leading academics.

In traditional 12-Step Programs, the second step is to acknowledge the presence of a higher power. Academic luminaries and Nobel Laureates serve as the higher power for investors. They have provided us with Nobel Prize-winning research and hundreds of peer-reviewed published papers that collectively discredit the myth that an active investor can consistently beat the market. Instead, their research supports the argument that a globally diversified, low-cost strategy maximizes returns at given levels of risk.

In the painting titled, *Whom Should You Trust?,* the dilemma of the investing public is illustrated. On one side is the slick salesman of Wall Street products. Tugging on the other side is an academic who provides valuable research that does not require the facade of a polished, packaged advertising campaign. The investors are caught in the middle, torn between the forces providing information. Hopefully, they will listen to the academic.

WALL ST.
Academic

Problems

Investors Rely On Lady Luck

The most significant problem for active investors is their reliance on factors other than empirical research in selecting investments. They speculate heavily and depend on Lady Luck, rather than on the science of investing. In addition, they often chase the recent success of a manager, stock, time, or investment style. The great majority of investors are unaware of the tremendous amount of academic brain power that has been applied to investing. This lack of awareness makes investors more susceptible to the lure of active management, so they engage in risks they do not understand and cannot quantify.

Solutions

Center For Research In Security Prices

Milestones of achievement in modern finance have accelerated over the last several decades, as advancements in technology have enabled sophisticated calculations and analysis of hundreds of thousands of data points. At the heart of these analyses and computations is the renowned Center for Research in Security Prices (CRSP).

In 1960, University of Chicago Professor James Lorie was asked by Merrill Lynch to determine how well most people performed in the stock market relative to other investments. His research led to the creation of CRSP, a database of total returns, dividends and price changes for all common stocks listed on the NYSE from 1926 to the present. The CRSP database has made the University of Chicago's Booth School of Business the premier institution for financial and stock market research, boasting 26 out of 69 Nobel Laureates in Economics who have either attended or taught at the university as of 2011.

The CRSP database plays such a pivotal role in portfolio construction that Rex Sinquefield, co-founder of Dimensional Fund Advisors, said this about its creation: "If I had to rank events, I would say this one is probably slightly more significant than the creation of the universe."[19] Having celebrated its 50th anniversary in 2010, CRSP is now the leading provider of historical stock market data to nearly 500 institutions around the world.

The Nobel Prize In Economics

Since 1969, the Nobel Prize in Economic Sciences has been awarded to honor contributions in the fields of economic policy, development economics, international trade, and the use of financial resources. The groundbreaking accomplishments of academics provide the knowledge that active investors need to free them from the delusion they can beat a market.

A Timeline Of The Science Of Investing

Truly successful investing is built on the pillars of academic research. The following milestones demonstrate how strongly the creativity, determination and tireless research of thousands of individuals have influenced the development of this 12-Step Recovery Program for Active Investors.

NEW YORK STOCK EXCHANGE

Adam Smith

1776 – The Wealth Of Nations

In his 1776 landmark book, *The Wealth of Nations*,[20] Adam Smith asserted that countries that embrace free markets would prosper while others would not. His assertion was illustrated with the visual image of the invisible hand representing free market forces. Smith believed that individuals who acted in their own self-interest would benefit society as a whole. By allowing buyers and sellers to set prices, a free market economy would ensure the allocation of resources in the most efficient manner. Similarly, investing is based on the idea that market prices constantly shift to reflect current market conditions.

Louis Bachelier

1900 – The Random Walk Theory

In his 1900 doctoral thesis, "The Theory of Speculation," Louis Bachelier set forth his revolutionary conclusion that "there is no useful information contained in historical price movements of securities." Therefore, the expected return of speculation is zero (minus costs). Bachelier's theory was rejected by his peers and sat untouched for 60 years until economist Paul Samuelson discovered it. Samuelson, Eugene Fama and others would expand on Bachelier's findings with the ensuing and revolutionary Random Walk Theory, which asserts that stock prices continuously react to new information and therefore move in a random and unpredictable fashion.

WISDOM

Francis Galton

1906 – The Wisdom Of The Crowds

English scientist Francis Galton was a statistician who developed the important concepts of correlation and regression toward a mean. He discovered in the early 1900s that the collective wisdom of many is more accurate than the wisdom of a few. Galton arrived at his discovery of "The Wisdom of the Crowds" at a livestock convention, where a crowd of almost 800 people were asked to guess the correct weight of a butchered ox. Surprisingly, the average guess of the entire crowd was very close to the ox's actual weight, only one pound off. No one individual came as close to the correct answer. In a 1906 *Nature* Magazine article titled, "Vox Populi" (Voice of the People), Galton concluded that a group of individuals making independent guesses would make a more accurate assessment than an individual would on their own. The world's equity markets support Galton's discovery, as millions of investors independently estimate a stock's value by agreeing upon a price.

In 2005, *New York Times* journalist and author James Surowiecki eloquently detailed the accuracy of the collective wisdom of all of us in his popular book, *The Wisdom of Crowds: Why the Many Are Smarter Than the Few and How Collective Wisdom Shapes Business, Economies, Societies and Nations.*[21] His book describes and affirms Galton's findings that large groups of people are smarter than the elite few.

Paul Samuelson

1965 – Prices Are Random

In 1970, MIT Professor of Economics Paul Samuelson was the first American to be awarded a Nobel Prize in Economics. Samuelson has long been credited with contributing more than any other contemporary economist to raising the analytical and methodological levels of economic science. Influenced greatly by Louis Bachelier, Samuelson proved, expanded and refined Bachelier's work in his famous paper, "Proof that Properly Anticipated Prices Fluctuate Randomly,"[22] published in 1965. His findings can be summarized as follows: a) market prices are the best estimates of value; b) price changes follow random patterns; and c) future news and stock prices are unpredictable. Samuelson's wisdom is reflected in his words, "Investing should be dull, like watching paint dry or grass grow. If you want excitement, take $800 and go to Las Vegas. It is not easy to get rich in Las Vegas, at Churchill Downs, or at the local Merrill Lynch office." The painting on the right illustrates Samuelson's belief that investing should provide as much excitement as watching grass grow.

Eugene Fama

1965 – Efficient Markets

University of Chicago professor Eugene Fama is widely viewed as the "Father of Modern Finance." Fama set out to explain why stock market prices fluctuate randomly, and his findings led to his coining of the phrase "Efficient Market." In "The Behavior of Stock

Market Prices,"[23] published in 1965, Fama examined the prevailing assumption that the tremendous resources available to any major brokerage firm, including industry trends, effects of interest rates, accounting data, and access to managers of firms consistently allow fund managers and security analysts to outperform a randomly selected portfolio of securities with similar general risk levels. However, the study determined no such advantage existed beyond that attributed to chance alone. In 1970, Fama published his Efficient Market Hypothesis in "Efficient Capital Markets: A Review of Theory and Empirical Work,"[24] in which he concluded equity markets consistently incorporate all available information into their prices, and trends in capital markets cannot be identified in advance. He found that an agreement between a buyer and a seller reflects the most accurate value of a security, resulting in an environment where the only way an investor can beat market returns is by taking on greater than market levels of risk.

Kenneth French

Eugene Fama and Kenneth French's 1992 paper, "The Cross-Section of Expected Stock Returns,"[25] expanded upon the Nobel-Prize winning research of Harry Markowitz and William Sharpe that delivered Modern Portfolio Theory. They determined that exposure to market, size and value risk factors explained as much as 97% of historical returns in diversified stock portfolios. Their discoveries serve as the foundation for constructing indexes that efficiently capture risks and returns based on five independent risk factors, including term and default for fixed income.

Rex Sinquefield

1973 – The Birth Of Index Funds

Shortly after earning his MBA from the University of Chicago, Rex Sinquefield convinced his then employer, American National Bank of Chicago, to develop the first market-cap-weighted S&P 500 Index Fund. Established in 1973, the fund was only available to institutions, and the New York Telephone Company became its first major investor. In 1976, Sinquefield teamed up with Roger Ibbotson to co-author "Stocks, Bonds, Bills and Inflation," an annually updated study that is widely recognized as the most comprehensive empirical study of stock market returns available. Also in 1973, David Booth helped develop a market-cap-weighted S&P 500 Index Fund for Wells Fargo Bank.

Sinquefield and Booth teamed up in 1981 to launch Dimensional Fund Advisors, a mutual fund company committed to the construction of passive funds that efficiently capture the specific market risk factors identified by Fama and French. Sinquefield has been an eloquent and outspoken advocate for passive investing. At a 1995 Charles Schwab conference, Sinquefield said, "It is well to consider, briefly, the connection between the socialists and the active managers. I believe they are cut from the same cloth. What links them is a disbelief or skepticism about the efficacy of market prices in gathering and conveying information… so who still believes markets don't work? Apparently it is only the North Koreans, the Cubans and the active managers."

THE WALL STREET JO
THE WALL STREET JOURNAL

Burton Malkiel

1973 – A Random Walk

Economist, author and Princeton Professor of Economics Burton Malkiel is a leading proponent of Fama's Efficient Market Hypothesis. In his 1973 book, *A Random Walk Down Wall Street* (now in its 10th edition),[26] Malkiel challenged the financial services industry to provide the investing public a better way to invest. "Fund spokesmen are quick to point out you can't buy the market averages," he wrote. "It's time the public could." He also quipped, "A blindfolded monkey throwing darts at a newspaper's financial pages could select a portfolio that would do just as well as one carefully selected by the experts." Two years after his book was published, the Vanguard Group was formed to create the first index fund available to individual investors. Vanguard founder John C. Bogle refers to Malkiel as the "spiritual leader of the [indexing] crusade."[27]

Friedrich von Hayek

1974 – A Case For Capitalism

In his book, *The Road to Serfdom*,[28] Austrian economist Friedrich von Hayek (1899 to 1992) made the case for free market capitalism as a superior economic model to communism or socialism. He and his mentor Ludwig von Mises were influential figures in the Austrian school of political economy. He postulated that centralized planning by a government is not democratic and that market economies are the result of spontaneous order, resulting in a more efficient allocation of societal resources than any other system could achieve. Building on the work of Adam Smith, Mises, and others, Hayek argued that in socialist or communist societies, an individual or a small group of people unreliably determines the distribution of resources. The findings of his research support the concept that prices in a free market, such as the New York Stock Exchange, are set by information that is available to market participants and serve as a means of communication between buyers and sellers. Hayek was awarded the Nobel Memorial Prize in Economics in 1974 and the Presidential Medal of Freedom in 1991 by President George H.W. Bush.

John Bogle

1975 – First Retail Index Fund

On December 31, 1975, Princeton graduate John C. Bogle created Vanguard's First Index Investment Trust with just $11 million, the first index fund available to individual investors. Now known as the Vanguard 500 Index Fund, the fund was initially met with criticism, even earning the nickname, "Bogle's Folly." The fund became the security industry's largest mutual fund in 2000 and as of September 2011, managed more than $92 billion in assets.

Bogle is widely recognized as a vocal champion of the individual investor, even earning him the moniker of "St. Jack" for his unwavering commitment to keeping fees as low as possible and ensuring fund transparency and purity. Bogle has received significant accolades in recognition for his unselfish efforts. In 2004, *TIME* Magazine named Bogle one of the world's 100 most powerful and influential people, and *Institutional Investor* presented him with its Lifetime Achievement Award. In 1999, *Fortune* designated him as one of the investment industry's four "Giants of the 20th Century." In 1998, Bogle was presented the Award for Professional Excellence from the Association for Investment Management and Research, and he was inducted into the Hall of Fame of the Fixed Income Analysts Society, Inc. in 1999.

Bogle is also a prolific and best-selling author of many books, including *Common Sense on Mutual Funds* (2000); *Don't Count on it!: Reflections on Investment Illusions, Capitalism, "Mutual" Funds, Indexing, Entrepreneurship, Idealism, and Heroes* (2010); and *The Little Book of Common Sense Investing: The Only Way to Guarantee Your Fair Share of Stock Market Returns* (2007).

David Booth

1981 – A New Dimension Of Investing

David Booth earned his MBA from the University of Chicago in 1971, where he studied under great economic minds like Eugene Fama and Merton Miller. Booth suspected many investors were unaware of the importance of market efficiency and the benefits of size risk exposures. So in 1981, along with Rex Sinquefield, Booth founded Dimensional Fund Advisors (DFA), a highly regarded mutual fund company that applies passive asset class strategies to its wide range of fund choices, many of which provide a tilt toward small and value factors which have shown to deliver higher returns over time. DFA was one of the first fund companies to impart to its clients and advisors the concept that economic science demonstrated a direct relationship between risk and return. Booth's efforts have been amply rewarded, as DFA is widely regarded by independent investment advisors as a top mutual fund company with assets of $195 billion as of September 2011. Booth has generously shared his wealth to continue the advance of investing science. In 2008, Booth donated $300 million to the University of Chicago's School of Business, the largest gift in the University's history and the largest gift to any business school. In appreciation of the gift, the University of Chicago's business school has been renamed Chicago Booth School of Business.

1990 – Nobel Prize In Economic Sciences

After several decades of economic breakthroughs, the science of investing was recognized in 1990. The Sveriges Riksbank Prize in Economic Sciences in Memory of Alfred Nobel was awarded to three investment research pioneers for their collective work known as Modern Portfolio Theory: Harry Markowitz, for research regarding portfolio construction in relation to risk and return; William Sharpe, for his Capital Asset Pricing Model and the concept of beta; and Merton Miller, for modern corporate finance theory and the theory of company valuation with respect to dividends. After years of work, they were credited with collectively reforming the way the world invests and forming conclusions that continue to inspire financial economists today.

Harry Markowitz

When Harry Markowitz was a doctoral student at the University of Chicago in 1952, he concluded that investment diversification reduced risk. His groundbreaking paper, "Portfolio Selection,"[29] was the foundation of Modern Portfolio Theory and established him as a pioneer in the financial industry. He is commonly referred to as the "Father of Modern Portfolio Theory." Markowitz's contributions showed assets should be evaluated not only for their individual characteristics, but also for their effect on a portfolio as a whole. He has mathematically supported efficient portfolios that have provided the highest expected return for a given level of risk.

William Sharpe

Stanford professor William Sharpe presented the Capital Asset Pricing Model (CAPM), or single factor asset-pricing model, in his 1963 paper, "A Simplified Model for Portfolio Analysis."[30] In his 1964 paper, "Capital Asset Prices: A Theory of Market Equilibrium under Conditions of Risk,"[31] he theorized risk is volatility relative to the market and found an asset's sensitivity to market risk (known as beta) determines an investor's expected return and the cost of capital of a firm. Stocks that carry higher risk (a beta of more than one) are more volatile than the market and therefore should have higher expected returns. CAPM is often used as the asset-pricing model for evaluating the risk and expected return of securities and portfolios.

Merton Miller

Merton Miller derived two vital invariance theorems with the help of Frank Modigliani, now aptly named the MM theorems. Through his work an important lesson was ascertained: a firm's value is unrelated to its dividend policy, and policy is an unreliable guide for stock selection. The MM theorems have since established themselves as the comparative norm for theoretical and empirical analyses in corporate finance.

The Higher Power For Investors

The above vignettes are brief snapshots of an enormous treasure trove of substantive information that can provide every investor the opportunity to invest for a better financial future. The research and findings of financial scientists, academics and Nobel Laureates are indeed the higher power for investors, enabling them to invest with an abundance of knowledge that will enable them to better fund their own retirement, not their broker's retirement.

IBM
40
16
YHOO
MSFT
GOOG
CSCO
GE
8
3

Step 3: Stock Pickers

"Active management is little more than a gigantic con game."

– Ron Ross, Ph.D. , *The Unbeatable Market*, 2002

"By day we write about 'Six Funds to Buy NOW!'... By night we invest in sensible index funds. Unfortunately, pro-index fund stories don't sell magazines."

– Anonymous, *Fortune* Magazine, 1999

"If there are 10,000 people looking at the stocks and trying to pick winners, well, one in 10,000 is going to score, by chance alone, a great coup, and that's all that's going on. It's a game, it's a chance operation, and people think they are doing something purposeful... but they're really not."

– Merton Miller, Ph.D., Nobel Laureate, PBS *Nova* Special, "The Trillion Dollar Bet," 2000

"Very little evidence [was found] that any individual [mutual] fund was able to do significantly better than that which we expected from mere random chance."

– Michael Jensen, Ph.D., "The Performance of Mutual Funds in the Period 1945-1964," *Journal of Finance*, 1968

Stockaholics search for the best stock to choose,
but end up cryin' the Speculation Blues.
– The Speculation Blues

One of the potholes in the road that jolts investors off the recovery wagon is also a glamorous aspect that attracts them to active investing in the first place: Stock Picking. The term is pretty self-explanatory. As *The Big Casino* painting illustrates, stock picking is the same as throwing dice and hoping for the big bucks—sheer gambling. What's not to like about stock picking? You have stock picker thespians like Jim Cramer appearing in Hollywood blockbusters, such as *Iron Man*, where he plays the same role he does on his highly rated cable TV show. One should ask themselves, "Are they both acts?" Then there is *Wall Street*, a movie depicting a high octane, push-it-to-the-limit lifestyle that seems exciting and a bit dangerous in a cool kind of way. The real danger occurs when investors are influenced by the speculative stories and recommendations these stock pickers throw around.

Problems

Stock Pickers Fail

Stock prices are quickly moved by news that is available to all market participants at the same time. Because news is utterly unpredictable and random by nature, we come to the unavoidable conclusion that movements of stock prices are also unpredictable and random. Therefore, the current stock

MUSE
MUSE
YHOO
181

price is always the best estimate of the stock's fair price. This means those celebrity stock pickers appearing on television and the silver screen are no different than a team captain calling a coin toss before a big game. It's a blind guess as to whether the stock will go up or down in the short term because these events will occur based on news that is unknowable in advance. This means your portfolio, if based on a few hand-picked stocks, will rise or fall on the whims of the daily news.

Ever since the first stock market trade, traders have been looking for ways to predict future stock market movements. They have studied reams of data, looking for patterns in the prices of securities. In 2000, a *Nova* television special, "The Trillion Dollar Bet,"[32] reported that a group of academics in the 1930s decided to find out if traders really could predict how prices moved. Since they could not find any scientific basis for the belief, they decided to run a series of experiments. In one of them, they created a random portfolio of stocks by throwing darts at *The Wall Street Journal* while blindfolded. After one year, they were stunned to discover the dartboard portfolio had outperformed the portfolios of Wall Street gurus. The academics arrived at a devastating conclusion: The success of top traders was simply due to luck, and patterns in prices appeared by chance alone.

In 1992, 63 years after the stock market crash, John Stossel of ABC's *20/20*[33] program conducted some follow-up research on the dart throwing. He determined the economists' findings from more than six decades prior remained true. Stossel interviewed Princeton Professor Burton Malkiel, author of *A Random Walk*

Down Wall Street. Professor Malkiel reminded viewers that stock markets have historically delivered a performance of 9.5% to 10% per year. "To beat the average, should an investor listen to the Wall Street professionals?" Stossel asked. "No," replied Malkiel. "All the information an analyst can learn about a company, from balance sheets to marketing material, is already built into the stock price because all of the other thousands of analysts have the same information. What they don't have is the knowledge that will move the stock such as news events, which are unpredictable and impossible to forecast."

Lack Of Market Knowledge

Stock pickers presume there are mispriced stocks that can be identified in advance and exploited for profit. They don't realize that virtually all of the information about a stock, a sector, or an economy is very quickly digested by the totality of market participants and swiftly embedded into the price. This market efficiency ensures the prices agreed upon between willing buyers and willing sellers are the best estimate of fair market values. In other words, available information and news is "baked in the cake," meaning nobody has access to anything "special" that is not already included in the price, unless investors have inside information. No single trader can know more or have a consistent advantage over the millions of other market participants around the world. Markets reward investors, not speculators.

Tenets of market efficiency do not state that at any given time there are no mispriced securities in the marketplace. Rather, these

P R
NEWS

CE
MUSE
YHOO
YHOO
WORLD

tenets assert that because prices reflect all known information, mispriced securities cannot be identified in advance.

Stock Pickers' Poor Behavior

Stock pickers are very confident, harboring biases about their abilities to pick winning stocks. In a study titled, "Are Investors Reluctant to Realize Their Losses?,"[34] Terrance Odean, professor of finance at the University of California, Berkeley, analyzed the activity of 10,000 discount brokerage accounts. Odean's findings, published in the October 1998 issue of *Journal of Finance*, showed that investors habitually overestimated the profit potential of their stock trades. In fact, they would often engage in costly trading, even though their profits did not even cover their transaction costs. Odean's research showed investors believed they had unique information which would give them an edge, when in reality they operated under widely disseminated information. On average, the stocks investors bought underperformed the stocks they sold.

In a follow-up paper, "Trading is Hazardous to Your Wealth: The Common Investment Performance of Individual Investors,"[35] Odean joined Brad Barber of University of California, Davis to analyze 66,465 individual trading accounts. They found that from 1991 to 1996, investors who traded most earned annualized returns of 11.4%, while in the same period the market earned annualized returns of 17.9%. The tendency for these investors to trade excessively resulted in an erosion of returns compared to the market.

A Stock Picker's Defeat

Even professional stock pickers can fall hard. One infamous story shows how a former Morningstar "Fund Manager of the Decade"[36] lost his Midas touch after a well known winning streak. Bill Miller's Legg Mason Value Trust Fund (LMVTX) is portrayed in Figures 3-1, 3-2 and 3-3, showing the risk and return results of his fund for three different time periods, compared to various indexes and index portfolios: Figure 3-1 for the decade of the 90s through 2000; Figure 3-2 for the ten years from 2001 to 2010; and Figure 3-3 for the 28 years and 8 months since the inception of the LMVTX fund.

As the first chart clearly shows, LMVTX did earn higher returns than the S&P 500 and the index portfolios during the

Figure 3-1

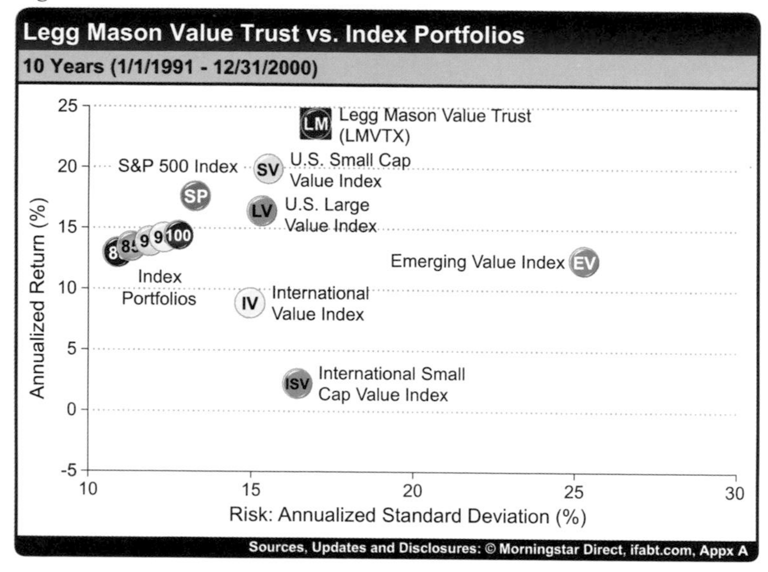

90s, but with significantly higher risk—a risk that eventually caught up with Miller. In a January 6, 2005 article in *The Wall Street Journal*, Miller accounted for his winning streak saying, "As for the so-called streak, that's an accident of the calendar. If the year had ended on different months it wouldn't be there. At some point, mathematics will hit us. We've been lucky. Well, maybe it's not 100% luck—maybe 95% luck."[37]

Figure 3-2 shows just how hard the mathematics did hit Miller. Despite the fact that his "so-called streak" showed him to outperform the S&P 500 for a 10-year period, Miller's subsequent 10-year returns from 2001 to 2010 pale in comparison to the indexes and index portfolios shown. Miller's outperformance and subsequent underperformance were the result of his excessively

Figure 3-2

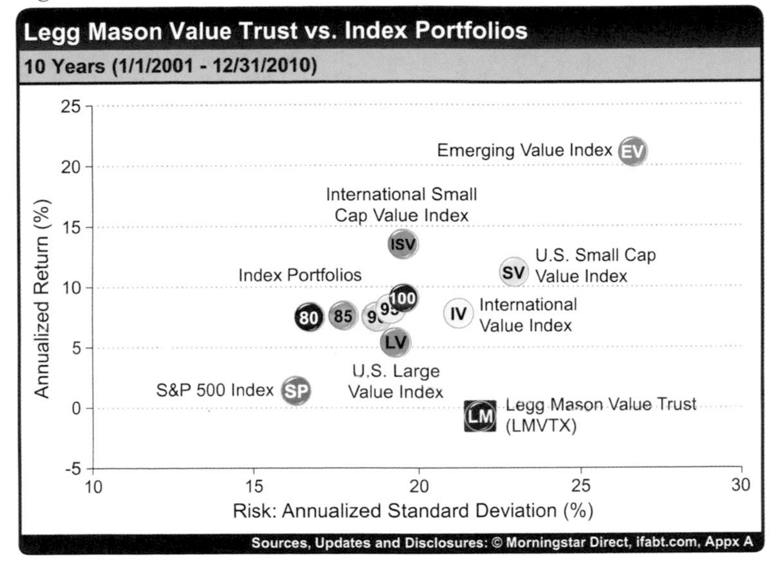

risky bets on concentrated investments among highly correlated stocks. While equity index portfolios invest across many asset classes and invest in as many as 12,000 companies in 40 different countries, Miller's strategy was to "place big bets on stocks other investors feared," cites a *Wall Street Journal* article, "The Stock Picker's Defeat." According to the December 2008 article, "Mr. Miller was in his element [a year ago] when troubles in the housing market began infecting financial markets. Working from his well-worn playbook, he snapped up American International Group Inc., Wachovia Corp., Bear Stearns Cos. and Freddie Mac. As the shares continued to fall, he argued that investors were overreacting. He kept buying." The article continued, "What he saw as an opportunity turned into the biggest market crash since the Great Depression. Many Value Trust holdings were more or less wiped out. After 15 years of placing savvy bets against the herd, Mr. Miller had been trampled by it." Miller stated, "The thing I didn't do, from Day One, was properly assess the severity of this liquidity crisis… I was naïve… Every decision to buy anything has been wrong… It's been awful."[38] Not only did the assets themselves plummet, but investors bailed on the fund pushing its assets down from its apex of $21 billion to around $4.2 billion.

At one point, Miller said, "The S&P 500 is a wonderful thing to put your money in. If somebody said, 'I've got a fund here with a really low cost, that's tax efficient, with a 15 to 20-year record of beating almost everybody, why wouldn't you own it?'"

Figure 3-3 shows that over the lifetime of the LMVTX, several indexes and index portfolios outperformed the LMVTX with lower risk than the LMVTX, and the more appropriate benchmark of U.S. Large Cap Value beat Miller with less risk.

Miller's so-called streak was based on bad benchmarking. LMVTX was far riskier than the S&P 500, a reality most investors certainly did not understand—especially investor Peter Cohan who lamented to the *Wall Street Journal*, "Why didn't I just throw my money out the window and light it on fire?"[39]

Morningstar ranked Miller's fund as one of the top 3 losers for fund performance in June 2011. Bloomberg News reports that Russel Kinnel, Morningstar director of mutual fund research said, "People assume because certain managers have had good streaks that they are always going to be a step ahead of the market. It never works out that way."[40]

Figure 3-3

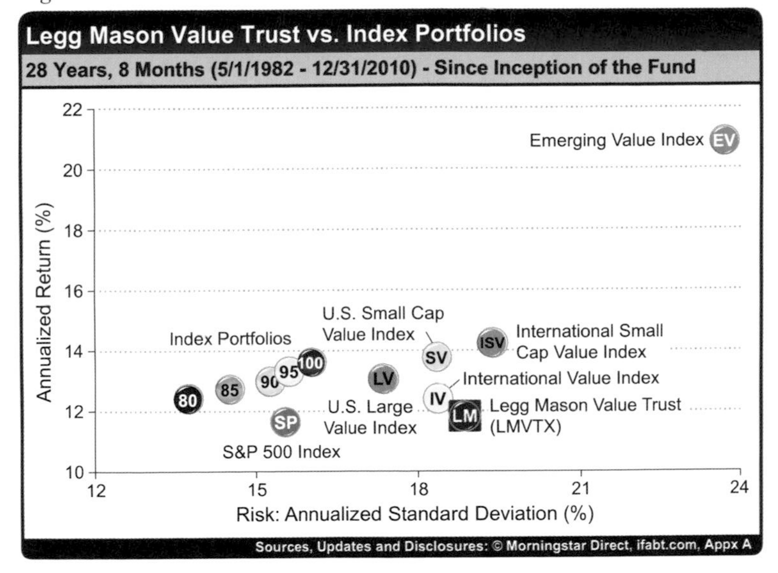

Stock Pickers' Graveyard

The media loves a good story. Who can blame them? It's their job to present the latest and greatest news. So when a stock picker happens upon a sector that turns red hot, the media adorns this lucky stock picker with guru status—until, of course, that red-hot sector turns cold and the guru torch is handed over to the next lucky stock picker. In fact, the stock picking graveyard is crammed with wildly successful stock pickers and companies who have perished from the exchanges.

The financial press largely focuses on the daily movements of stocks and markets, showering rewards on those who are lucky enough to be in the right place at the right time. But luck is not a repeatable skill. This reality is clearly spelled out in

Mark Hulbert's 2008 *New York Times* article, "The Prescient are Few."[41] Hulbert details the findings of a study[42] by Professors Laurent Barras, Olivier Scaillet and Russell Wermers about the performance of 2,076 mutual fund managers over a 32-year time period. It found that from 1975 to 2006, 99.4% of these managers displayed no evidence of genuine stock picking skill, and the 0.6% of managers who did outperform the index were "statistically indistinguishable from zero," or as Hulbert puts it, "just lucky." Figure 3-4 depicts the study's results.

A statistical test called the Student's t-test was introduced in 1908 by William Sealy Gosset, referred to as the "Student," while working for the Guinness brewery in Dublin, Ireland

Figure 3-4

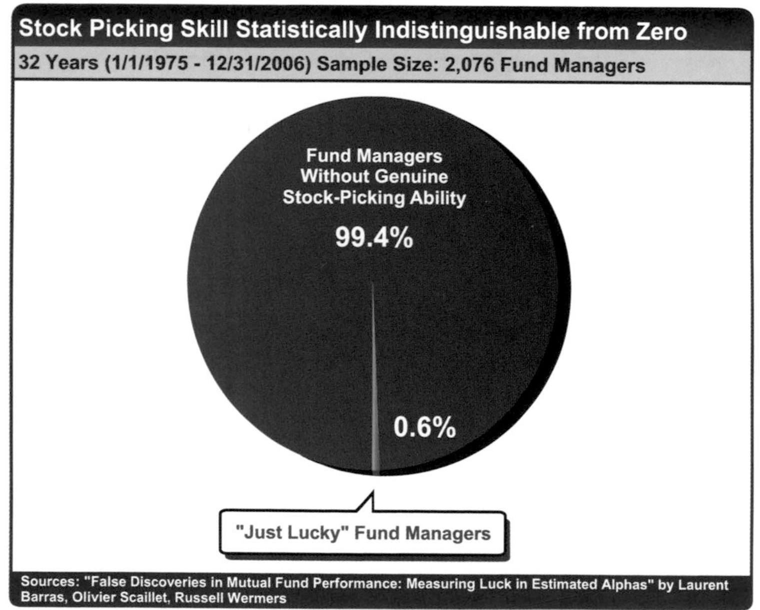

to evaluate the quality of the brewery's ingredients. The t-test can be used to determine if a series of historical returns is reliably superior–showing a t-statistic of 2 or higher–to a risk-equivalent benchmark. This can determine whether alpha (any return above the benchmark return) is due to luck or skill. In Figure 3-5, the t-test is applied to U.S. equity funds in six different style classifications over a 10-year period. Out of 614 mutual funds, only one (0.16%) had a t-stat greater than or equal to 2 (signifying skill), but that t-stat dropped below 2 (signifying luck) when that fund was analyzed from its 1991 inception date. See the Step 5 Solutions section for a further explanation of the t-stat.

Figure 3-5

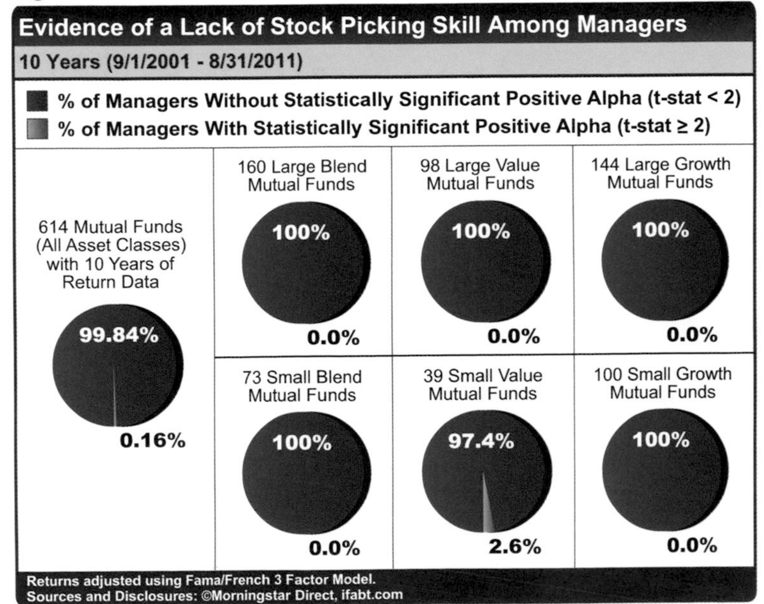

LOOKING FOR A NEEDLE IN A HAYSTACK

Everyone wants to find the next Google or Apple, but picking a stock that will do better than the market index over the long haul is virtually impossible. Vanguard Group founder John Bogle has accurately described the practice of stock picking as "looking for a needle in a haystack." Even if you are lucky enough to pick a stock that outperforms the market, there is no certainty of success, or even survival, in the future.

In their book, *Creative Destruction*,[43] McKinsey & Company consultants Richard Foster and Sarah Kaplan analyzed the companies of the original S&P 500 Index from 1957. Their findings shown in Figure 3-6 revealed that only 74 companies remained on the list in 1997, and just 12 of them ended up

Figure 3-6

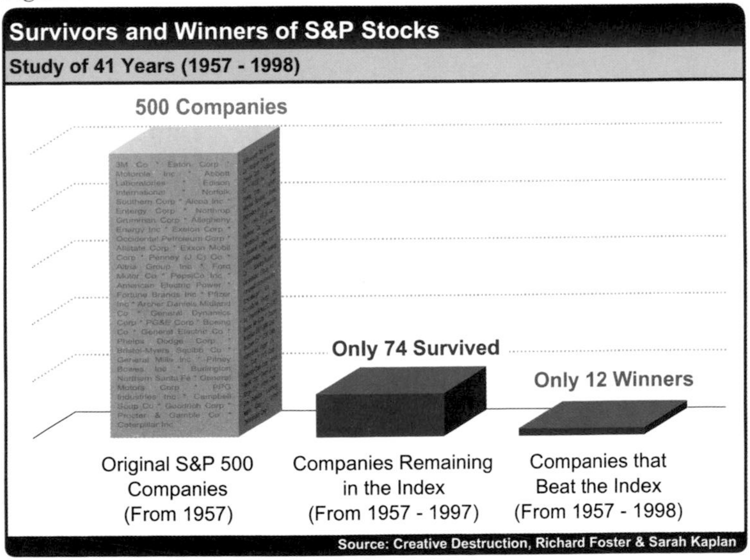

Survivors and Winners of S&P Stocks

Study of 41 Years (1957 - 1998)

500 Companies

Only 74 Survived

Only 12 Winners

Original S&P 500 Companies (From 1957)

Companies Remaining in the Index (From 1957 - 1997)

Companies that Beat the Index (From 1957 - 1998)

Source: Creative Destruction, Richard Foster & Sarah Kaplan

with returns that outperformed the index for the 41-year period through 1998. "As the '80s passed and we made our way through the '90s, both of us observed that almost as soon as any company had been praised in the popular management literature as excellent or somehow super durable, it began to deteriorate," the authors wrote. "Searching for excellent companies was like trying to catch light beams; they were easy to imagine, but so hard to grasp," they concluded.

Figure 3-7 takes stock pickers for a short walk down Misery Lane, reminding them of the ten largest bankruptcies from January 1981 through October 2011. Few industries escaped, as companies such as Lehman Brothers, Washington Mutual, GM, and MF Global Holdings ultimately failed and succumbed

Figure 3-7

The Ten Largest Bankruptcies

30 Years and 10 Months (1/1/1981 - 10/31/2011)

	Companies	Date	Total Assests Pre-Bankruptcy
1.	Lehman Brothers Holdings,Inc.	09/15/08	$691,063,000,000
2.	Washington Mutual, Inc.	09/26/08	$327,913,000,000
3.	WorldCom, Inc.	07/21/02	$103,914,000,000
4.	General Motors Corporation	06/01/09	$91,047,000,000
5.	CIT Group, Inc.	11/01/09	$80,448,000,000
6.	Enron Corporation	12/02/01	$65,503,000,000
7.	Conseco, Inc.	12/17/02	$61,392,000,000
8.	MF Global Holdings, Ltd.	10/31/11	$40,541,000,000
9.	Chrysler, LLC	04/30/09	$39,300,000,000
10.	Thornburg Mortgage, Inc.	05/01/09	$36,521,000,000

Year	2006	2007	2008	2009	2010
Number of Total Business Bankruptcies	19,695	28,322	43,546	60,837	56,282

Sources: BankruptcyData.com. New Generation Research, Inc., American Bankruptcy Institute

to bankruptcy. The number of bankruptcies dramatically increased from 19,695 in 2006 to 56,282 in 2010.

Great Companies Don't Make Great Investments

Remember Peter Lynch's advice about buying companies whose products you like? It turns out this advice is not as good as it sounds. Great companies don't make great investments. You may love Apple's iPad, but this doesn't mean Apple is a great stock to buy. In fact, the opposite is usually true. Distressed companies have earned higher returns than those of companies with lots of hype or goodwill. Unfortunately, investors generally avoid investing in distressed companies, because it seems counterintuitive to buy perceived losers.

Finance Professors Meir Statman and Deniz Anginer wrote a 2010 study called "Stocks of Admired Companies and Spurned Ones."[44] Their study was based on *Fortune* Magazine's annual list of "America's Most Admired Companies" from 1983 to 2007. *Fortune's* annual surveys ranked companies on eight attributes of reputation:

- Quality of management
- Quality of products or services
- Innovativeness
- Long-term investment value
- Financial soundness
- Ability to attract, develop and keep talented people
- Responsibility to the community and the environment
- Wise use of company assets

From these ratings, Statman and Anginer constructed two portfolios, each consisting of one half of the *Fortune* stocks. The "admired" portfolio (often referred to as growth stocks) contained the stocks with the highest *Fortune* ratings, and the "spurned" portfolio (often referred to as value stocks) contained the stocks with the lowest *Fortune* ratings. For example, the list of admired companies included The Walt Disney Company, UPS and Google. Spurned companies included Jet Blue, Bridgestone and Stanley Works.

The results of the study are of no surprise to value investors. "Stocks of admired companies had lower returns, on average, than stocks of spurned companies." Figure 3-8 shows the 16.12% annualized return of the spurned portfolio and the 13.81% annualized return of the admired portfolio over the 24-year, 9-month period.

Figure 3-8

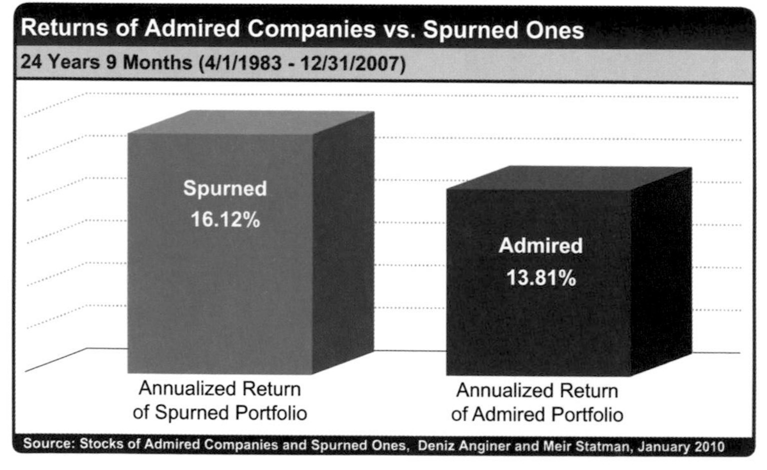

Why have value stocks delivered higher returns to their investors? The market perceives value companies to be riskier, driving down stock prices so their expected returns are high enough to attract investors. That is difficult for most investors to grasp since they prefer to believe growth stocks are better investments than value stocks. After all, investors looking for a stock tip want to hear the name of the next Apple, not the next JCPenney. As you will see in Step 8, the data indicates that investors should be interested in great investments (value stocks), not just great companies (growth stocks).

Fortune Kookie

I analyzed *Fortune's* "Ten Most Admired Companies" (2001) as a whole portfolio and as individual companies, comparing them to 10 index portfolios for the 10-year period from February 2001 through January 2011. The results of the study are shown in Figure 3-9, indicating the equal-weighted "Fortune Most Admired Portfolio" significantly underperformed every index portfolio—even Index Portfolio 10 which has 80% fixed income. Despite the fact that the "Fortune Most Admired Portfolio" carried slightly higher risk than the riskiest Index Portfolio 100, it had a negative return for the time period. In contrast, Index Portfolio 100 grew to $226,000, while the "Fortune Most Admired Portfolio" shrank to $95,000. The story gets worse for the "Fortune" tellers. In fact, nine of the ten stocks underperformed substantially, and seven of the ten ended up with a negative return for the period. Even Warren Buffett's widely touted Berkshire Hathaway stock failed to compensate investors for risk, closely delivering the

Figure 3-9

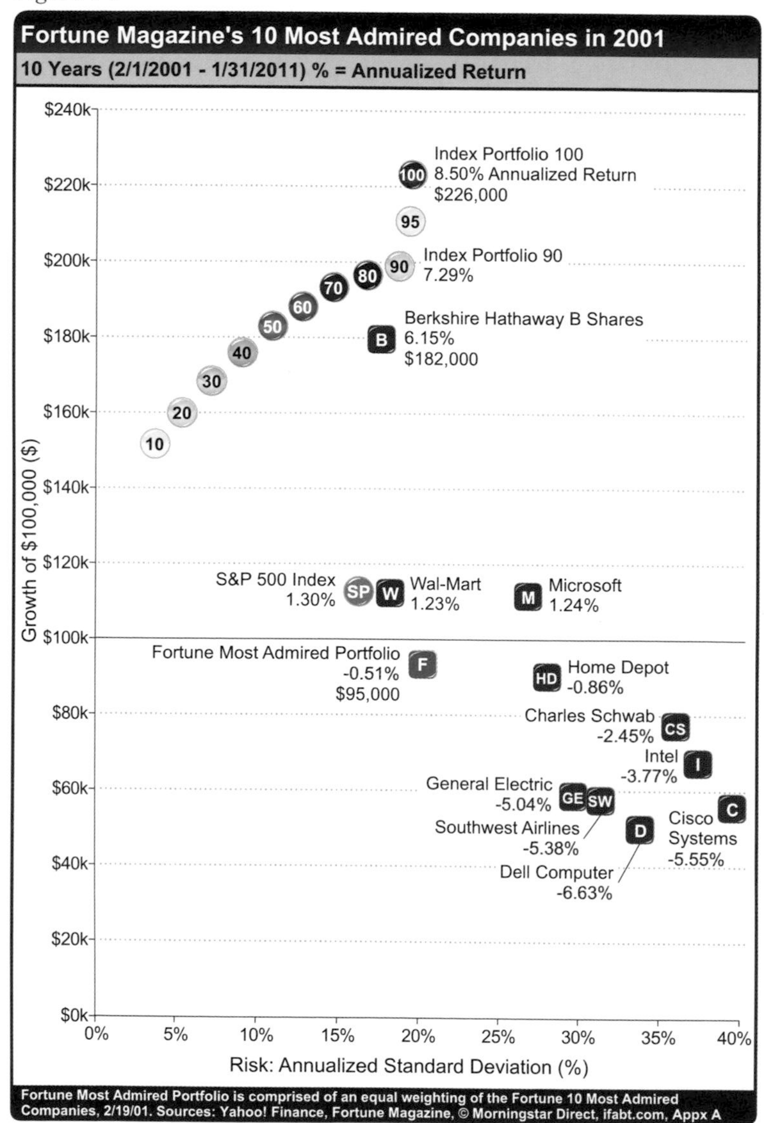
Fortune Magazine's 10 Most Admired Companies in 2001
10 Years (2/1/2001 - 1/31/2011) % = Annualized Return
$240k
$220k
$200k
$180k
$160k
$140k
$120k
$100k
$80k
$60k
$40k
$20k
$0k
Growth of $100,000 ($)
0%
5%
10%
15%
20%
25%
30%
35%
40%
Risk: Annualized Standard Deviation (%)
Index Portfolio 100
8.50% Annualized Return
$226,000
100
95
90
80
70
60
50
40
30
20
10
Index Portfolio 90
7.29%
Berkshire Hathaway B Shares
6.15%
$182,000
B
S&P 500 Index
1.30%
SP
W
Wal-Mart
1.23%
M
Microsoft
1.24%
Fortune Most Admired Portfolio
-0.51%
$95,000
F
HD
Home Depot
-0.86%
Charles Schwab
-2.45%
CS
Intel
-3.77%
I
General Electric
-5.04%
GE
SW
Southwest Airlines
-5.38%
D
Dell Computer
-6.63%
C
Cisco
Systems
-5.55%
Fortune Most Admired Portfolio is comprised of an equal weighting of the Fortune 10 Most Admired Companies, 2/19/01. Sources: Yahoo! Finance, Fortune Magazine, © Morningstar Direct, ifabt.com, Appx A

returns of an Index Portfolio 50, despite the fact that it took greater risk than an Index Portfolio 80.

This sort of data begs the question: If stock picking is such a fruitless endeavor, why do magazines keep selling this elusive dream? The answer is quite basic: Pro-index funds stories don't sell magazines. No big brokerage house would take out a full-page ad that says, "Don't hire us to trade your portfolio—just index and relax." Nonetheless, this is a poor reason to perpetuate the myth that financial journalists or "Fortune Tellers" can pick the handful of stocks to achieve wealth. In fact, by the looks of it, the best way to lose a fortune is to follow *Fortune*.

Bond Pickers

The benefits of passive investing also apply to the fixed income portion of an investor's portfolio. The first major study of bonds funds was conducted by Blake, Elton, and Gruber and was called "Fundamental Economic Variables, Expected Returns, and Bond Fund Performance."[45] It examined 361 bond funds for the period starting in 1977. They compared the actively managed bond funds to a simple index alternative. The results of the study are that the actively managed bond funds underperformed the proper benchmark by 0.85% per year, before federal and state taxes. A set of 12 fixed income studies are shown in Figure 3-10, revealing that across multiple fixed income investment funds, including municipal, government long-term, short-term and high yield, the indexes overwhelmingly outperformed the active managers. No matter how you slice it, passive beats active.

Figure 3-10 [46]

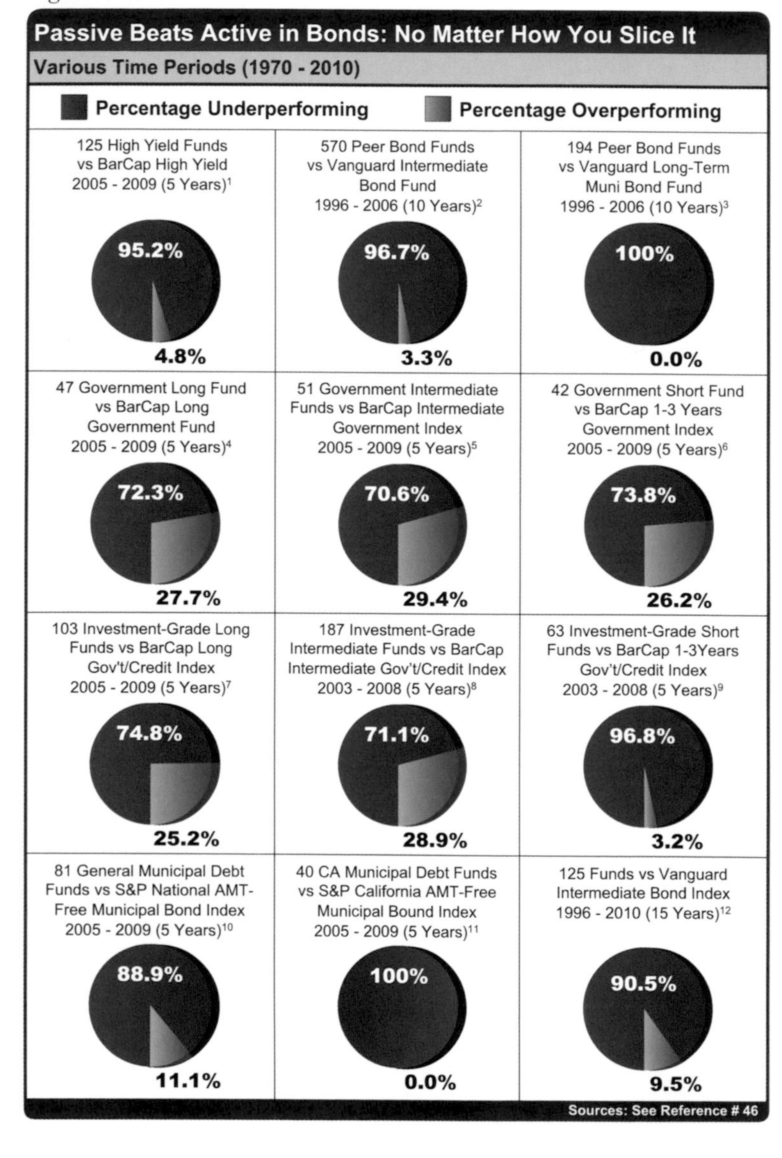

Solutions

Looking for a needle in a haystack is not the answer. Picking stocks is an ill-fated pursuit that wastes time, energy and money. Would you bet your money in Vegas because you have a gut feeling the roulette ball will land on 12-black? You know by now that it is impossible to predict the future.

The better solution is to buy the haystack, keep costs low and maintain risk-appropriate exposures in globally diversified index portfolios.

Step 4: Time Pickers

"If I have noticed anything over these 60 years on Wall Street, it is that people do not succeed in forecasting what's going to happen to the stock market."

– Benjamin Graham, Interview with Hartman L. Butler, "An Hour with Mr. Graham," 1976

"Statistical research has shown that, to a close approximation, stock prices seem to follow a random walk with no discernible predictable patterns that investors can exploit. Such findings are now taken to be evidence of market efficiency… Only new information will move stock prices…"

– Zvi Bodie, *Investments*, 2004

"Market timing is a wicked idea. Don't try it—ever."

– Charles D. Ellis, Ph.D., *Winning the Loser's Game*, 2002

"There are two kinds of investors, be they large or small: those who don't know where the market is headed, and those who don't know that they don't know. Then again, there is a third type of investor… whose livelihood depends upon appearing to know."

– William Bernstein, Ph.D., M.D., *The Intelligent Asset Allocator*, 2000

Market timers dream of makin' a killin' on a trend,
but buyin' and holdin' wins out in the end.
– The Speculation Blues

P.T. BARNUM IS OFTEN CREDITED with coining the phrase, "There's a sucker born every minute." History buffs argue the famed circus founder instead stated, "There's a customer born every minute." However, for investors subscribing to market-timing services, the words "sucker" and "customer" are virtually interchangeable.

Time Pickers or market timers claim the ability to predict the future movement of the stock market, moving into the market before it goes up and getting out before it goes down. However, numerous studies from industry and academic experts demonstrate market timers have no such ability to beat the market, and they should be avoided just like the lion's cage at Barnum's circus. According to Eugene Fama, "Market timing is a flimsy, dangerous occupation."[47]

PROBLEMS

GURUS ARE INACCURATE TOO OFTEN

How often does a market-timing guru need to be right to beat an index? Nobel Laureate William Sharpe set out to answer that very question in his 1975 study titled, "Likely Gains from Market Timing."[48] Sharpe wanted to identify the percentage of time a market timer would need to be correct to break even relative to a benchmark portfolio. He concluded a market timer must be correct 74% of the time in order to outperform a passive portfolio at a comparable level of risk. In 1992, SEI Corporation updated Sharpe's study to include the average 9.4% stock market return from the period 1901-1990. This study determined that gurus must be right at least 69% and as high as 91% of the time, depending on the timing of the moves.[49]

What percentage of times do market timing gurus get it right? CXO Advisory Group tracks public forecasts of self-proclaimed market-timing gurus and rates their accuracy by assigning grades as "correct," "incorrect" or "indecisive." Figure 4-1 depicts CXO's percentage grades for 37 well-known market-timing gurus who made a collective 3,541 forecasts from as early as December 28, 1998 through August 15, 2011.[50] The study shows that not one of the self-proclaimed gurus was able to meet Sharpe's requirement of 74% accuracy, or SEI's minimum 69%, thereby failing to deliver accuracy sufficient to beat a simple index portfolio.

At first glance, the 11 gurus who had percentage accuracy of more than 50% might look appealing to a time picker—but beware, the opportunity costs associated with a time picker's proclivity toward holding cash in some up years creates a higher hurdle as they will have to make up those superior returns foregone by stocks. Transaction costs associated with market timing add another hurdle for market timers to break even.

In *The Big Investment Lie*,[51] Michael Edesess explains why market timing is so difficult, "The stock market can turn on a dime and always does. Prices are constantly twisting and turning without trend or predictable pattern. Their recent movement gives you nothing to go on."

Figure 4-1

Forecast Accuracy: 74% Required to Beat the Market

Forecasts Range From 12/28/1998 to 8/15/2011

Name	Accuracy
Accuracy required to outperform the market [1]	74%
Jon Markman	67%
Jack Schannep	66%
Ken Fisher	64%
Cabot Market	62%
The Aden Sisters	61%
Louis Navellier	61%
Steve Sjuggerud	60%
Jason Kelly	59%
Carl Swenlin	57%
Richard Moroney	54%
Gary Kaltbaum	53%
James Dines	50%
Bernie Schaeffer	49%
Clif Droke	48%
Stephen Leeb	48%
Jeremy Grantham	48%
Carl Futia	47%
Gary Savage	47%
Marc Faber	46%
Gary D. Halbert	45%
Dennis Slothower	45%
Jim Jubak	44%
Nadeem Walayat	44%
Tim Wood	44%
Comstock	43%
Bill Cara	43%
Price Headley	42%
Linda Schurman	40%
John Mauldin	40%
Bob Hoye	38%
Bill Fleckenstein	37%
Richard Russell	37%
Abby Joseph Cohen	35%
Robert McHugh	32%
Curt Hesler	31%
Steven Jon Kaplan	27%
Steve Saville	26%

Sources:1.William F. Sharpe "Likely Gains From Market Timing,"Financial Analysts Journal, March/April 1975, pp. 60-69.www.cxoadvisory.com/gurus/ Copyright: CXO Advisory Group LLC: Reproduced with permission

Studies Prove Time Picking Doesn't Work

A study by University of Utah Professor John Graham and Duke University Professor Campbell Harvey is titled, "Market Timing Ability and Volatility Implied in Investment Newsletters' Asset Allocation Recommendations."[52] The massive 51-page study tracked 15,000 predictions made by 237 market-timing newsletters from June 1980 to December 1992. By the end of the period, 94.5% of the timing newsletters had gone out of business with an average life span of just four years. "There is no evidence that newsletters can time the market," the study concluded. "Consistent with mutual fund studies, 'winners' rarely win again and 'losers' often lose again."

"Sure, it'd be great to get out of stocks at the high and jump back in at the low," observed John Bogle in an April 2008 interview with *Money*[53] Magazine. "[But] in 55 years in the business, I not only have never met anybody who knew how to do it, I've never met anybody who had met anybody who knew how to do it."

Missing The Best And Worst Days

Almost all big stock market gains and drops are concentrated in just a few trading days each year. Missing only a few days can have a dramatic impact on returns. Figure 4-2 illustrates how an investor who hypothetically remained invested in the S&P 500 Index throughout the 20-year period from 1991 to 2010 (5,043 trading days) would have earned a sizable 9.14% annualized return, growing a $10,000 investment to $57,512. By missing only the five best-performing days in that time period, the annualized return shrank to 6.93%, with $10,000 growing to $38,167. Even worse, if an investor missed just the one day a year (on average) with the largest gains, the returns were cut down to just 2.99% a year. If an average of just two of the biggest days a year were missed, an investment in the S&P 500 turned negative, with $10,000 eroding in value to just $8,243, a loss of $1,757!

Many market timers will tell you their aim is to miss the worst days, which is an even bigger issue than the problem of missing the best days. The predicament, however, is that the worst days are equally concentrated and just as difficult to identify in advance as the best days. If someone could have avoided the worst days, they would have obtained true guru status. Figure 4-3 illustrates the value of missing the worst-performing days in the 20-year period from 1991 to 2010. If the

Figure 4-2

The Problem with Market Timing: Missing the Best Days

20 Years (1/1/1991 - 12/31/2010)

$10,000 Invested in the S&P 500 Index	S&P 500 Annualized Return	Value of $10,000 at the End of the Period	Gain/ Loss	Impact of Missing Days
All 5,043 trading days	9.14%	$57,512	$47,512	--
Less the 5 days with the biggest gains	6.93%	$38,167	$28,167	-41%
Less the 10 days with the biggest gains	5.42%	$28,724	$18,724	-61%
Less the 20 days with the biggest gains	2.99%	$18,020	$8,020	-83%
Less the 40 days with the biggest gains	-0.96%	$8,243	-$1,757	-104%

Source: Yahoo! Finance

40 worst-performing days of the S&P 500 Index were missed, an investor's increased return would have been 769% more than investors who stayed in the market every day throughout the entire 20 years. The problem, however, is finding the crystal ball that can forecast the 40 worst performing days out of 5,043 days. This shows how market timing can be tempting and alluring.

University of Michigan Professor H. Nejat Seyhun analyzed 7,802 trading days for the 30 years from 1963 to 1993 and concluded that just 90 days generated 95% of all the years' market gains—an average of just three days per year.

As MIT Professor Fisher Black says, "The market does just as well, on average, when the investor is out of the market as it does when he is in. So he loses money, relative to a simple buy-and-hold strategy, by being out of the market part of the time."

Figure 4-3

The Allure of Market Timing: Missing the Worst Days

20 Years (1/1/1991 - 12/31/2010)

$10,000 Invested in the S&P 500 Index	S&P 500 Annualized Return	Value of $10,000 at the End of the Period	Gain/ Loss	Impact of Missing Days
All 5,043 trading days	9.14%	$57,512	$47,512	--
Less the 5 days with the biggest losses	11.52%	$88,479	$78,479	65%
Less the 10 days with the biggest losses	13.35%	$122,583	$112,583	137%
Less the 20 days with the biggest losses	16.32%	$205,672	$195,672	312%
Less the 40 days with the biggest losses	20.59%	$422,666	$412,666	769%

Source: Yahoo! Finance

Goddess Fortuna

Many investors believe market watchers and financial journalists have a special ability to forecast future movements of markets, but history tells a different story. Take the first half of 2009, when market forecasters largely dismissed the rise in stock prices that began in mid-March 2009 as an aberration that would soon be rectified. Only market timers who had the Goddess Fortuna, also known as Lady Luck, whispering in their ears might have predicted that outcome.

The Goddess Fortuna offers a cornucopia of gold coins and delicious treats, but she is sitting on a bubble that floats in the ocean, reminding us how fleeting luck can be. Also, her flowing scarf reminds worshipers that their fortune can change like the wind.

News Is Devoured In Minutes

In *Analysis for Financial Management,*[54] Robert C. Higgins portrays how market participants instantly devour new information, which serves as the inspiration for the painting on the following pages. "The arrival of new information to a competitive market can be likened to the arrival of a lamb chop to a school of flesh-eating piranhas," Higgins writes. "The instant the lamb chop hits the water there is turmoil as the piranhas devour the meat. Very soon, the meat is gone, leaving only the worthless bone behind, and the water returns to normal… no amount of gnawing on the bone will yield any more meat, and no further study of old information will yield any more valuable intelligence."

A 1969 study titled, "The Adjustment of Stock Prices to New Information,"[55] was conducted by Eugene F. Fama, Lawrence Fisher, Michael Jensen, and Professor Richard Roll at the University of California, Los Angeles. The study concluded it takes five to sixty minutes for market prices to completely reflect new information. Fund managers try to exploit whatever slight gain might be had by reacting quickly to a news story, but the likelihood of them consistently being on the right side of a trade in reaction to the news is extremely low.

Solutions

Going or Gone?

When discussing the direction of the market, it's important to use the past-tense verb. During times of high market volatility, people commonly make the mistake of saying, "The market is going down (or up)." Although it appears harmless, this statement implies that the direction of market prices is knowable. People making this statement often use it as the impetus for major investment decisions. Such decisions usually do not fare well, because they are based on the fallacy that one can predict the direction of future price movements. Investors can avoid this pitfall by understanding Eugene Fama's finding that security prices move in a random walk. At any point in time, we only know the current and past price of any given security. Where the price will be even a second later is unknown. The market continuously sets prices in response to news, which by its very nature is unpredictable. Investors will accomplish an important step when they can say, "the market has gone down (or up)" without even having to think about it.

Free Market Forces

The job of free markets is to set prices so that investors are rewarded for the risks they take. To help explain this important statement, I created the Hebner Model, which attempts to simplify market forces into three variables: Price, Expected Return and Uncertainty. Prices move in the opposite direction of economic uncertainty so that expected returns at a specified level of risk can remain essentially constant, resulting in a fair price. From fair prices we expect fair returns, meaning that investors should be compensated for their risk exposure over time.

The reason people invest is to get a return. At the time of a trade, buyers pay a price that reflects the risk associated with capturing the expected return. In other words, a fair price equals a fair expected return.

This model is based on Eugene Fama's Efficient Market Hypothesis, which states that prices fully reflect all available information or news, economic uncertainty and probabilities of future events, thus implying that market prices are fair.

The Hebner Model illustrated in the following painting attempts to diagram the three variables of Uncertainty, Expected Return and Price, resulting in a distribution of returns shown at the bottom. The diagram shows the essentially constant expected return for a given investment portfolio. In this case Index Portfolio 50 is shown at the fulcrum of the teeter-totter, and the period specific expected return can be estimated based

GOOD NEWS
Er
Er
UNCERTAINTY
Er
SELLERS
BAD NEWS
50
PRICE
RETURN
BUYERS

on 30, 50 or 83 years of simulated returns, the Fama French Three or Five Factor Model, or any methods an investor chooses. Current news impacts uncertainty and is represented on the left side of the teeter-totter. This economic uncertainty includes the probabilities of future events. The price agreed upon by willing buyers and sellers is on the right side. When an investment's price has fallen by 2%, one could infer that uncertainty has increased by about 2%. Alternatively, when the price has increased by 2%, without knowing the news, one could deduct that uncertainty has decreased by 2%. In other words, prices react to shifts in uncertainty so that expected returns remain essentially the same.

From a fair price investors should expect: 1) a fair outcome, which would be a risk-appropriate or fair return; 2) an equal chance of being greater than or less than that fair return; and 3) the farther the actual return is from the expected return, the lower the probability of its occurrence.

So before you trade, ask yourself: 1) Who is on the other side of my trade? 2) Do I think I know more than they do? 3) Am I paying a fair price? In my opinion, your answers are as follows: 1) You don't know; 2) It's highly unlikely; and 3) If there are many willing buyers and sellers, by definition, it is a fair price.

For these reasons, market timing offers no advantage. Time pickers cannot forecast the direction of the market. There is no competitive edge that exists. The best way to earn the market's superior return is to simply remain invested at all times in a low-cost, passively managed index portfolio.

Step 5: Manager Pickers

"I have become increasingly convinced that the past records of mutual fund managers are essentially worthless in predicting future success. The few examples of consistently superior performance occur no more frequently than can be expected by chance."

– Professor Burton G. Malkiel, Ph.D.
A Random Walk Down Wall Street, 1973

"Wall Street's favorite scam is pretending that luck is skill."

– Ron Ross, Ph.D.,
The Unbeatable Market, 2002

"You will almost never find a fund manager who can repeatedly beat the market. It is better to invest in an indexed fund that promises a market return but with significantly lowered fees."

– John Bogle, *Economist*, July 3, 2003, quoted in
The Little Book on Common Sense Investing, 2007

"The number of funds that have beaten the market over their entire histories is so small that the False Discovery Rate test can't eliminate the possibility that the few that did were merely false positives."

– Russell Wermers, Ph.D., quoted in "The Prescient are Few," *New York Times*, July 13, 2008

Everyone knows there ain't no free lunch,
the pickers keep thinkin' they can win from a hunch.
– The Speculation Blues

CADDYSHACK *II*, BATMAN *&* ROBIN, THE GODFATHER *III*... all of these movies have one thing in common: they all were abysmal sequels to blockbuster movies. We long to regenerate scenarios when everything comes together perfectly and the stars align, but that kind of success is rarely duplicated. In the world of money managers, success means blockbuster performance... every year! Managers who are successful in the short term are considered the current financial heroes, despite the fact that every reputable study of mutual fund performance over the past 30 years has found there is no reliable way to know if past superior managers will win again in the future. This is why some variation of the disclaimer "past performance is no guarantee of future results" must appear in all mutual fund advertisements and prospectuses. Even still, unwitting investors select these managers to handle their portfolios, and the dangerous practice of manager picking begins.

Sometimes managers can duplicate their success a few years in a row, but it just doesn't last. At least with movies, the directors are somewhat in control of the elements that are used in creating their sequels. Money managers have no such control over the news that drives the markets. As hard as it is to duplicate success in the film world, it is even more difficult for these all-star money managers to duplicate their past success.

Problems

Track Record Investing

"Most investors follow the crowd down the path to comfortable mediocrity," says David Swensen in *Pioneering Portfolio Management.*[56] Anxious to capture the financial gains that come with a winning mutual fund manager, manager pickers blindly chase the hot performing mutual fund manager's recent track record, failing to realize their odds for future success have vastly diminished.

Figure 5-1 shows the results of a study using Morningstar data about the performance of active fund managers for the 12 years from 1999 to 2010. The chart depicts how an average of only 13.2% of the top 100 fund managers repeated their performance

Figure 5-1

the following year. In the years 2000, 2008 and 2009, none of them repeated their previous year's top performance.

These variations in manager performance are a function of luck and the random rotation of the style of their fund. When a particular manager's investment style is rewarded by the market, that manager is often credited with brilliance and skill. As market conditions change, however, so does the performance of fund managers. Figures 5-2 and 5-3 track the rankings of the top 10 mutual fund managers in a given year and subsequent time periods. These charts reveal how quickly a "top" fund manager can slide to the bottom. For example, Figure 5-2 shows that the ProFunds UltraJapan Inv A had the highest performance out of 5,629 mutual funds in 2005. In 2006, however, the fund slipped to 2,320th place. Investors found themselves at the bottom in 2007 when the fund slipped to 6,744 out of 6,765. The data contained in these two figures reveal many other examples of fund performance that sharply declined.

Top-performing funds in 2005 also failed to maintain their position throughout a subsequent 4-year period. As Bob Dylan said, "the first ones now will later be last, for the times they are a changin."[57]

An analysis of the Morningstar database of 204 mutual funds with 10 years of returns is shown in Figure 5-4. The top graph shows the performance rankings of these 204 funds from best to worst (left to right) for the first 5-year period from 2001 to 2005. Then the same order of fund rankings is maintained in the bottom graph in order to see if fund performance was repeated in the years 2006 to 2010. Based on the above studies,

Figure 5-2

2005 Top Ten Managers and Subsequent Performance

6 Years (1/1/2005 - 12/31/2010)

Fund Name	Annual Rankings 2005	2006	2007	2008	2009	2010
ProFunds UltraJapan Inv A	1	2,320	6,744	7,106	5,805	7,243
ING Russia A	2	7	250	7,103	20	566
Nationwide Glbl Nat Res A	3	988	150	6,284	989	5,186
Guinness Atkinson Glb Eng	4	3,415	79	6,197	378	2,288
T.Rowe Price Latin America	5	15	36	6,937	35	1,899
T.Rowe Price Em EurMedi	6	156	297	7,119	23	194
Matthews Korea	7	2,587	677	6,807	388	1,369
Black Rock Glb Res Inv A	8	4,576	220	6,833	178	608
iShares SP Latin 40	9	54	38	6,325	81	3,594
Fidelity Latin America	10	35	72	6,896	78	2,045
Total Number of Mutual Funds:	5,629	6,122	6,765	7,770	7,646	7,950

Source: Morningstar Principia 2010, Universe limited to distinct portfolios.

Figure 5-3

2006 Top Ten Managers and Subsequent Performance

5 Years (1/1/2006 - 12/31/2010)

Fund Name	Annual Rankings 2006	2007	2008	2009	2010
Dreyfus Prem Grt China A	1	16	6,960	31	4,290
iShares FTSE/Xinhua China	2	21	6,393	905	6,320
Oberweis China Opp	3	19	7,063	17	2,107
Old Mutual Cl Fn China A	4	39	6,279	332	4,323
JHancock Grt China Opp A	5	41	6,815	483	4,348
Columbia Grt China A	6	20	6,630	489	3,006
ING Russia A	7	250	7,103	20	566
Nationwide China Opp A	8	7	6,948	414	515
AllianceBer Grt China97Ad	9	30	6,922	497	4,540
Matthews China	10	9	6,519	166	2,539
Total Number of Mutual Funds:	6,122	6,765	7,770	7,646	7,950

Source: Morningstar Principia 2010, Universe limited to distinct portfolios.

it should come as no surprise that many of the managers who outperformed their peers in the first 5-year period did not do so in the second 5-year period, and vice versa.

Another tracking mechanism that can cause confusion is the reporting of mutual fund returns, often inflated when compared to actual long-term returns. The discrepancy arises from neglecting to account for funds that have closed or merged, resulting in the higher average returns of only surviving funds included in calculations. When funds go under, their records are stricken from databases, creating a survivorship bias. This

Figure 5-4

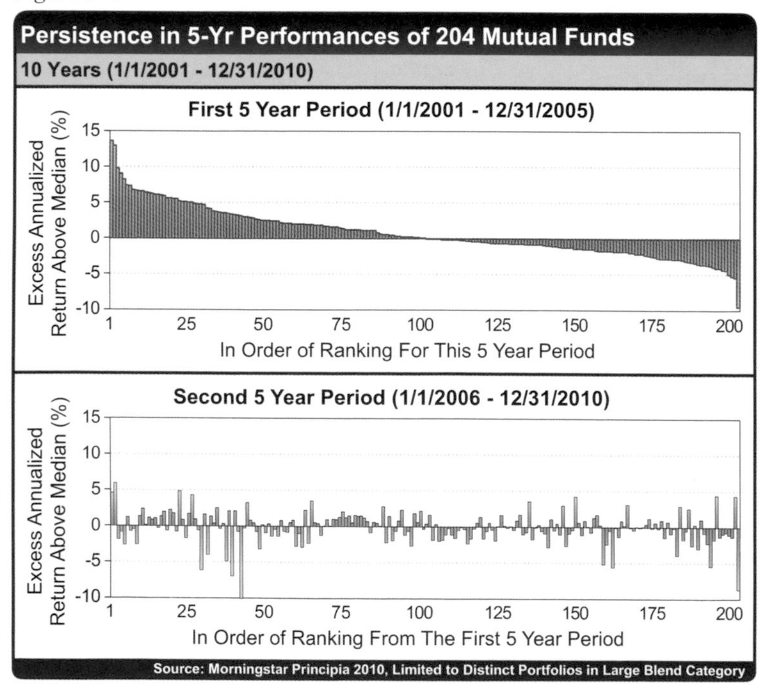

bias inflates the remaining funds' average returns by 19% of the return, according to the Center for Research on Securities Prices (CRSP). Out of the 44,888 mutual funds in CRSP's database from 1962 to 2010, 17,565 of them went under—an astounding 39%.

The Fired Beat The Hired

Even large institutions and pension plans chase performance, much to their detriment. A study conducted by Amit Goyal of Emory University and Sunil Wahal of Arizona State University found that manager hiring and firing decisions made by consultants, board members and trustees were a waste of time and money.

The study, "The Selection and Termination of Investment Management Firms by Plan Sponsors,"[58] reveals the negative impact of manager picking. Goyal and Wahal analyzed hiring and firing decisions made by approximately 3,700 plan sponsors, representing public and corporate pension plans, unions, foundations, and endowments. Figure 5-5 shows the results of hiring 8,755 managers over a 10-year period from 1994 through 2003. Note that investment manager performance is measured by average annualized excess returns over a benchmark. The chart illustrates that managers that were hired had outperformed their benchmarks by 2.91% over the three years before being hired. However, over the following three years the managers on average underperformed their benchmarks by 0.47% per year when adjusted for management fees and transition costs. Plan sponsors often proceeded to fire managers who had underperformed in favor of other recent top performers, only to repeat the cycle

Figure 5-5

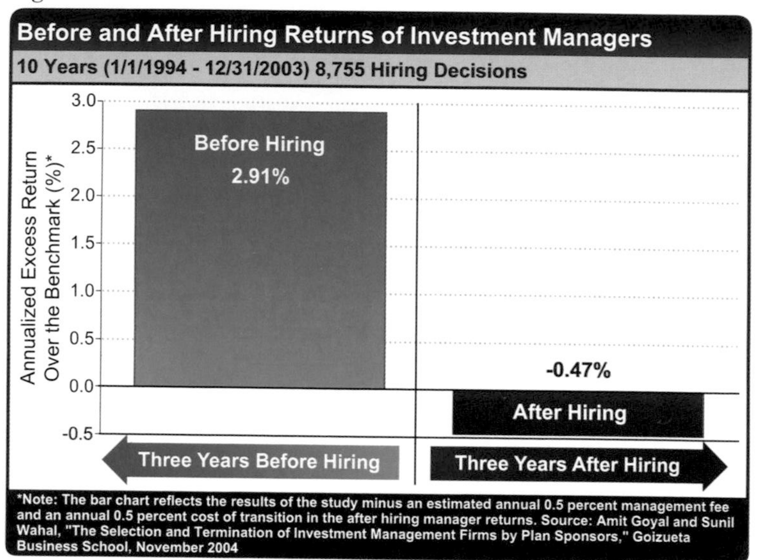

again. The study concluded, "In light of such large transaction costs and positive opportunity costs, our results suggest that the termination and selection of investment managers is an exercise that is costly to plan beneficiaries."

Using data from the same study by Goyal and Wahal, Figure 5-6 also conveys the tendency for investment committees or plan sponsors to hire investment managers with a history of above-benchmark returns and fire managers with lower performance. The chart shows that after managers were hired, their post-hiring excess returns were indistinguishable from zero, and the managers that were fired actually performed better than the hired managers. The plan sponsors should have just bought index funds and forgotten about manager picking in the first place.

Figure 5-6

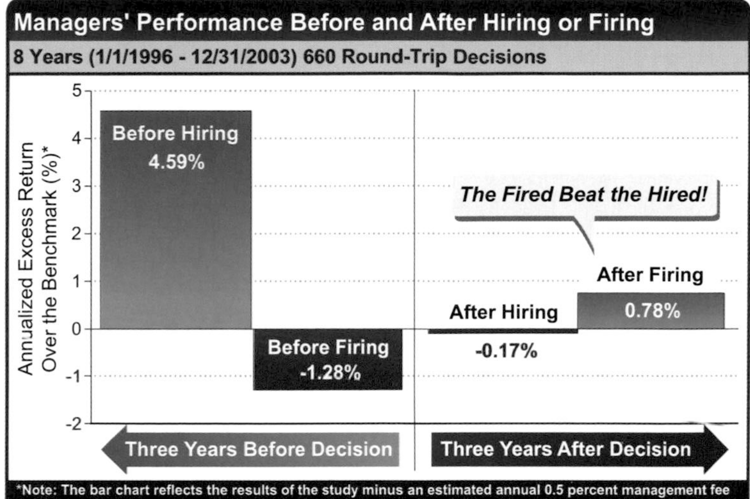

Pension-Gate

In the 2009 edition of *Pioneering Portfolio Management: An Unconventional Approach to Institutional Investment*,[59] Yale Endowment Chief Financial Officer David Swensen states, "Active management strategies, whether in public markets or private, generally fail to meet investor expectations." However, "In spite of the daunting obstacles to active management success," he continues, "the overwhelming majority of market participants choose to play the loser's game."

Despite Swensen's admonition, active manager selection and termination remains a common practice among state and municipal pension plans. Plan sponsors rely on investment consultants to recommend fund managers whom they anticipate will deliver above benchmark returns. Because these consultants are paid to conduct searches for winning managers, they are inherently conflicted, likely finding it difficult to advise their clients to abandon the losing game of active management and opt instead for a passive portfolio. Might these consultants know too well that their presumed necessity would fade away once plan sponsors embrace the merits of low-cost passive investing? As Upton Sinclair so keenly observed, "It is difficult to get a man to understand something when his salary depends upon his not understanding it."[60]

An investigative journalist for *St. Petersburg Times*, approached Index Funds Advisors (IFA) and a handful of other investment experts to collect some in-depth analysis of the risks and returns of the Florida State Pension Plan for various periods of time relative to various index portfolio strategies. The research results were revealed in a July 31, 2011 article titled, "Easy investments beat state's expert pension planners,"[61] which concluded that a simple index portfolio would have outperformed the Florida state pension plan's investment performance over the last ten years.

"The professionally managed SBA [State Board of Administration] performed worse—by more than a percentage point—than seven index-fund portfolios for the decade ending Dec. 31, 2010," the article reports. "On average, a $100 investment in an index portfolio grew to $184, while Florida's pension delivered just $157," the reporter concluded.

The findings prompted further query for IFA. If Florida's $124 billion pension plan fared so poorly against the index portfolios, what about the other states? IFA has attempted to analyze the employee retirement systems in all 50 states. Data on over 40 state pension plans have been received to date, yielding similar results with varying degrees of underperformance relative to the index portfolios.

Figures 5-7 through 5-10 show the annual risk and return of various state pension plans, net of fees, compared to 7 passively managed index portfolios comprised of a blend of diversified asset allocations. A best effort was made to estimate fees in states that report returns before fees are deducted. States were analyzed for both 10 or 11-year periods and 23 or 24-year periods and were charted based on either a June 30th or December 31st year-end date. The data show only one state succeeded to outperform, albeit negligibly, relative to the index portfolios. For data sources, go to pension-gate.com.

Directors of these pension plans have access to so-called "top" money managers and investment consultants, which would lead one to believe that these plans fired their very best shots at earning above-benchmark returns, only to fall short. This analysis reveals that the widely implemented and costly process of using consultants to recommend the hiring and firing of investment managers for state pension plans has overwhelmingly delivered a negative payout relative to a risk-appropriate set of index benchmarks.

Figure 5-7 [62]

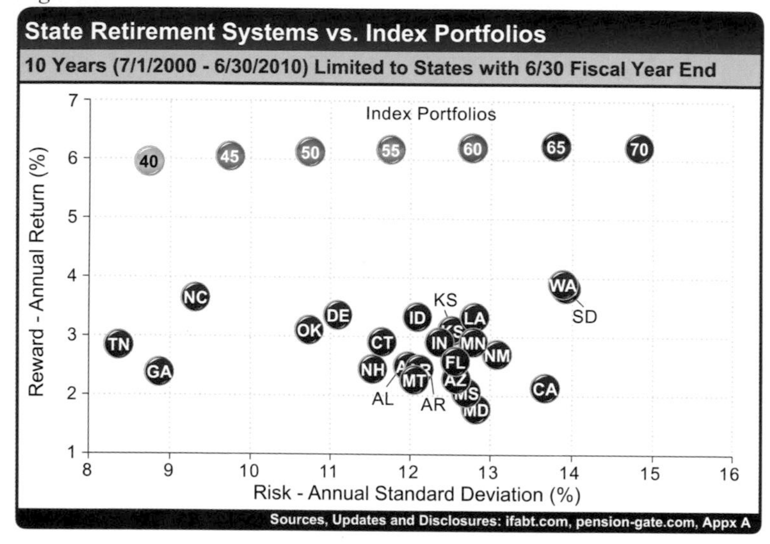

Figure 5-8 [63]

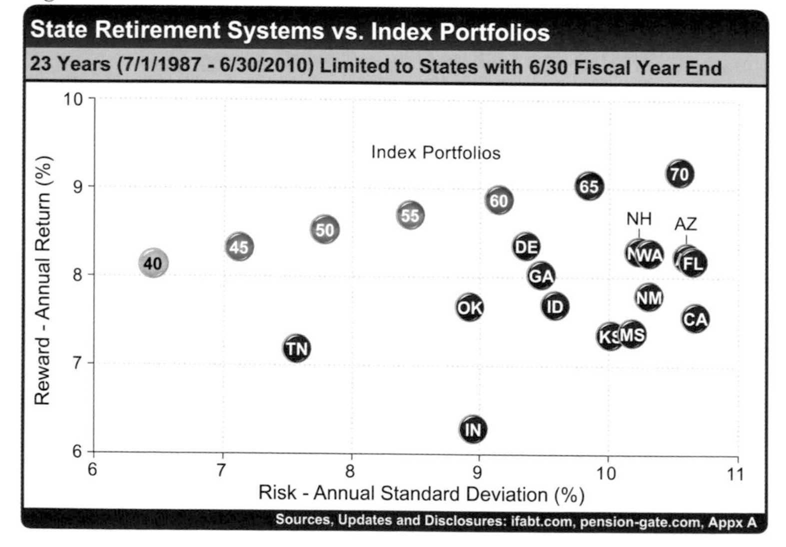

Figure 5-9 [64]

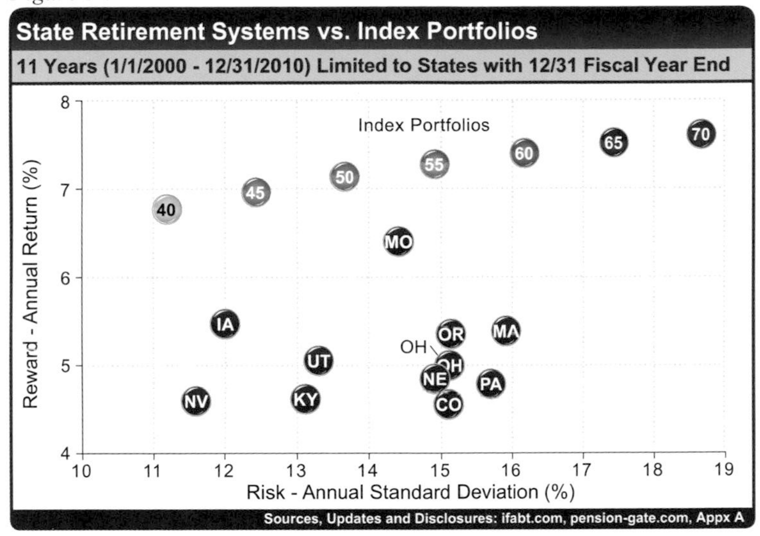

Figure 5-10 [65]

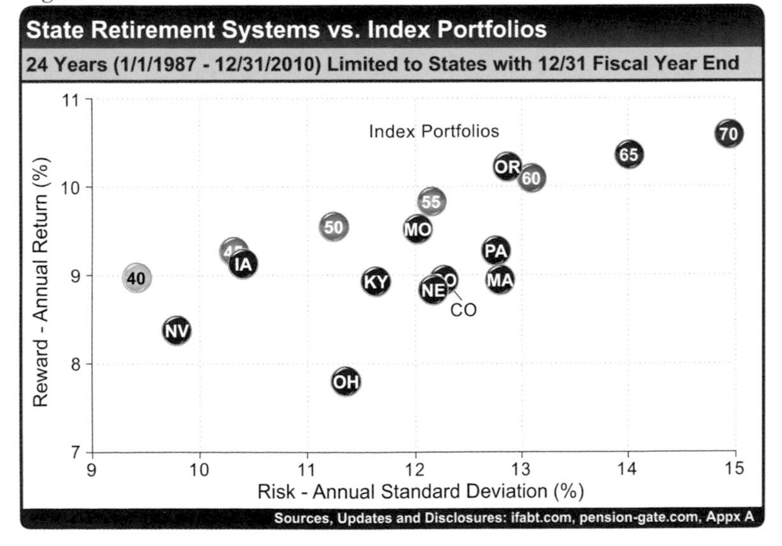

Solutions

One solution to test the claim that a manager can beat a market is to see if we have enough years of performance data to be statistically significant. A measurement called a t-stat of 2 or higher indicates that we are at least 95% confident that the manager actually earned a return higher than his benchmark due to skill, with up to a 5% chance that it was due to luck. Figure 5-11 shows the formula to calculate the number of years needed for a t-stat of 2.

The first step is to determine the excess returns the manager earned above an appropriate benchmark. Then we determine the regularity of the excess returns by calculating the standard deviation of those returns. Based on these two numbers, we can then calculate how many years we need to support the manager's claim.

Using the study previously shown in Figure 3-5 as an example, 614 mutual funds were compared to their risk-appropriate benchmarks over a 10-year period. Only 80 of the 614 fund managers had positive excess returns and only one appeared to have skill (a t-stat of 2), but when the time period was extended back to the fund's November 1991 inception, the t-stat dropped below 2, indicating that skill evaporated.

Of those 80 fund managers, the average excess return was 0.84% and the standard deviation was 5.64%. You can find the intersection of the average excess return (0.84%) and standard deviation (5.64%) in Figure 5-12, and then follow the line, concluding that 180 years of returns data are needed to establish skill as the reason for the higher returns. Obviously, no manager has ever managed a fund for 180 years; therefore, we are unable

Figure 5-11

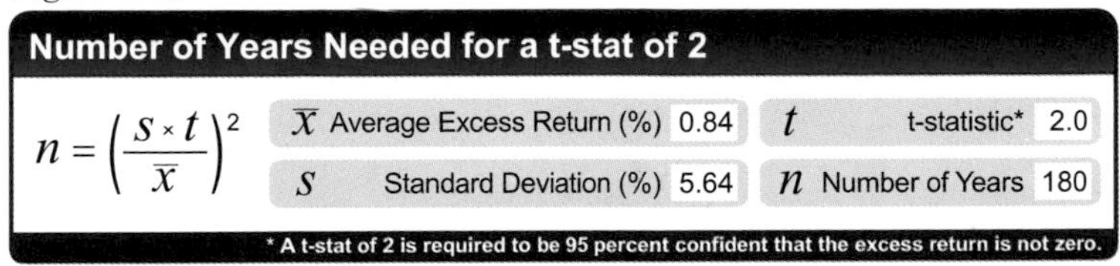

Figure 5-12

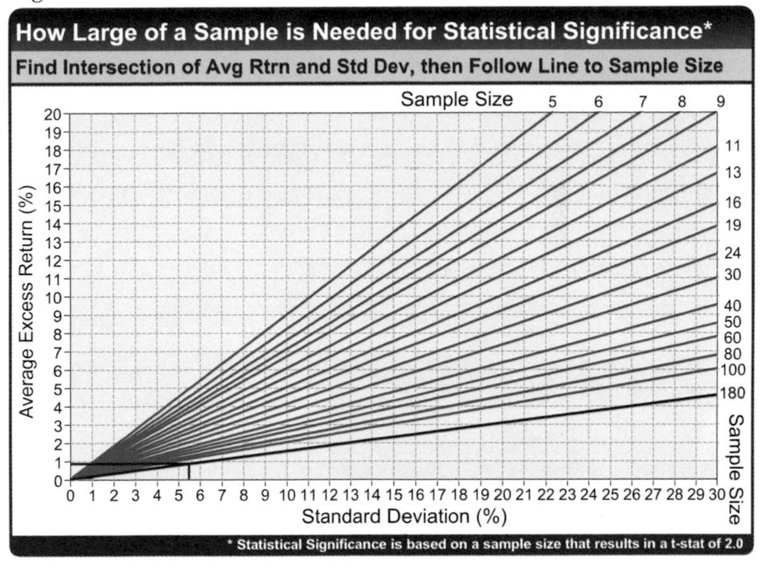

to accept the manager's claim. Alas, managers are mere mortals.

In "Challenge to Judgment," Paul Samuelson dismisses investors who claim they can find benchmark-beating managers by saying, "They always claim that they know a man, a bank, or a fund that does do better. Alas, anecdotes are not science. And once Wharton School dissertations seek to quantify the performers, these have a tendency to evaporate into the air—or, at least, into statistically insignificant t-statistics."[66]

STEP 6: STYLE DRIFTERS

"Style drift is a serious problem [for investors] because it distorts asset allocation and undermines performance when styles rotate. Value managers who have drifted over the past three years [1998–2000] toward more favored growth stocks are regretting those moves, but not as much as their [investors]."

– Ron Surz, President, PPCA Inc. "Get the Drift," 2001

"One thing is clear. Style drift happens to a sizable percentage of mutual funds.. For [investors or] planners seeking to create portfolios tapping into consistently different equity styles, style drift presents a significant concern."

– Craig L. Israelsen, Ph.D., "Drift Happens," Financial Planning Interactive, 1999

"The SEC deems it a fraud if performance results are compared to an inappropriate index, without disclosing the material differences between the index and the accounts under management."

– Robert J. Zutz, "Compliance Review," Schwab Institutional, Vol 10, Issue 8, August, 2001

Traders oughta learn from Nobel Laureates,
but they keep on makin' them long and short bets.
– The Speculation Blues

When you buy a box of Corn Flakes, you expect corn flakes in your cereal bowl. It is a safe and reasonable assumption that you are getting what you think you are buying. You know you are not buying granola or oatmeal. The name on the box is true to the box's contents.

This is not the case with Style Drifting. A style can refer to the asset class, index, market segment, or classification that a mutual fund states as its objective, described as the fund's investment purpose. When active managers engage in Style Drifting, they do not stay true to the type or name of a fund in which your money is invested. They do this by drifting from a fund's stated style into another style that no longer represents the fund's objective. For example, you may be intentionally invested in a growth fund; then unbeknownst to you, your active manager takes 30% of your large cap stock fund and puts it in cash and bonds. This changes the composition of your growth fund by altering the risk exposure, return and time horizon of your investment. The fund no longer matches its name or style. In passive investing with index funds, the name of a fund corresponds to the contents of that fund, described as "style pure."

Problems

Style Drift Alters Risk Exposure

There are different risk characteristics among the many categories of investment styles. An index or asset class is designed to carry a particular risk exposure, a key identifying factor for any fund. Market capitalization styles include large cap, mid cap, small cap, and micro cap stocks. A growth style commonly pertains to stocks that have experienced rapid growth in earnings, sales or return on equity, as well as low book-to-market ratios (BtMs). A value style, on the other hand, refers to stocks that have carried low price earnings ratios, high BtMs, and are often labeled as "distressed." Beyond these broad descriptions, funds are sorted into categories such as domestic, international, emerging markets, select technology, health care, energy, and others.

No industry-wide standards exist for defining these terms, making it hard for proper benchmarks to define what constitutes value, growth, large cap, small cap, international, or emerging market stocks. To make matters even more difficult, carefully crafted fund prospectuses give active fund managers significant leeway to deviate from their fund's stated investment style. As a result, companies with divergent risk and return characteristics are often lumped together into the same style.

Style Picking

When active fund managers assume their fund's investing style will underperform, they often abandon their stated strategies to chase the returns of other investment styles. For example, when small company fund managers project a slump in small company stocks, they may start buying large cap stocks in hopes of beating small cap benchmarks. Multiple studies, including one by Standard and Poor's[67] revealed that approximately 40% of actively managed funds utilize investments that do not reflect their stated objectives.

Fidelity is an example of a mutual fund company repeatedly charged with changing its investing style. In November 1998, *Boston Globe* columnists Steven Syre and Steve Bailey exposed Fidelity's Emerging Growth Fund for including giant companies like Microsoft and MCI WorldCom.[68] The SEC compelled Fidelity to change the fund's name to the Aggressive Growth Fund, along with the prospectus's spurious claim that the fund focused on smaller stocks.

The Elements Of Style

The next three charts reveal the difficulty of identifying a winning style in advance. Figure 6-1 displays the Periodic Table of Investment Returns for the 20-year period from 1991 through 2010 and shows that high and low returns of key market indexes follow no discernible pattern. Figures 6-2 and 6-3 show the same is true for the historical returns of various countries and industrial sectors. Investors who attempt to overweight or underweight specific styles based on speculation about future market movement undermine their ability to achieve the risk-adjusted returns that result from maintaining a proper asset allocation made up of a consistent blend of investment styles.

Figure 6-1

Annual Returns of 13 Indexes

20 Years (1/1/1991 - 12/31/2010)

← Highest — Sorted by Annual Returns — Lowest →

Year													
1991	EM 69%	SC 48%	SV 45%	EV 40%	LC 33%	LV 31%	ES 25%	RE 23%	5F 13%	IV 10%	1F 9%	IS 5%	ISV 4%
1992	SV 31%	SC 20%	RE 15%	LV 14%	ES 9%	LC 7%	5F 6%	1F 5%	EM 3%	EV -5%	IV -11%	IS -21%	ISV -22%
1993	EV 106%	ES 90%	EM 89%	ISV 45%	IV 40%	IS 34%	SV 23%	RE 19%	LV 17%	SC 14%	5F 12%	LC 10%	1F 4%
1994	IS 14%	EV 14%	ISV 8%	IV 9%	1F 2%	ES 3%	LC 1%	SV 1%	SC -1%	LV -5%	5F -4%	RE -8%	EM -11%
1995	LV 38%	LC 37%	SV 31%	SC 30%	5F 16%	RE 12%	IV 12%	1F 8%	EM 2%	ISV 1%	IS 0%	EV -8%	ES -10%
1996	RE 34%	SV 24%	LC 23%	LV 20%	SC 18%	EM 11%	EV 12%	5F 11%	IV 8%	1F 6%	ES 5%	IS 2%	ISV 1%
1997	LC 33%	SV 33%	LV 28%	SC 24%	RE 19%	5F 8%	1F 6%	IV -3%	EV -16%	EM -19%	ES -22%	ISV -23%	IS -24%
1998	LC 29%	IV 15%	LV 12%	IS 8%	5F 8%	ISV 5%	1F 6%	EV -1%	SV -3%	ES -4%	SC -6%	EM -9%	RE -15%
1999	ES 85%	EV 84%	EM 72%	SC 25%	IS 22%	LC 21%	ISV 19%	IV 16%	SV 13%	1F 5%	LV 5%	5F 4%	RE -2%
2000	RE 28%	SV 25%	LV 10%	1F 7%	5F 7%	SC 2%	IV 0%	ISV -3%	IS -5%	LC -9%	EM -29%	ES -32%	EV -34%
2001	SV 18%	RE 13%	SC 13%	1F 6%	5F 6%	LV 4%	EV -1%	ES -3%	ISV -5%	EM -7%	IS -11%	LC -12%	IV -15%
2002	5F 10%	ISV 6%	RE 4%	1F 4%	IS 2%	ES 0%	EV -2%	IV -9%	EM -9%	SV -10%	LV -15%	SC -19%	LC -22%
2003	EV 76%	ES 73%	ISV 66%	EM 60%	IS 59%	SV 54%	SC 51%	IV 50%	RE 36%	LV 34%	LC 28%	5F 3%	1F 2%
2004	EV 40%	ISV 35%	RE 32%	IS 31%	EM 30%	ES 29%	IV 29%	SV 25%	LV 18%	SC 18%	LC 11%	5F 3%	1F 1%
2005	EV 31%	EM 30%	ES 26%	ISV 23%	IS 22%	IV 15%	RE 13%	LV 10%	SV 9%	SC 6%	LC 5%	1F 2%	5F 2%
2006	ES 37%	EV 38%	RE 35%	IV 34%	EM 29%	ISV 28%	IS 25%	LV 20%	SV 20%	SC 17%	LC 16%	1F 5%	5F 4%
2007	EV 46%	ES 38%	EM 36%	IV 10%	LC 5%	5F 5%	IS 6%	1F 5%	ISV 3%	LV -3%	SC -3%	SV -8%	RE -19%
2008	1F 4%	5F 4%	SV -34%	LC -37%	SC -36%	RE -40%	LV -41%	ISV -42%	IS -44%	IV -46%	EM -49%	EV -54%	ES -55%
2009	ES 100%	EV 92%	EM 72%	IS 42%	ISV 40%	IV 39%	SC 36%	RE 33%	SV 32%	LV 30%	LC 27%	5F 4%	1F 2%
2010	ES 30%	SC 31%	SV 29%	IS 24%	RE 24%	EV 22%	EM 22%	LV 20%	ISV 18%	LC 15%	IV 11%	5F 5%	1F 1%

LC U.S. Large Company; LV U.S. Large Value; SC U.S. Small Company; SV U.S. Small Cap Value; RE Real Estate Securities; IV Int'l Value; IS Int'l Small Cap; ISV Int'l Small Cap Value; EM Emg. Market; EV Emg. Market Value; ES Emg. Market Small; 1F One-Year Fixed Income; 5F Five-Year Global Fixed Income

Sources, Updates, and Disclosures: ifabt.com, Appx A

Figure 6-2

Annual Returns of 13 Country Indexes

16 Years (1/1/1995 - 12/31/2010)

← Highest — Sorted by Annual Returns — Lowest →

Year													
1995	USA 38%	SWE 34%	GBR 21%	CAN 19%	DEU 17%	FRA 15%	AUS 12%	JPN 1%	CHE -3%	BRA -19%	CHN -21%	RUS -27%	IND -31%
1996	RUS 153%	BRA 43%	SWE 38%	CHN 37%	CAN 29%	GBR 27%	USA 24%	FRA 22%	AUS 18%	DEU 14%	IND -2%	CHE -14%	JPN -15%
1997	RUS 112%	USA 34%	BRA 27%	DEU 25%	GBR 23%	SWE 13%	CAN 13%	FRA 12%	IND 11%	CHE 6%	AUS -10%	JPN -24%	CHN -25%
1998	FRA 42%	USA 31%	DEU 30%	GBR 18%	SWE 15%	AUS 7%	JPN 5%	CAN -6%	IND -21%	CHE -28%	BRA -40%	CHN -42%	RUS -83%
1999	RUS 247%	IND 87%	SWE 81%	BRA 67%	JPN 62%	CAN 54%	CHE 39%	FRA 30%	USA 22%	DEU 21%	AUS 19%	CHN 13%	GBR 12%
2000	CAN 6%	FRA -4%	AUS -9%	BRA -11%	GBR -12%	USA -13%	CHE -15%	DEU -15%	IND -22%	SWE -21%	JPN -28%	RUS -30%	CHN -31%
2001	RUS 56%	AUS 3%	CHE -3%	USA -12%	GBR -14%	BRA -17%	IND -19%	CAN -20%	DEU -22%	FRA -22%	CHN -25%	SWE -27%	JPN -29%
2002	RUS 16%	IND 8%	AUS 0%	JPN -10%	CAN -13%	CHN -14%	GBR -15%	CHE -20%	FRA -21%	USA -23%	SWE -30%	BRA -31%	DEU -33%
2003	BRA 115%	CHN 88%	CHE 84%	IND 78%	RUS 76%	SWE 66%	DEU 65%	CAN 55%	AUS 51%	FRA 41%	JPN 36%	GBR 32%	USA 29%
2004	SWE 37%	BRA 36%	AUS 32%	CHE 29%	CAN 23%	IND 19%	GBR 20%	FRA 19%	DEU 17%	JPN 16%	USA 11%	RUS 6%	CHN 2%
2005	RUS 74%	BRA 57%	IND 38%	CAN 29%	JPN 26%	CHE 22%	CHN 20%	AUS 18%	SWE 11%	FRA 11%	DEU 11%	GBR 7%	USA 6%
2006	CHN 83%	RUS 56%	IND 51%	BRA 46%	SWE 45%	DEU 37%	FRA 35%	AUS 33%	GBR 31%	CHE 29%	CAN 18%	USA 15%	JPN 6%
2007	BRA 80%	IND 73%	CHN 66%	DEU 36%	CAN 30%	AUS 30%	RUS 25%	CHE 24%	FRA 14%	GBR 8%	USA 6%	SWE 1%	JPN -4%
2008	JPN -29%	CHE -35%	USA -37%	FRA -43%	DEU -45%	CAN -45%	GBR -48%	AUS -50%	SWE -49%	CHN -51%	BRA -56%	IND -65%	RUS -74%
2009	BRA 129%	RUS 105%	IND 103%	CHE 87%	AUS 77%	SWE 66%	CHN 63%	CAN 57%	GBR 43%	FRA 33%	USA 27%	DEU 27%	JPN 6%
2010	CHE 44%	SWE 35%	IND 21%	CAN 21%	RUS 19%	USA 15%	JPN 15%	AUS 15%	DEU 9%	GBR 9%	BRA 6%	CHN 5%	FRA -3%

AUS Australia; BRA Brazil; CAN Canada; CHE Chile; CHN China; FRA France; DEU Germany; IND India; JPN Japan; RUS Russia; SWE Sweden; GBR United Kingdom; USA United States

Source: http://mscibarra.com/products/indices/global_equity_indices/performance.html

Figure 6-3

Annual Returns of 9 Sector Indexes

20 Years (1/1/1991 - 12/31/2010)

← Highest — Sorted by Annual Returns — Lowest →

Year									
1991	F 63%	R 62%	H 62%	CS 45%	M 30%	T 29%	U 24%	CD 18%	E 7%
1992	CD 38%	F 31%	R 15%	T 10%	M 10%	U 8%	E 5%	CS 5%	H -15%
1993	CD 44%	F 24%	T 21%	M 17%	E 14%	U 13%	R -1%	CS -3%	H -7%
1994	T 18%	H 7%	M 6%	E 3%	CS 2%	F -4%	R -8%	U -11%	CD -15%
1995	H 57%	F 45%	T 43%	CS 36%	M 31%	U 32%	E 28%	CD 15%	R 12%
1996	F 34%	T 31%	E 27%	M 26%	CS 23%	R 19%	H 17%	CD 15%	U 7%
1997	F 70%	R 41%	H 38%	CS 32%	U 28%	CD 28%	M 24%	T 22%	E 20%
1998	T 63%	R 56%	H 38%	CD 30%	U 11%	CS 10%	F 8%	M 6%	E -2%
1999	T 81%	F 42%	M 24%	R 20%	E 20%	H -3%	CD -4%	CS -15%	U -14%
2000	U 52%	H 38%	CS 23%	E 22%	F 15%	M 1%	CD -17%	R -18%	T -38%
2001	R 12%	CD 7%	CS 0%	M -7%	E -7%	U -11%	H -12%	F -15%	T -25%
2002	CS -2%	M -7%	E -9%	CD -15%	R -22%	H -23%	U -23%	F -24%	T -38%
2003	F 49%	T 48%	CD 49%	M 33%	R 29%	E 26%	U 26%	H 22%	CS 20%
2004	E 33%	U 25%	M 16%	R 11%	CS 10%	F 10%	CD 9%	T 5%	H 0%
2005	E 34%	F 21%	U 17%	M 7%	R 5%	H 5%	CS 2%	T 1%	CD -20%
2006	F 35%	CD 22%	E 21%	U 21%	M 19%	CS 18%	T 9%	R 8%	H 8%
2007	E 32%	M 21%	U 19%	T 16%	CS 12%	H 4%	CD -3%	F -4%	R -6%
2008	H -17%	R -21%	CS -24%	U -29%	E -34%	M -41%	T -42%	CD -59%	F -59%
2009	CD 80%	T 58%	F 53%	M 35%	R 30%	CS 26%	H 21%	E 15%	U 15%
2010	CD 51%	M 26%	E 20%	CS 19%	R 17%	T 15%	U 8%	F 6%	H 5%

CS Consumer Staples
CD Consumer Discretionary
E Energy
F Financials
H Healthcare
M Manufacturing
R Retail
T Technology
U Utilities

Source: http://mba.tuck.dartmouth.edu/pages/faculty/ken.french/

Style Drifters

In the 1980s, Fidelity's Magellan fund and its then-manager Peter Lynch were touted for outpacing the S&P 500 Index. However, Lynch had achieved his big returns by concentrating 25% of the large cap blend fund's holdings in foreign stocks. In so doing, his investors were unwittingly exposed to a higher level of volatility that was not in line with their investment objectives. Magellan's returns looked good when measured against the S&P 500 Index, an inappropriate benchmark that included no foreign stocks. The appropriate benchmark for Magellan would have been a blended index of both foreign and domestic equities.

In the mid-1990s, Jeffrey Vinik took over the fund's helm. In February 1996, Vinik tinkered with Magellan's style by selling off a large share of stocks, moving 20% of the equity fund's holdings into bonds and 10% into cash equivalents. His bet that bonds and short-term marketable securities would outperform equities backfired, as equities soared to new highs and bonds fell in value. As a result, investors suffered from lower returns and higher capital gains taxes.

Figure 6-4 illustrates the style drift of Fidelity's Magellan fund from January 1, 1984. The scale on the vertical axis represents the fund's relative exposure to different styles, and the different colors represent different investing styles. In June 1995, the fund looks like a large value fund, but by February 2000, it would have been seen as a large growth fund. This shift from large value to large growth caused the fund's investors to unwittingly be exposed to risks substantially different from what they might have planned.

Figure 6-4

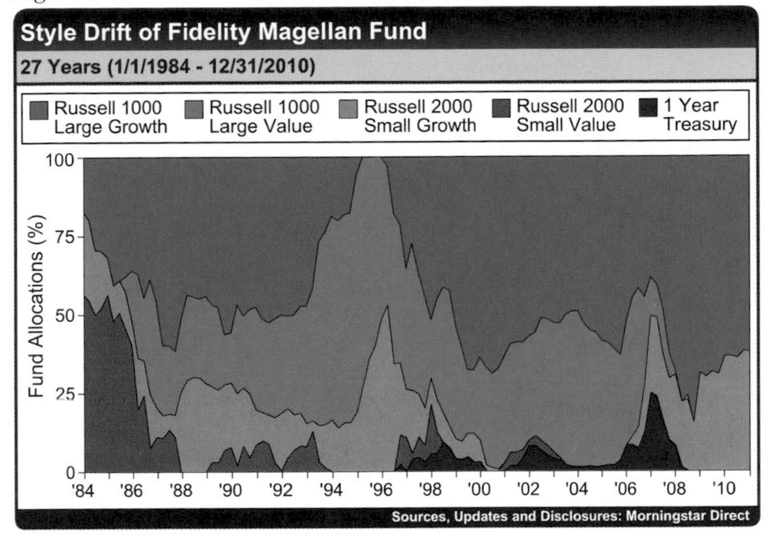

One way to analyze style drift is to measure the exposure to different indexes at sequential times. Figure 6-5 displays the style drift of the Vanguard Explorer Fund, which is designated by Vanguard as a small growth fund. The scale on the left designates the relative exposure to different styles. Note that the orange zone is a small growth index, and the brown is a small value index. The fund experienced a spike in exposure to small value in the early 1990's, shifting it away from its original allocation and altering its risk exposure for its investors.

Similarly, Figure 6-6 illustrates the style drift of the Growth Fund of America, which is designated as a large growth fund. Note the lack of style consistency as the various indexes in the fund seem to move up and down like a roller coaster. Both of these funds did not stay true to their identity.

Figure 6-5

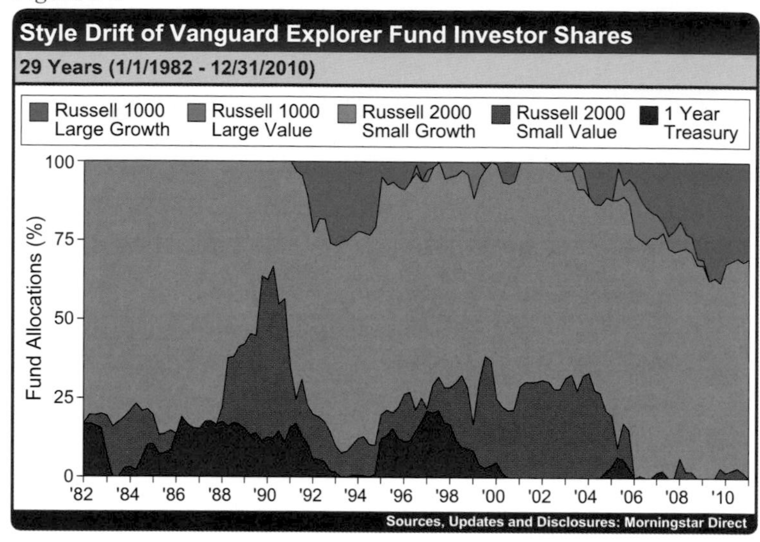

Figure 6-6

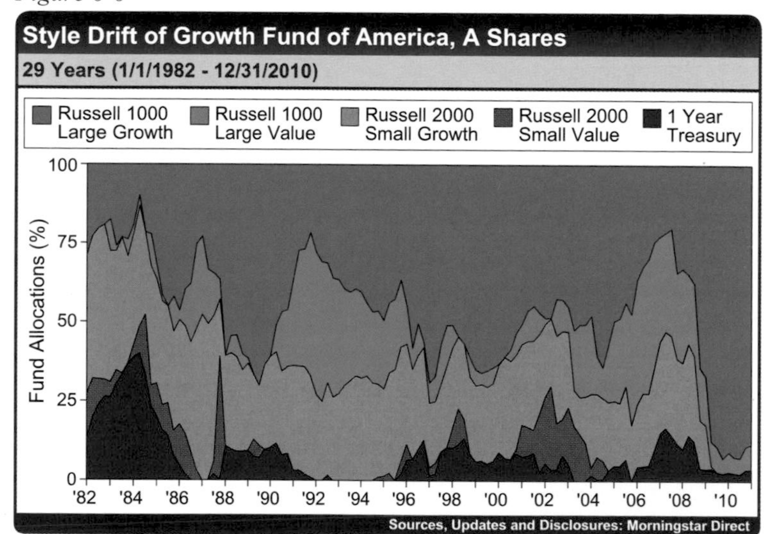

Solutions

Style Purity

There is a stark contrast between the loose style definitions held by actively managed mutual funds and the strict definitions used by indexers. Indexes are created according to specific criteria, allowing for accurate tracking and prevention of style drift. Figure 6-7 shows the style purity of a large company index over a 27-year period. In contrast to the drift of Fidelity's Magellan Fund, the index maintained relatively constant exposure to large growth and large value equities over the entire period.

The "Standard & Poor Indices versus Active Funds Scorecard"[69] (SPIVA®) is a report that provides information on the consistency or "persistence" of funds staying true to

Figure 6-7

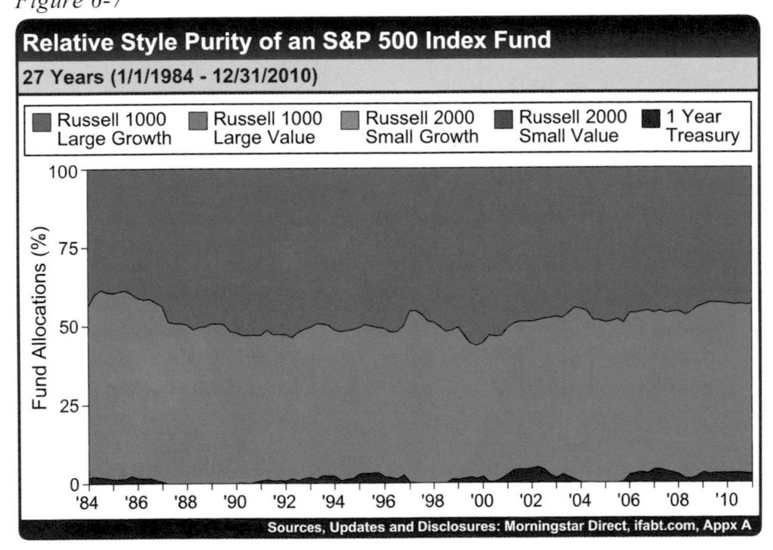

their styles. Data from the 2010 report is shown in Figure 6-8, revealing the inconsistency or lack of persistence in the list of funds from 2006 to 2010. When considering how to minimize style drift and maximize returns, investors should look beyond nebulous fund labels. Instead, they should carefully read all prospectuses and other available material to determine if a fund has a history of adhering to its stated investment style. Because passively managed index funds adhere to their styles, they provide investors with consistent risk exposure and the assurance that their funds will stay pure and true to their purpose.

Figure 6-8

Style Consistency Data from SPIVA

5 Years (1/1/2006 - 12/31/2010)

Fund Category	No. of Funds at Start	Survived the Period (%)	Style Consistency (%)
All Domestic Funds	2,077	75.59	50.89
All Large Cap Funds	668	72.90	57.04
All Mid Cap Funds	353	75.92	45.04
All Small Cap Funds	457	78.12	57.77
All Multi Cap Funds	599	76.46	42.24
Large Cap Growth Funds	200	66.00	58.50
Large Cap Blend Funds	269	70.63	51.30
Large Cap Value Funds	199	82.91	63.32
Mid Cap Growth Funds	168	67.86	48.81
Mid Cap Blend Funds	100	79.00	46.00
Mid Cap Value Funds	85	88.24	36.47
Small Cap Growth Funds	183	71.04	56.28
Small Cap Blend Funds	191	83.25	64.40
Small Cap Value Funds	83	81.93	45.78
Multi Cap Growth Funds	132	73.48	37.12
Multi Cap Core Funds	312	77.88	47.76
Multi Cap Value Funds	155	76.13	35.48
Real Estate Funds	77	87.01	87.01

Source: SPIVA Scorecard Year-End 2010

Tactical Asset Allocation

Tactical asset allocation refers to the practice of changing the composition of a portfolio based on market conditions. An example would be selling a portion of the portfolio's bonds and buying stocks when the earnings yield on stocks has risen above a benchmark interest rate. Of course, the parties on the other side of these trades are well aware of these changed market conditions, so the prices paid and received by the tactical allocator are fair and impart no expectation of an additional risk-adjusted return. Figure 6-9 displays the results of a study of the 18 mutual funds with a 20-year record based on tactical asset allocation as of June 30, 2011. As the chart shows, only three funds plot above the line of index portfolios. While 3 of 18 (16.7%) is rather

Figure 6-9

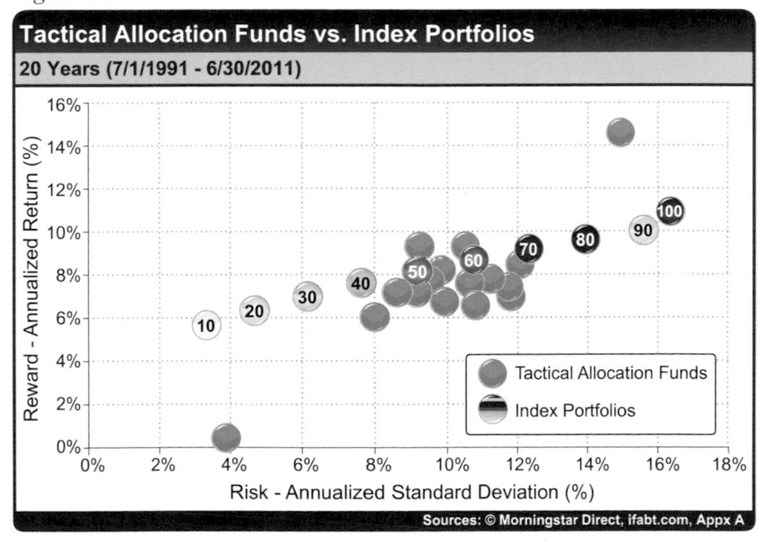

dismal to begin with, the true percentage is much lower because we are only looking at funds that survived for the last 20 years. An investor who chose a tactical allocation fund 20 years ago had a very small chance of both keeping the same fund and beating a risk-appropriate allocation of index funds.

Bottom Line

Wise investors avoid the pitfalls of style drift in two different ways. First, they resist the temptation to overweight or underweight asset classes that may be touted or spurned based on speculation or hype from so-called experts or the financial media at any particular time. Second, they steer clear of actively managed funds that are notorious for this style inconsistency as they also participate in this overweighting or underweighting behavior as they attempt to beat the market. Instead, wise investors avoid style drift by holding a consistent allocation of index funds appropriate to their risk capacity, allowing them the full benefits of style purity.

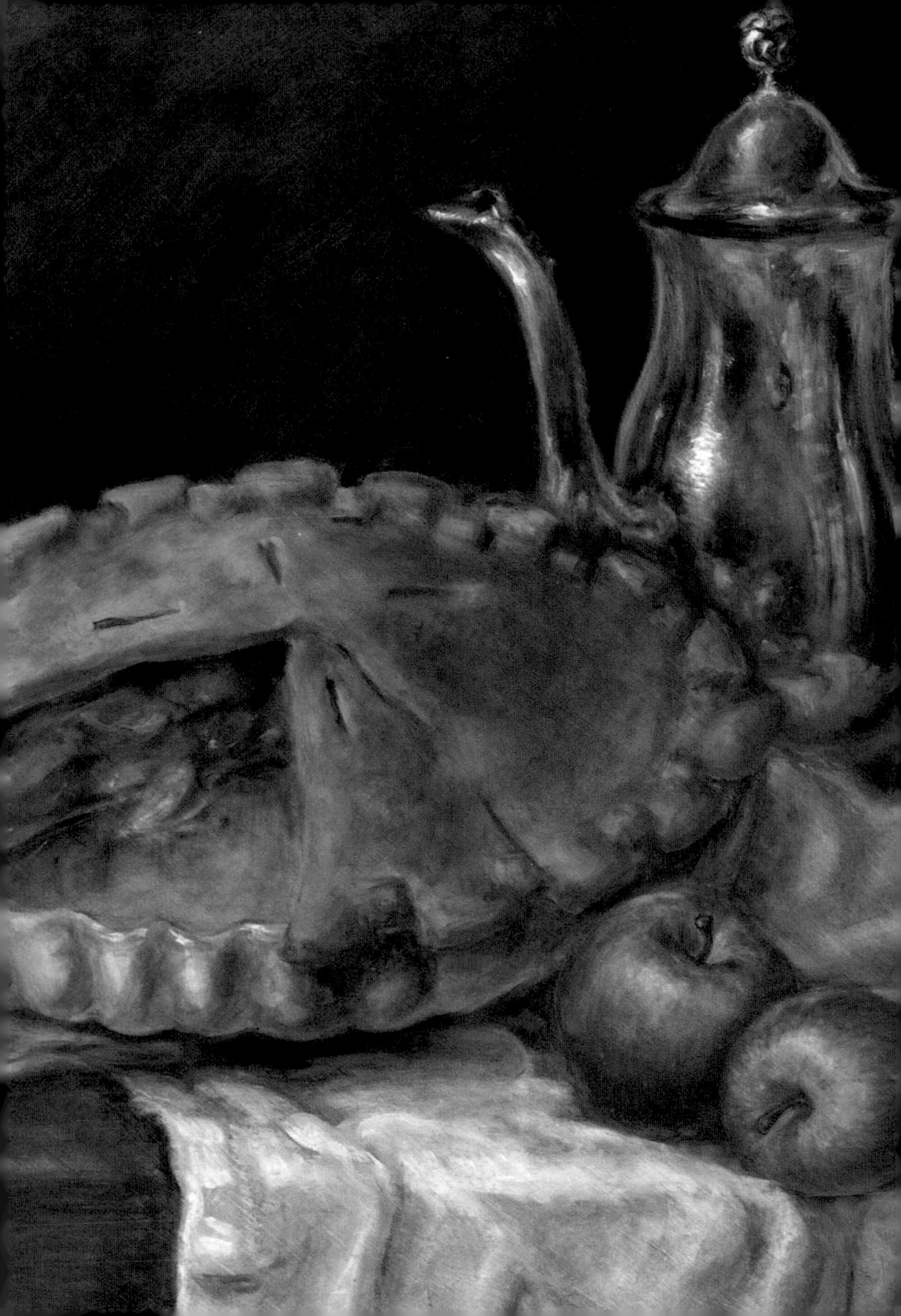

Step 7: Silent Partners

"It is difficult to systematically beat the market. But it is not difficult to systematically throw money down a rat hole by generating commissions (and other costs)."

– Michael C. Jensen, Ph.D., Harvard University, *Forbes* Magazine, 1984

"Fund returns are devastated by costs, taxes and inflation."… "The miracle of compounding returns is overwhelmed by the tyranny of compounding costs."

– John Bogle, *The Little Book of Common Sense Investing*, 2007

"For the taxable investor, indexing means never having to say you're sorry."

– William Bernstein, Ph.D., M.D., *The Intelligent Asset Allocator*, 2002

"It's not brains or brawn that matter in taxable investing; it's efficiency. Taxable investing is a loser's game. Those who lose the least—to taxes and fees—stand to win the most when the game's all over."

– James P. Garland, President, The Jeffrey Company, 1997

Silent partners are havin' a feast on most investors,
but they suck the least from savvy indexers.
– The Speculation Blues

THINK OF A TAPEWORM. It silently absorbs nutrients intended for your body's health. You may not notice what's happening at first. The tapeworm takes a little here and a little there, not being much of a bother. However, before you know it, the doctor is surgically removing a 25-foot parasite out of your intestines. A similar scenario occurs with active investing. There are silent partners sucking money out of your portfolio little by little. As they slowly siphon off fees and transfer costs, they become fatter and happier like a well-nourished tapeworm.

Silent partners are those who share in your realized or unrealized gains. In any other situation, a silent partner would provide some sort of contribution to aid in your venture, but in the case of your investments, these silent partners lurk in the shadows, adding no value. There are numerous silent partners that take a bite out of realized and unrealized gains on investments. The many sources, individuals and entities that benefit from eating away at an investor's pie of wealth are represented in the painting on the right, *The Feast.* As the family members stand idly in the background looking hungry with perplexed expressions on their faces, their wealth is voraciously consumed with greed and gluttony.

Consider these silent partners:

- The sales agent or stock broker who earns a commission or load for individual stock and mutual fund trades
- Federal and state income tax agencies that tax realized gains
- The fund manager who actively invests the stocks in a mutual fund
- Accountants
- Firms that charge investment advisory fees
- Market makers who earn a bid-ask spread on transactions
- Transfer agents who handle the share transfers for all those trades
- Mutual fund distributors
- The brokerage firm that earns interest on margin accounts

Problems

The Silent Feast

According to a 15-year study conducted by Vanguard founder John Bogle, investors kept 47% of the cumulative return of an average actively managed equity mutual fund, but they kept 87% in a market index fund, as reflected in Figure 7-1. This means $10,000 invested in the average actively managed equity fund grew to $49,000 versus $90,000 in an index fund. That's a $41,000 drain that pads the pockets of the silent partners in the form of transaction costs, sales commissions, expense ratios, taxes, and cash drag (cash that is unnecessarily carried in a portfolio which can negatively affect performance because the mutual fund or portfolio is not optimally invested).

Figure 7-1

Taxes

A later study[70] by Bogle analyzed the returns and tax implications of the average equity investor vs. an investor in an S&P 500 Index Fund. Figure 7-2 details the end results for the 25 years from January 1, 1981 to December 31, 2005. The chart shows that $10,000 invested in the average managed equity fund would have grown to post-tax results of only $71,700.

Figure 7-2

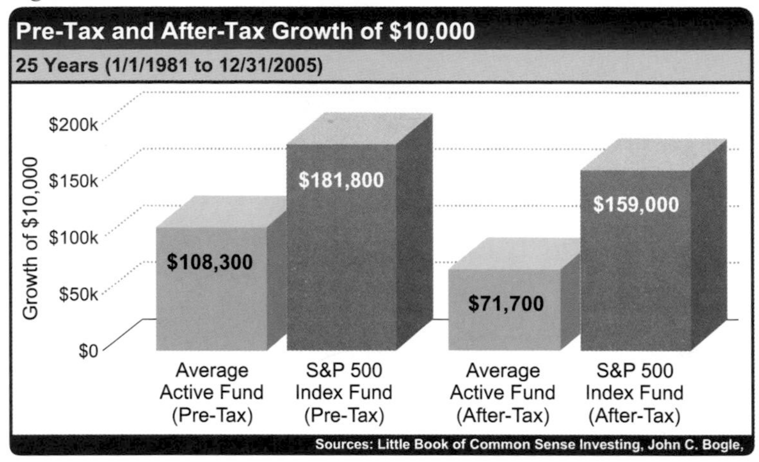

The same amount invested in the S&P 500 Index Fund would have grown to a much larger post-tax sum of $159,000.

Figure 7-3 further reveals the contrast between the post-tax returns of both Vanguard index funds and their respective Morningstar categories. From October 1996 through September 2011, a $100,000 investment in the Vanguard 500 Index Fund lost only $13,593 to taxes, while the Morningstar Large Blend category lost $31,395, a $17,802 difference. Looking at another index at the bottom of the chart, the Vanguard Total International Index Fund lost $14,713 to taxes, while the Morningstar Foreign Large Blend category lost $27,759, a $13,046 difference. Note that the annualized returns for the Morningstar categories are upwardly biased due to the impact of survivorship bias. Such contrasts in taxes reveal why passive investing with index funds makes for one very sad Uncle Sam, as seen in the next painting.

Figure 7-3

Value Lost to Taxes: Index Funds with 15 Years of Data				
15 Years (10/1/1996 - 9/30/2011)				
Fund/Category	Pre-Tax Annualized Return	Post-Tax Annualized Return	Difference	Value Lost to Taxes on $100,000
Vanguard 500 Index Investor	5.15%	4.69%	0.46%	$13,593
Morningstar Large Blend	4.87%	3.71%	1.16%	$31,395
Vanguard Value Index Inv	5.16%	4.10%	1.06%	$29,929
Morningstar Large Value	5.01%	3.43%	1.58%	$42,322
Vanguard Small Cap Index Inv	6.58%	5.52%	1.06%	$36,224
Morningstar Small Blend	7.14%	5.56%	1.58%	$56,229
Vanguard Total Intl Stock Index Inv	3.71%	3.09%	0.61%	$14,713
Morningstar Foreign Large Blend	3.48%	2.23%	1.25%	$27,759

Source: © Morningstar Direct

Turnover Is Costly In Taxable Accounts

A number of studies show the average active mutual funds have high turnover rates, creating tax liabilities that erode returns. Figure 7-4 shows just how carried away fund managers can get with buying and selling equities. The Prasad Growth Fund had 598% turnover in 2010, as compared to the Schwab S&P 500 Index at 3% turnover.

In another study analyzing trading between 1963 and 1992, researchers at Stanford University determined a passively invested dollar would have grown to $21.89 in a tax-deferred account such as an IRA. In contrast, they found a dollar invested by a high tax-bracket individual in an actively managed fund, in a taxable account, grew to just $9.87, almost 55% less! Passive index fund managers minimize portfolio turnover, thereby maximizing unrealized capital gain, and tax-managed index funds virtually eliminate short term capital gains.

Figure 7-4

Turnover Ratio of Various Funds	
1 Year (1/1/2010 - 12/31/2010)	
Fund Name	**Turnover Ratio**
Schwab S&P 500 Index	3%
Vanguard 500 Index Investor	12%
DFA US Small Cap Value I	21%
DFA US Large Cap Value I	29%
Fidelity Magellan	39%
Fidelity Contrafund	58%
Vanguard Windsor Adm	61%
Fidelity Growth & Income	98%
Brandywine	225%
Prasad Growth	598%

Source: Morningstar Principia

Inflation

Unlike investment costs and taxes, nothing can be done about inflation. Inflation is an equal opportunity destroyer of an individual's purchasing power. Inflation has averaged 2.34% per year over the last ten years, which does not seem too significant. However, a 2.34% inflation rate is only negligible in the short term but is terribly erosive in the long term, with purchasing power being cut by 21% for the ten years ending December 2010 and by 39% for the 20-year period with the same ending date. A certain amount of loss from inflation is incurred whether assets are invested in stocks or bonds, but investing as large a portion of an investment portfolio in stocks as soon as possible—and for as long as possible—is the best way to outpace inflation. Stocks have grown in value more than bonds over the years and have been the best antidote for inflation.

Fees

Part of the disparity in ending wealth is due to active managers charging higher fees than passive managers as compensation for their perceived "skill." Figure 7-5 reveals the disparity in expense ratios determined from simple averages of all share classes of funds tracked by Morningstar. The figure portrays the differences of average expense ratios between actively managed funds, passively managed funds, exchange-traded funds (ETFs), and a 60% stocks/40% fixed income Index Portfolio 50. As the chart indicates, the average actively managed mutual fund is nearly twice as costly as the average passively managed mutual fund and is about four times more costly than the index portfolio. The expense ratio for the average passive mutual fund is higher than the average exchange-traded fund because the former includes high-cost index funds such as the Nationwide S&P 500 Fund.

Figure 7-5

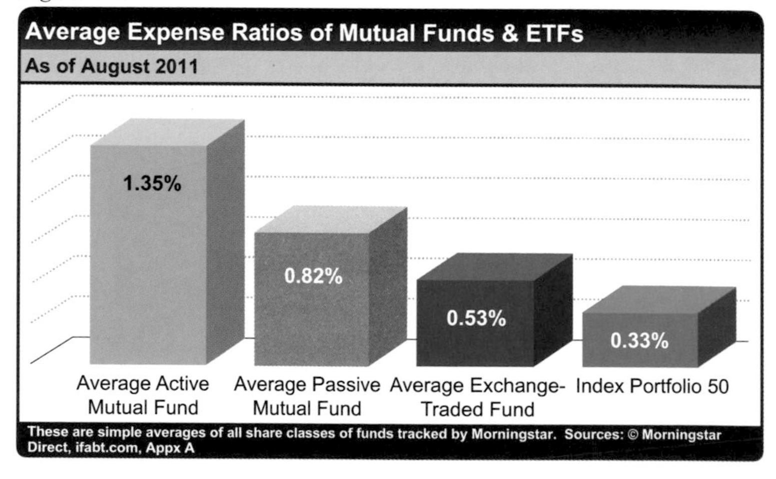

Solutions

Tax-Managed Funds

Most index funds are tax efficient by their very nature. However, some indexes can be further tax-managed to save you even more in taxes. These tax-managed index funds are very efficient at offsetting realized gains with realized losses, deferring the realization of net capital gains and minimizing the receipt of dividend income. The result is maximized unrealized capital gains that have not yet been realized for tax purposes. Taxes are not paid until a future date when withdrawals are made and the gains then become realized. The benefit is that the unrealized capital gains (profits) remain a growing part of the net asset value of a fund rather than being distributed to the investor. This tax benefit assists in overall wealth accumulation.

Minimize The Silent Partners

Buy-and-hold index funds provide an excellent opportunity to seek high returns while minimizing the negative impact of silent partners. Dimensional and Vanguard are leading providers of tax-managed index funds with offerings in many different equity categories. While fees, transaction costs and taxes eat up active investors' returns, index funds investors maximize asset growth by avoiding the major impacts of costs and taxes. No investment is completely free from silent partners, but passive investors use index funds to retain as much money as possible. Remember, it's not just what you make, it's what you keep that counts.

Step 8: Riskese

"The most important questions of life are, for the most part, really only problems of probability."

– Marquis de Laplace,
Théorie Analytique des Probabilités, 1814

"The average long-term experience in investing is never surprising, but the short-term experience is always surprising. We now know to focus not on rate of return, but on the informed management of risk."

– Charles Ellis, Ph.D.,
Investment Policy, 1985

"If your broker [or investment advisor] is not familiar with the concept of standard deviation of returns, get a new one."

– William Bernstein, Ph.D., M.D.,
The Intelligent Asset Allocator, 2000

"Odds are you don't know what the odds are."

– Gary Belsky and Thomas Gilovich,
Why Smart People Make Big Money Mistakes, 2000

"The probable is what usually happens."

– Aristotle

So before investing your hard earned green,
catch a good vibe for the variance and the mean.
– The Speculation Blues

Do you speak riskese? Citizens of Japan speak Japanese, lawyers speak legalese, and leading investment advisors, casino statisticians and insurance actuaries speak riskese. Riskese is the essential language of investing and is used to discuss topics of risk, return and time. Returns and risk go hand in hand. You cannot expect high returns without taking risk. People are perfectly comfortable talking about the returns portion of the investment process, but how squeamish do they get when they realize they may lose money on their investments? After the crash of 2008, people are far more aware of this possibility, but they are still looking for that perfect investment with small risk and big returns. People are also still looking for a weight loss pill that will allow them to continue eating country fried steak, massive cinnamon buns and ice cream on a regular basis. Neither exists.

Problems

Lack Of Understanding

One of the primary deterrents to investors earning market rates of returns is their lack of understanding of the relationship between risk and return. The natural tendency of investors is to want returns without the risk. Because risk is the source of returns, investors would be better served to be more concerned with the risk level of their investments.

The overall concept of the risk/return relationship is that when risk increases, the expected return on the asset should also increase as a result of the risk premium earned. Investors should not expect high returns on an investment if they aren't taking a high degree of risk. If you bet on last year's defending champions to win the World Series, your neighborhood bookie will give you much lower odds than if you bet on Major League Baseball's cellar dweller from last season. You are obviously taking a lot more risk by putting your money on the last place team.

Solutions

Risk Defined

Blaise Pascal

Modern finance began with the realization that risk needed to be measured and managed. In 1654, French mathematicians Blaise Pascal and Pierre de Fermat tried to predict the future outcome of a game of chance. Their questions led to Pascal's Theory of Probability, which quantifies the numerical likelihood of future events. Pascal's Triangle was the foundation for learning how to manage the uncertainty of future outcomes, such as investment returns.

Every investment carries an expected return. The risk of an investment is quantified by the degree to which the returns of the investment deviate from the average return during specific periods of time. Higher risk investments carry a wider range of short-term outcomes but also carry higher expected returns, compensating investors for withstanding short-term volatility. In contrast, investments that carry a narrow range of outcomes will provide more consistent returns in the short term with the trade-off of lower expected returns. For example, an all-bond index portfolio provides a small but consistent return, while an all-equity index portfolio provides a much greater expected return, but with erratic short-term movements. Higher expected returns are the reward for an investor's willingness to accept this volatility. In other words, risk is the source of returns and therefore should not be thought of as a dirty four letter word.

Standard Deviation Of Returns

An effective method to measure the deviation of investment returns from the average is the standard deviation of returns. Standard deviation provides a statistical measure of historical volatility and sets forth a distribution of the ranges of probable outcomes. In investing, measuring standard deviation of returns shows the extent to which returns (daily, monthly or annual) are distributed around the average return, estimating a range of probable outcomes and establishing a likely framework of risk and return trade-offs.

The normal distribution in the form of a bell-shaped curve shown in Figure 8-1 illustrates the concept of standard deviation. The curve represents the set of outcomes. In this case, let's say the outcomes are the monthly returns of an investment.

Figure 8-1

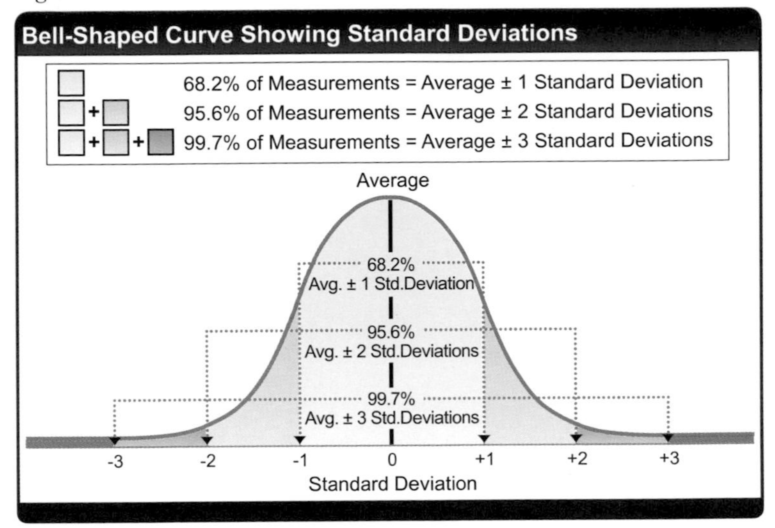

The yellow area covered in one standard deviation away from the average in both directions accounts for approximately 68% of the outcomes in a period. The area within two standard deviations from the average, the yellow and green shaded areas, accounts for 95.6% of outcomes, and the area up to three standard deviations away from the mean, illustrated by the yellow, green and orange shaded areas, accounts for 99.7% of all outcomes. The higher an investment's standard deviation, the greater the chance that future returns will lie farther away from the average return.

Francis Galton, an English mathematician who was an expert in many scientific fields, created his "Quincunx" machine to demonstrate how a normal distribution is formed through the occurrence of multiple random events. He expressed his

4 ft. 4 in.
8 ft.

Francis Galton

fascination with this phenomenon by stating, "I know of scarcely anything so apt to impress the imagination as the wonderful form of cosmic order expressed by the 'Law of Frequency of Error.' It reigns with serenity... amidst the wildest confusion. The huger the mob, and the greater the apparent anarchy, the more perfect is its sway. It is the supreme law of Unreason. Whenever a large sample of chaotic elements are taken in hand and marshalled in the order of their magnitude, an unsuspected and most beautiful form of regularity proves to have been latent all along."[71]

I recently commissioned the creation of the Probability Machine to better educate investors about the probability of outcomes that result from a series of random events. In the case of the market, the random events are news stories about a company or about capitalism in general. The random falling of the beads ultimately forms a normal distribution in the shape of a bell curve. The distribution of the beads bears a striking resemblance to the distribution of monthly returns shown in red behind the beads, also shown in Figure 8-2 which reflects 600 monthly returns (50 years) for an all-equity index portfolio. Like the Probability Machine's normal distribution, the all-equity index portfolio carries a wide range of outcomes or a high standard deviation. It maintains an approximate normal distribution that accumulates to about a 1% monthly return over the 600 months, but with a standard deviation of about 4.7%, which is a high level of short-term volatility.

Note the comparison to Figure 8-3, which shows a lower-risk index portfolio comprised of 80% fixed-income funds and 20% stocks with a narrow range of outcomes. The 100% equity index portfolio in Figure 8-2 experienced greater price swings but had higher returns. Over the simulated 50-year period, a dollar invested in the low risk index portfolio would have grown to $30.30, while a dollar invested in the higher risk index portfolio would have grown to $468.12. This historical data supports the presumption that investors who have the capacity to hold higher risks are expected to earn substantially higher returns.

Not All Risks Are Rewarded

While higher expected returns can only result from accepting increased risk, not all risks are rewarded at the same rate. Financial economists have long sought to identify the factors that explain stock market returns. With the help of CRSP, ground-breaking progress has been made. As previously mentioned in Step 2, Nobel Laureate William Sharpe presented the Capital Asset Pricing Model (CAPM), a financial model that explains approximately 70% of all stock portfolio returns. CAPM enabled investors to quantify expected returns based on how investments fluctuate relative to the market as a whole. It concluded that investments which fluctuate more than the market as a whole carry more risk than the market and therefore should also carry higher expected returns. Sharpe asserted however, that some investments carry increased risk without providing the trade-off of higher expected returns. To clarify, he divided risk into two categories: systematic and unsystematic.

Figure 8-2

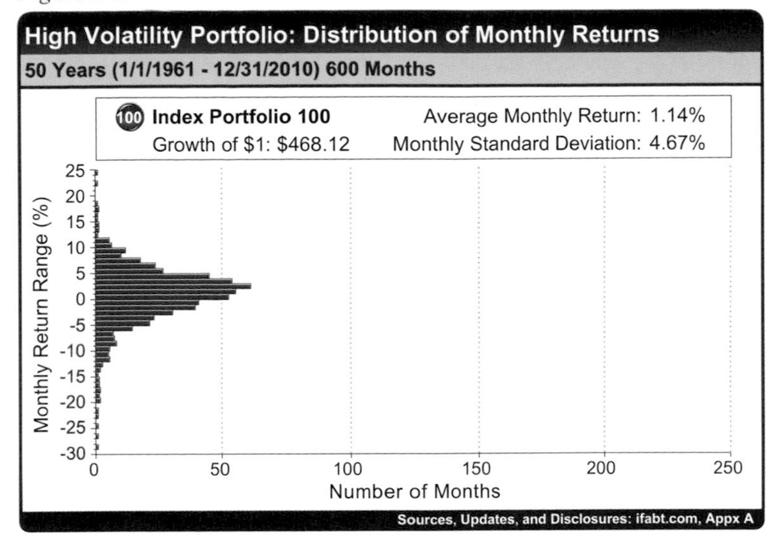

Figure 8-3

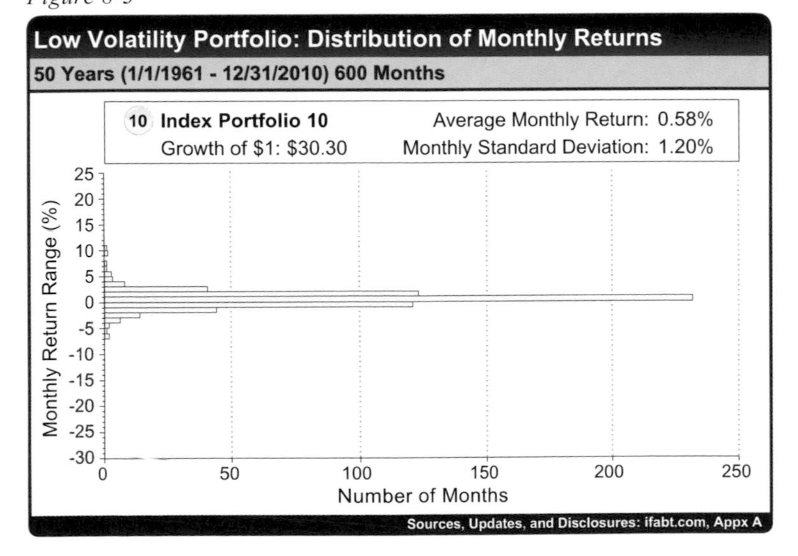

The entire market is exposed to unavoidable systematic risk, such as war, recession, inflation, and government intervention. In contrast, unsystematic risk refers to threats specific to individual companies, such as lawsuits, fraud and competition. A summary of these different risks is presented in the top portion of Figure 8-4. Systematic risk—the risk of investing in capitalism itself—has rewarded investors with an approximate 9.5% annualized return over the last 83 years. However, an investment in unsystematic risk, such as buying individual stocks, does not increase expected returns. Unsystematic risk should be avoided through diversification, thereby maximizing portfolio efficiency and returns at each level of risk.

Figure 8-5 illustrates the lack of increased expected returns when investors accept the additional concentrated and unsystematic risk of individual stocks. The additional risk of buying individual stocks is not expected to carry additional returns.

The Trade-Off Between Risk And Return

Even when all non-compensated risk has been eliminated from a portfolio, an investor cannot escape the systematic risks inherent in the market itself. As previously mentioned, history shows an investment in the market as a whole has delivered about 9.5% a year on average for the last 83 years, but not without major uncertainty. Risk and return go hand in hand. To obtain greater equity returns, the trade-off is suffering significant short-term volatility, such as investors experienced in 2008.

Figure 8-4

SYSTEMATIC RISK

- Market Wide Risk
  - War
  - Recession
  - Inflation
  - Government Intervention
- Capitalism Risk
- Non-Diversifiable
- Expected Return of Capitalism is About 9.5% Per Year

UNSYSTEMATIC RISK

- Company Specific Risk
  - Lawsuits
  - Fraud
  - Management
  - Unique Circumstances
- Unrewarded Risk
- Diversifiable
- No Additional Expected Return
- Increased Volatility
- Speculative

STOCKS
Risk Factors That Explain Returns

An investor's expected return is determined by their exposure to the five risk factors shown below.

FIXED INCOME
Risk Factors That Explain Returns

MARKET

- The stock market has higher expected returns than the risk free T-bills.
- The annual average return of the market over T-bills from 1928 to 2010 was 7.62%.

SIZE

- Stocks with low market capitalization or small companies have higher expected returns than large companies.
- The annual average return of the bottom 30% of companies over the top 30% of companies ranked by size from 1928 to 2010 was 3.30%.

VALUE

- Stocks priced closer to their book value have higher expected returns than stocks priced far above their book value.
- The less goodwill in the stock price, the higher expected returns.
- The annual average return of bottom 30% goodwill stocks over the top 30% goodwill stocks from 1928 to 2010 was 4.92%.

TERM

- Longer terms have higher yields.
- Longer terms have higher volatility.
- Terms beyond 5 years have increased volatility, but offer little increased expected returns.
- The average annual return for the term risk factor from 1928 to 2010 was 2.17%.

DEFAULT

- Lower credit ratings have higher expected returns.
- Lower credit ratings have higher volatility.
- Higher credit ratings have lower returns.
- 30-day T-bills have returns approximating inflation, i.e. zero risk = zero return.
- The average annual return for the credit risk factor from 1928 to 2010 was 0.29%.

Figure 8-5

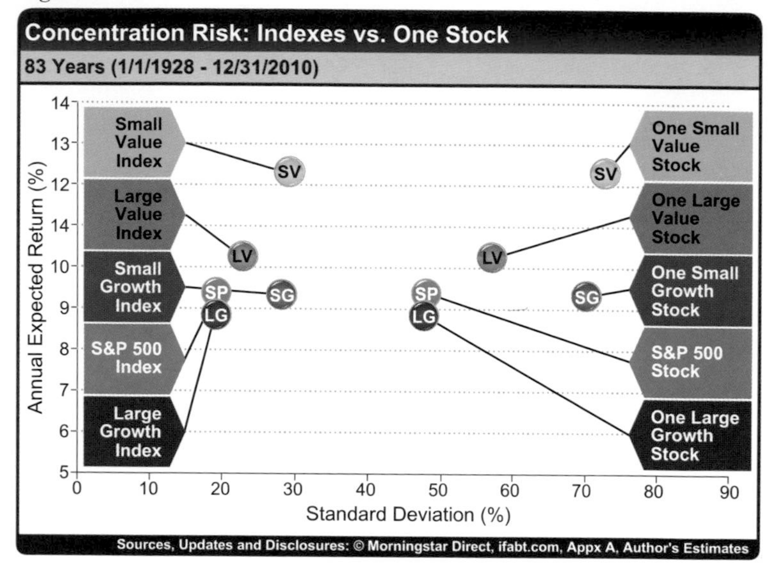

The Dimensions Of Investment Returns

Sharpe's CAPM was widely held as the explanation of equity returns until 1992 when Eugene Fama and Kenneth French introduced their Fama/French Three Factor Model, identifying Market, Size and Value as the three factors that explain as much as 97% of the returns of diversified portfolios. Fama and French analyzed the CRSP database all the way back to 1962 to determine that equity returns can be explained by a portfolio's exposure to the market as a whole, as well as the exposure to small and value companies. Their data show that small and value companies have carried higher risk and that risk has been rewarded. These small and value excess returns have been shown to carry long-term persistence, but are not consistent in short periods of time. More than 83 years of risk and return data have confirmed their results.

Fama and French later expanded their model to include Fixed Income, identifying Term and Default as two additional risk factors that explain returns for fixed income. Thus, a Five Factor Model was created, as shown in Figure 8-6.

The relationship that exists between these five risk factors and a portfolio's expected return serves as a framework for designing investment portfolios. The five risk factors are portrayed on the following pages.

Figure 8-6

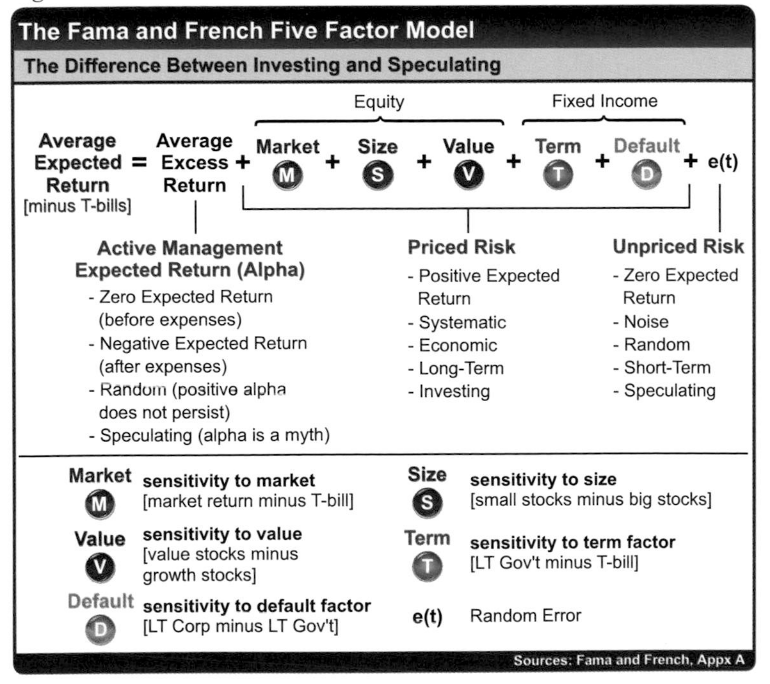

acer
vivendi
ORBIS
vodafone
IBM
Chevron
WAL★MART
HISCOX
Johnson
P&G
Allianz
Bank of
MARKET
BOEING
THE DEPARTMENT OF THE TREASURY
1789
30
25
5
20
DAYS
10
15
30 DAY T-BILLS

The Market As A Risk Factor

The first risk factor in the Fama/French Five-Factor Model is the market risk factor or the amount of an investor's exposure to the overall stock market compared to risk-free investments, such as the 30-day T-Bill. Investors take on market risk through all their different equity investments. Figure 8-6 plots the risk and return associated with the market risk factor for five allocations of the total U.S. stock market and U.S. Treasury bills. The highest market exposure, labeled 5, carries 100% exposure to the total U.S. market. The button labeled 0 is invested in 100% T-Bills. The chart reflects the differences in growth of $1 in the various market exposures over the 83-year period from January 1, 1928 through December 31, 2010.

Figure 8-6

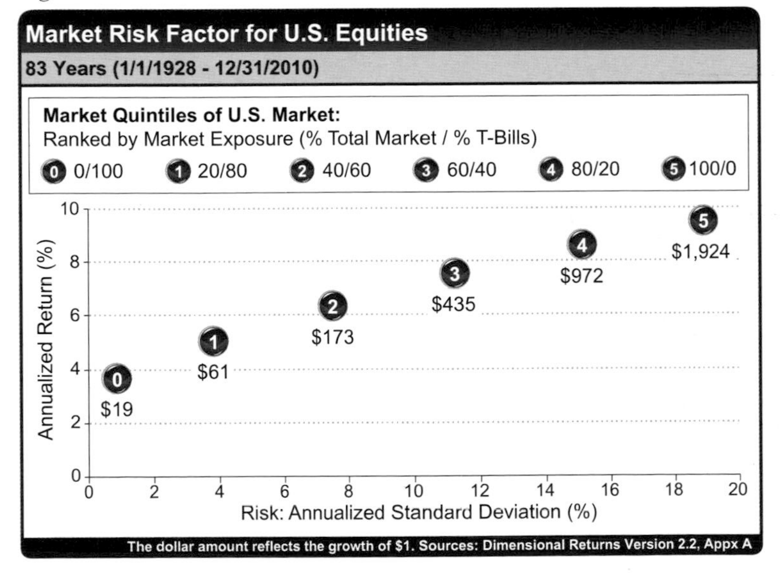

ACME

Size As A Risk Factor

The second risk factor in the Fama/French model is the size risk factor, referring to the level of a portfolio's exposure to small company stocks. Small companies are more volatile and riskier than larger companies because they have less business diversification, fewer financial resources and greater uncertainty of earnings than their large counterparts.

The image for the size factor contrasts General Electric with the small cap company Acme Packet. It is obvious that Acme is a riskier investment than GE, therefore the cost of capital for Acme and the expected return for its investors should be higher.

Figure 8-7 plots the risk and return of the S&P and U.S. companies according to size over an 83-year period.

Figure 8-7

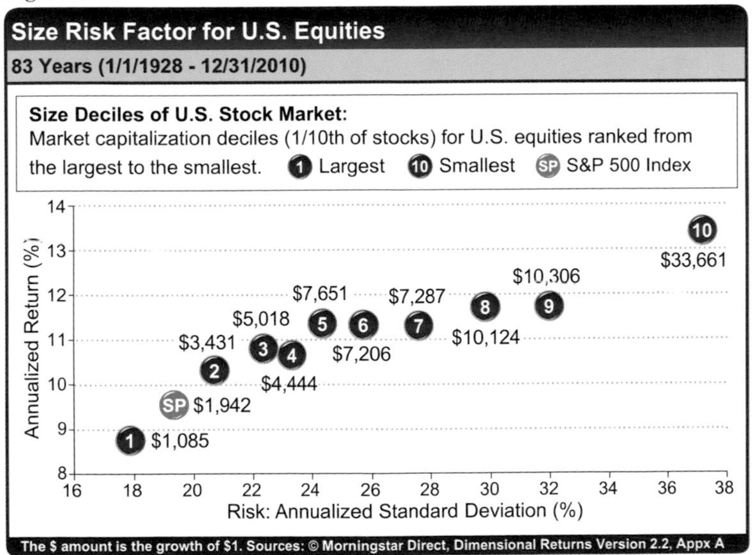

MOTOROLA
GROWTH

Hormel
SPAM
Hormel
VALUE

Value As A Risk Factor

The third risk factor in the Fama/French model is the value risk factor, which refers to the amount of a portfolio's exposure to value or low priced stocks relative to their book value. Value is measured by the book-to-market (BtM) ratio. The book value of a company is an accounting term for its net worth, its assets minus its liabilities. The market value of a company is its price per share times the number of shares outstanding. Stocks with higher BtM ratios are considered value stocks while stocks with lower BtM ratios are considered growth stocks. Figure 8-8 plots the risk and return characteristics of the value risk factor for the five quintiles of the U.S. stock market from 1928 to 2010.

Figure 8-8

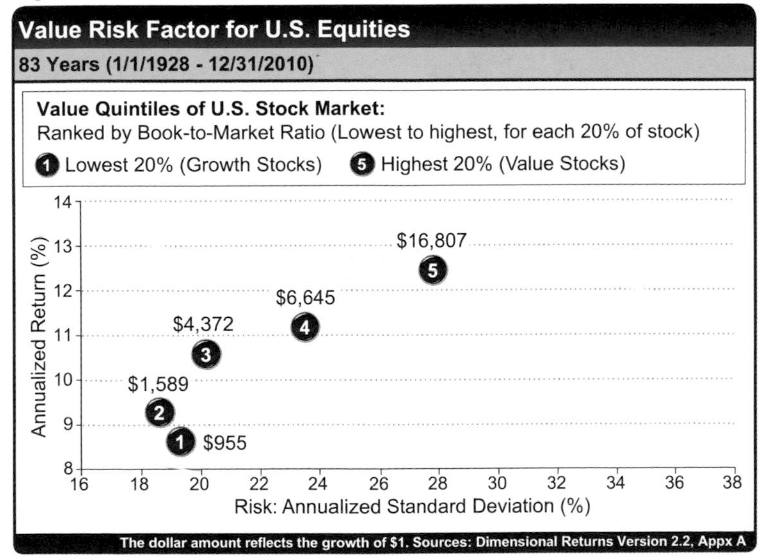

THE TREASURY DEPARTMENT
30
25
5
DAYS
20
10
15
30
25
5
YRS
20
10
15
DAYS
SHORT TERM
YEARS
LONG TERM

Term As A Risk Factor

Fixed income is also an important component to an investment portfolio. Since stocks and bonds frequently move in opposite directions, holding low-volatility bonds provides good diversification and will therefore level out a portfolio's performance by dampening stock volatility and providing short-term liquidity.

The term (maturity) risk factor refers to the difference in returns between long-term government bonds and short-term treasury bills. Longer-term bonds are riskier than shorter-term instruments and have yielded higher returns over the 83 years ending in 2010. Figure 8-9 shows six different fixed income allocations and their differences in risk and return.

Figure 8-9

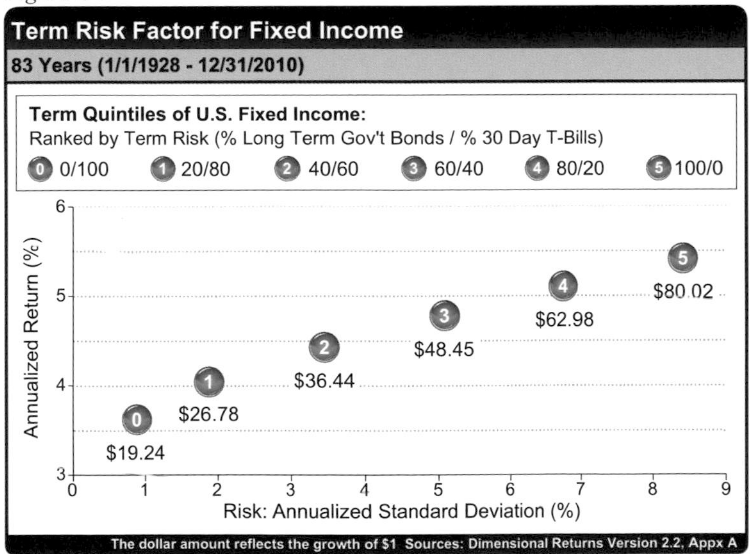

citi
THE TREASURY DEPARTMENT
30
25
5
20 YRS 10
15
LONG TERM
CORPORATE
BONDS
30
25
5
20 YRS 10
15
LONG TERM
GOVERNMENT
BONDS

Default As A Risk Factor

The last of the five risk factors is the default risk factor, which is associated with the credit quality of bonds. Instruments of lower credit quality are riskier than those of higher credit quality, thus yielding higher expected returns. Despite the August 2011 downgrade of U.S. government debt by Standard & Poors, the market still assigns a higher default risk to corporations over the U.S. government. The default risk factor refers to the additional expected return of corporate bonds over government bonds. Figure 8-10 shows the strong relationship between risk and return as the probability of default increases.

Figure 8-10

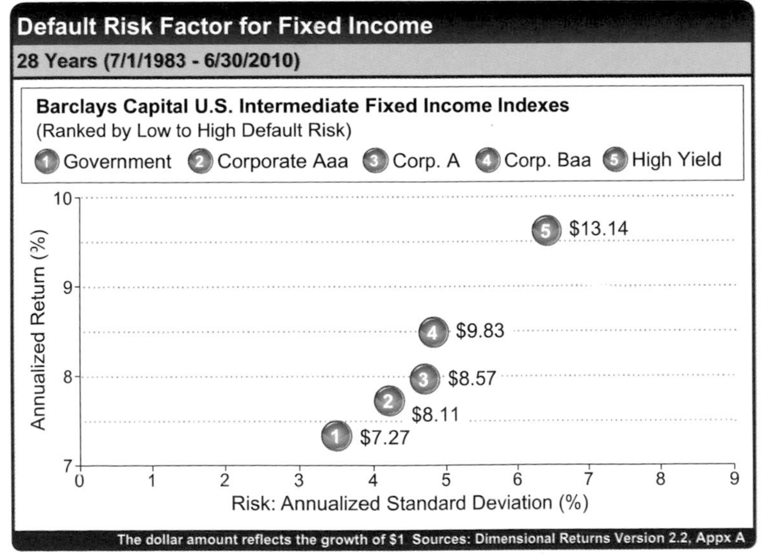

Figure 8-11

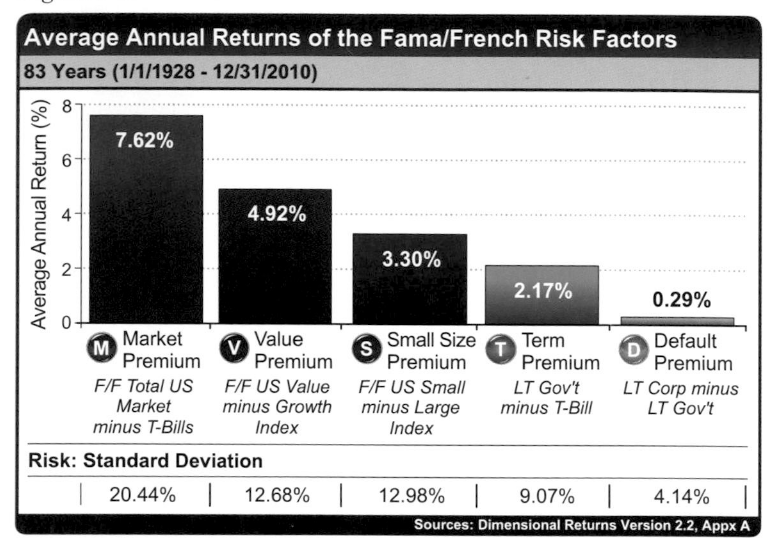

Figure 8-12

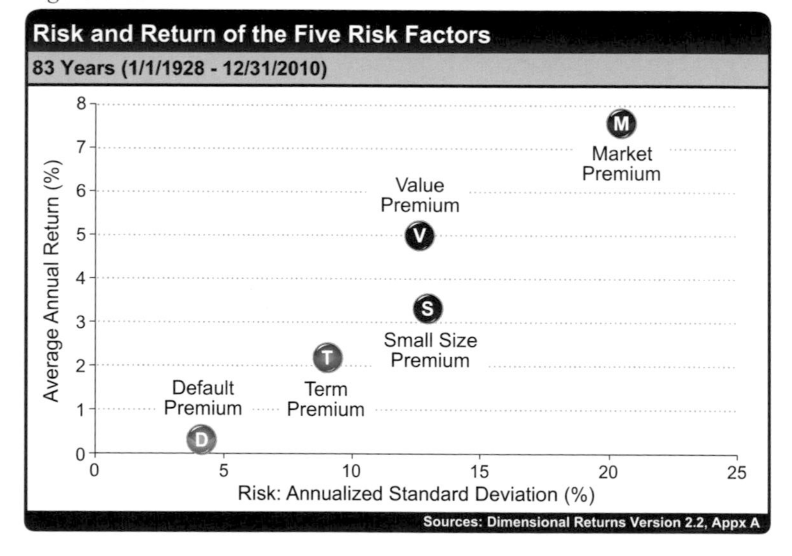

Implications Of The Five-Factor Model

A summary of the average annual returns for all five risk factors is presented in Figure 8-11. Both the risk and average annual returns for all five risk factors are shown in Figure 8-12.

The research of Eugene Fama and Kenneth French serves as a guiding protocol for both individual and institutional investing. Their Five-Factor Model has revolutionized how portfolios are constructed and analyzed.

As you have learned, three of the five factors apply to equities. The Three Factor Model is an invaluable tool for asset allocation and portfolio analysis. In his own words, Eugene Fama candidly explains the small-value story, among other subjects, in a November 2007 interview with *The Region*, the publication for the Federal Reserve Bank of Minneapolis. "So, small-cap stocks have higher average returns than large-cap stocks, and stocks with higher ratios of book value to market value have higher returns than low book-to-market stocks." He continues, "Low book-to-market stocks tend to be growth stocks. High book-to-market stocks tend to be relatively more distressed; they're what people call value stocks. That's given rise to what the finance profession—academic as well as applied—calls the size premium and the value premium. The value premium tends to be bigger," he added. "So, our model has three factors. Every asset pricing model says you need the market in there. Then they differ on how many other things you need. The CAPM says you only need the market. We basically say a minimum of two other factors seem to be necessary. And these two do a pretty good job."[72]

ENLIST NOW
1000
100
10
30s
40s
50s
60s
70s

Step 9: History

"It takes between 20 and 800 years of monitoring performance to statistically prove that a money manager is skillful rather than lucky—which is a lot more than most people have in mind when they say 'long-term' track record."

– Ted Aronson, "Confessions of a Fund Pro," *Money* Magazine, 1999

"While much has changed over the years, some things remain the same. There is still a strong relation between risk and expected return… Some things stand the test of time."

– James L. Davis, Ph.D., "Digging the Panama Canal," 2004

"Those who are ignorant of investment history are bound to repeat it. Historical investment returns and risks of various asset classes should be studied. Investment results, for an asset over a long enough period (greater than 20 years) are a good guide to future returns and risks of that asset."

– William Bernstein, Ph.D., M.D., *The Intelligent Asset Allocator*, 2000

"I know of no way of judging the future but by the past."

– Patrick Henry, Virginia Convention Speech, 1775

The smart money man is best served,
by checkin' out how the bell is curved.
– The Speculation Blues

I THINK WE CAN SAFELY SAY THAT MOST INVESTORS don't make decisions based on the long-term history of the stock market. They generally look at the most recent 1, 3 and 5-year returns and assume that recent past performance will persist. Unfortunately, they don't understand that short-term returns are based on random news and that investment decisions based on 50 years of data are more likely to enhance wealth than decisions based on 5 years of data.

Historical stock market data provide investors with a powerful set of tools for constructing portfolios that can maximize expected returns at given levels of risk. By analyzing the historical returns for various asset classes, including stocks, bonds, private equity, real estate, and even precious metals, an investor can see the difference between compensated and uncompensated risk over time. Statisticians require data from periods of at least 30 years to minimize the sampling error of short-term data and to provide a more reliable estimate of expected returns. Very few managers are able to provide 30 years of data to their clients.

Historical data serves as a testament to the enduring nature of capitalism. By considering and understanding long-term data, investors can use long-term risk and return data for various indexes to construct an asset allocation based on history and the science of investing, not on speculation.

PROBLEMS

INVESTORS FOCUS ON SHORT-TERM DATA

The first problem investors face is that the long-term history of stock market returns is not provided to them. Secondly, investors are not aware that long-term data has more value to them than does short-term data. When presented with 83 years of data, many investors deem the data irrelevant, because they do not have 83 years to live. This perspective overlooks the value of a large sample size. Investors who make decisions based on short-term data often later regret it.

When describing the risk and return of an index, significant errors are likely to occur when using a subset of the available data. For example, in the 10-year period from 2001 to 2010, the S&P 500 index had an annualized return of only 1.41%. Based on that low return, many investors would conclude that the S&P 500 was not a good investment. However, for the 20-year period ending 2010, the annualized return was 9.14%, very close to the annualized return of 9.55% for the 83-year period ending 2010. Also, it is quite close to the 50-year return of 9.75%. The S&P 500 consists of 500 of the most economically important U.S. companies, and it comprises between 70% and 80% of the total market capitalization of the US equity market. Therefore, an S&P index fund is still an important building block for a diversified index portfolio. When gathering information to identify the risk and return characteristics of the many asset class indexes that belong in a diversified portfolio, the more quality long-term data you have, the more accurate your conclusions.

Solutions

History Characterizes Risk And Return

The most complete historical database for stocks, bonds and mutual funds can be found at the Center for Research in Security Prices (CRSP) at the University of Chicago's Booth School of Business. Figure 9-1 shows the annualized rates of return for 24 different indexes. This table provides an interesting review of various indexes over several different time periods. Note the pattern of higher annualized returns of small cap and value stocks over large cap and growth stocks over time.

The time series construction in Figure 9-2 enables index funds investors to make investment decisions based on a statistically substantial and significant 83-year time frame. This time series construction simulates a fund's composition prior to its inception and allows for estimates of past performance data. The style purity of index funds investing allows for this exercise, providing an abundance of data. This time series construction carefully stitches together 83 years of risk and return data for the indexes referenced in this book, with the black-dotted outlined section representing the simulated indexes and the solid black lines representing live mutual fund data for investable asset class investments. While not a perfect representation, the data produced by the time series construction is a very useful tool. Statisticians who consider 30 years of risk and return data to be statistically significant would consider this collection of 83 years of data a feast!

Figure 9-1

Annualized Returns of Various Indexes

83 Years (1/1/1928 - 12/31/2010)

Indexes	1 Yr Ending 2010	3 Yrs 2008-2010	5 Yrs 2006-2010	20 Yrs 1991-2010	50 Yrs 1961-2010	83 Yrs 1928-2010
TM U.S. Total Market	17.22	-1.62	3.07	9.50	9.86	9.40
SP S&P 500	15.06	-2.86	2.29	9.14	9.75	9.55
LG U.S. Large Growth	17.16	-0.39	4.00	9.61	8.64	7.89
LV U.S. Large Value	20.17	-2.52	1.60	10.76	12.23	10.30
SC U.S. Small Company	30.70	4.47	5.21	12.35	11.68	10.95
MC U.S. Micro Cap	31.29	2.09	3.21	13.49	12.16	11.13
SG U.S. Small Growth	30.98	3.81	6.60	9.93	8.60	8.88
SV U.S. Small Cap Value	29.01	4.05	4.36	15.99	14.79	12.74
RE Real Estate Securities	23.79	-0.23	1.78	10.72	11.62	10.90
IV International Value	10.57	-6.12	4.12	8.27	11.54	9.89
IS International Small Company	23.91	-0.42	5.43	6.77	14.72	12.76
ISV International Small Cap Value	18.10	-1.32	4.90	7.63	15.89	13.39
EM Emerging Markets	21.82	2.06	13.31	13.59	17.53	13.97
EV Emerging Markets Value	22.06	2.63	16.77	16.72	18.81	15.11
ES Emerging Markets Small Cap	30.18	5.76	17.52	14.28	17.97	14.68
N NSDQ	16.91	0.01	3.76	10.30	8.86	9.16
TB One Month U.S. Treasury Bills	0.11	0.63	2.25	3.45	5.28	3.63
1F One-Yr Fixed Income	1.16	2.36	3.40	4.43	6.13	4.06
2F Two-Yr Global Fixed Income	1.75	2.63	3.52	4.85	6.12	4.75
3G Short Term Government	4.45	4.72	4.72	5.64	6.51	4.96
5F Five-Yr Global Fixed Income	5.30	4.51	4.52	6.25	6.52	4.96
GB Long-Term Government Bonds	10.14	5.65	5.57	8.50	7.10	5.42
CB Long-Term Corporate Bonds	12.44	8.01	5.94	8.17	7.35	5.86
CPI Inflation (Consumer Price Indx)	1.50	1.43	2.18	2.51	4.08	3.11

Sources, Updates and Disclosures: © Morningstar Direct, ifabt.com, Appx A

Figure 9-2

Time Series Construction of the IFA Indexes

83 Years (1/1/1928 - 12/31/2010) | Simulated Index | Live Mutual Fund

1928 1935 1940 1945 1950 1955 1960 1965 1970 1975 1980 1985 1990 1995 2000 2005 2010

Code	Index	Simulated Index	Live Mutual Fund
LC	Index Funds Advisors (IFA) U.S. Large Company Index	S&P 500 Index	DFUSX
LV	IFA U.S. Large Cap Value Index	Dimensional Fund Advisors (DFA) US Large Value Index	DFLVX
SC	IFA U.S. Small Cap Index	Dimensional Fund Advisors (DFA) US Small Cap Index	DFSTX
SV	IFA U.S. Small Cap Value Index	Dimensional Fund Advisors (DFA) US Targeted Value	DFFVX
RE	IFA Real Estate Index	50% (SC) & 50% (SV) / DJ U.S. Select REIT Index	DFGEX
IV	IFA International Value Index	IFA US Large Value Index (LV) / MSCI EAFE VALUE	DFIVX
IS	IFA International Small Company Index	IFA US Small Cap Index (SC) / DFA Int'l Small Cap Index	DFISX
ISV	IFA International Small Cap Value Index	IFA US Small Cap Value Index (SV) / DFA Int'l Small Cap Value Index	DISVX
EM	IFA Emerging Markets Index	50% (LV) & 50% (SC) / 50% (IV) & 50% (IS) / DFA EM Index	DFEMX
EV	IFA Emerging Markets Value Index	IFA US Small Cap Value Index (SV) / Fama/French EM Value Index	DFEVX
ES	IFA Emerging Markets Small Cap Index	IFA US Small Cap Index (SC) / Fama/French EM Small Index	DEMSX
1F	IFA One-Year Fixed Income Index	One-Month T-Bills / One-Year T-Note Index	DFIHX
2F	IFA Two-Year Global Fixed Income Index	5-Year T-Notes / ML US Treas. Index 1-3 Yrs / Citi World Gov't Bond	DFGFX
3G	IFA Short Term Government Index	5-Year T-Notes / BarCap Intermediate Gov't Bond Index	DFFGX
5F	IFA Five Year Global Fixed Income Index	IFA Short Term Government Index (3G) / Citi Global Gov't Bond	DFGBX

See additional details in Appendix A. Sources, Updates and Disclosures: ifabt.com

The Resilience Of Capitalism

Capitalism has proven to be resilient. Figure 9-3 shows the growth of a dollar in various indexes over the course of 83 years, marked with 15 major news events listed in Figure 9-4. While the major events had large short-term impacts on market prices, they proved to be largely inconsequential in the long-term as the market marched ahead. Despite several setbacks, capitalism has not only persevered, but thrived. This long-term history of quality data is the most useful tool for investors to construct risk appropriate portfolios.

Figure 9-3

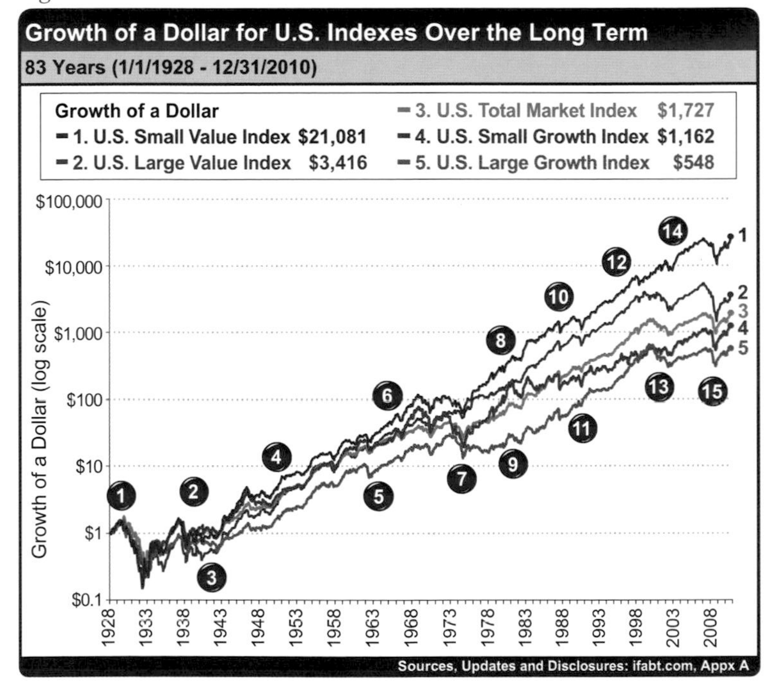

Figure 9-4

Market Turmoil and the Dow Jones Industrial Average

83 Years (1/1/1928 - 12/31/2010)

	Date	Event	DJIA Close Previous Day	DJIA Close	DJIA % Change	One Year Change
1	10/29/29	Black Tuesday	260.64	230.07	-11.73%	-17.10%
2	9/1/39	World War II Begins	134.41	135.25	0.62%	-4.07%
3	12/7/41	Japan Attacks Pearl Harbor	115.90	112.52	-2.92%	2.20%
4	6/25/50	North Korea Invades South Korea	224.35	213.91	-4.65%	14.67%
5	11/22/63	President Kennedy Assassinated	732.65	711.49	-2.89%	24.99%
6	1/31/65	Escalation of Vietnam War	902.86	903.68	0.09%	8.83%
7	8/9/74	President Nixon Resigns	784.89	777.30	-0.97%	5.98%
8	11/4/79	Iran Hostage Crisis Begins	818.94	812.63	-0.77%	17.29%
9	3/30/81	President Reagan Shot	994.78	992.16	-0.26%	-16.90%
10	10/19/87	Black Monday	2,246.73	1,738.74	-22.61%	95.93%
11	1/16/91	Operation Desert Storm Begins	2,490.59	2,508.91	0.74%	29.52%
12	4/19/95	Oklahoma City Bombing	4,179.13	4,207.49	0.68%	31.56%
13	9/11/01	Terrorist Attacks of 9/11	9,605.51	8,920.70	-7.13%	-3.81%
14	3/19/03	Operation Iraqi Freedom Begins	8,194.23	8,265.45	0.87%	23.24%
15	9/15/08	Lehman Declares Bankruptcy	11,421.99	10,917.51	-4.42%	-15.58%

Source: Yahoo! Finance

Monthly Rolling Periods

Despite the historic advance of equities and the proven resilience of capitalism, many investors still get nervous during extended or sharp down periods such as the one we endured in 2008. When market-moving news appears, many investors may question if the fundamental relationship between risk and return is still valid. However, when a larger data set is considered, the situation looks better for long-term investors.

Rolling period analysis enables investors to examine large sets of performance data by dividing returns into monthly rolling periods, instead of traditional calendar year periods with a January beginning and a December ending. This method provides Simulated Passive Investor Experiences (SPIEs) which begin at the 1st of each month throughout the designated period. Figure 9-5 shows 12 consecutive 12-year rolling periods beginning on January 1, 1959. Each rolling period can be thought of as representing the experience of a unique investor who started and ended on the dates specified in the period. Hence, the name Simulated Passive Investor Experiences.

The primary advantage of rolling periods is the large number of them that are embedded in a given time series of returns. For example, in a 50-year period, there are 589 rolling 12-month periods as opposed to 50 consecutive, non-overlapping

Figure 9-5

Explanation of 12-Year Monthly Rolling Periods

12 Years, 11 Months (1/1/1959 - 11/30/1971)

Periods			
1	January 1, 1959	12 years	December 31, 1970
2	February 1, 1959	12 years	January 30, 1971
3	March 1, 1959	12 years	February 28, 1971
4	April 1, 1959	12 years	March 31, 1971
5	May 1, 1959	12 years	April 30, 1971
6	June 1, 1959	12 years	May 31, 1971
7	July 1, 1959	12 years	June 30, 1971
8	August 1, 1959	12 years	July 31, 1971
9	September 1,1959	12 years	August 31, 1971
10	October 1, 1959	12 years	September 30, 1971
11	November 1, 1959	12 years	October 31, 1971
12	December 1, 1959	12 years	November 30, 1971

1959 1960 1961 1962 1963 1964 1965 1966 1967 1968 1969 1970 1971

12-month periods. One small disadvantage of rolling periods is the heavier weight given to returns that occur in the middle of the period and the lighter weight given to returns that occur at the beginning and end of the period, but this does not inherently bias the results.

Figure 9-6 charts the comparison of the performance of various equity indexes from 1928 through 2010 using this SPIE analysis. For example, the chart illustrates in the bottom left quadrant that over 985 1-year monthly rolling periods, a simulated passive investor in a Large Growth Index beat a simulated passive investor in a Large Value Index 44% of the time, causing investors to think it might be a toss-up between large growth and large value. Compounded by the financial media touting the benefits of large growth companies, investors tend to believe that large growth can perhaps be a good investment. But in 757 20-year monthly rolling periods, the large value indexer beat the large growth indexer 88% of the time. Over short periods, volatility and price swings confuse investors as to which indexes are better long-term investments, but the picture becomes much clearer when they consider longer periods.

Figure 9-7 tracks large, small, value, blend, and growth indexes from around the world. For U.S. markets, more than 83 years of data are shown. For non-U.S. developed markets, 36 years of data is available, and there are 22 years of data for emerging markets. In each case, it is worthwhile to note the lackluster annualized returns of both large and growth indexes, relative to the strong annualized returns delivered by all of the indexes labeled small or value.

Figure 9-6

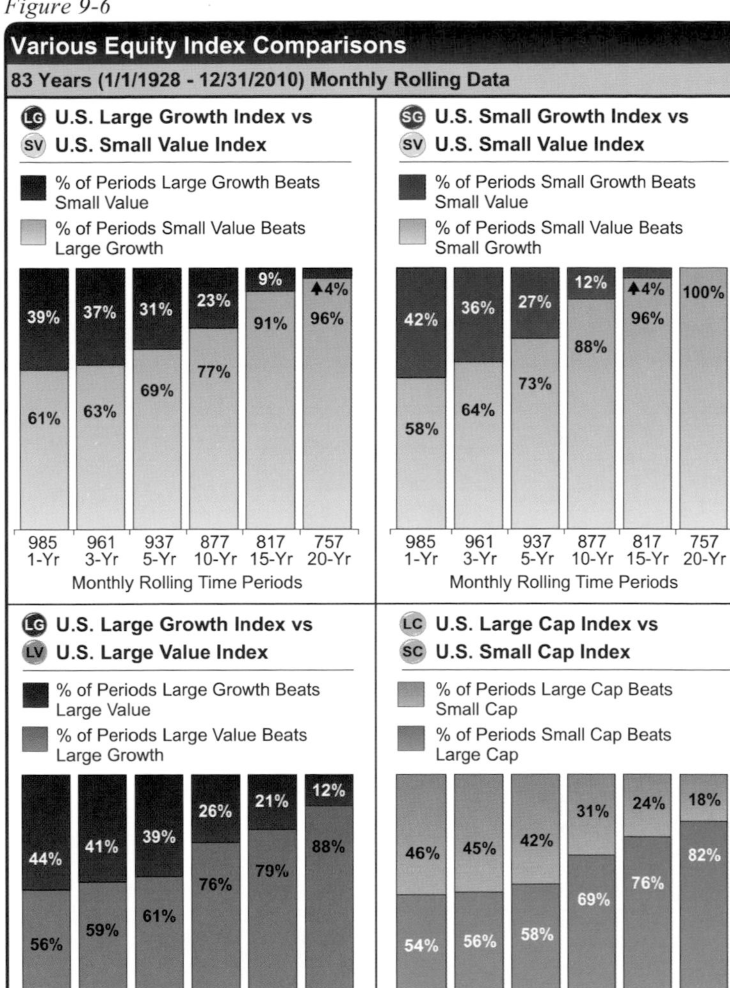
Various Equity Index Comparisons
83 Years (1/1/1928 - 12/31/2010) Monthly Rolling Data
LG U.S. Large Growth Index vs
SV U.S. Small Value Index
% of Periods Large Growth Beats Small Value
% of Periods Small Value Beats Large Growth
39% 37% 31% 23% 9% 4%
61% 63% 69% 77% 91% 96%
985 1-Yr 961 3-Yr 937 5-Yr 877 10-Yr 817 15-Yr 757 20-Yr
Monthly Rolling Time Periods
SG U.S. Small Growth Index vs
SV U.S. Small Value Index
% of Periods Small Growth Beats Small Value
% of Periods Small Value Beats Small Growth
42% 36% 27% 12% 4%
58% 64% 73% 88% 96% 100%
985 1-Yr 961 3-Yr 937 5-Yr 877 10-Yr 817 15-Yr 757 20-Yr
Monthly Rolling Time Periods
LG U.S. Large Growth Index vs
LV U.S. Large Value Index
% of Periods Large Growth Beats Large Value
% of Periods Large Value Beats Large Growth
44% 41% 39% 26% 21% 12%
56% 59% 61% 76% 79% 88%
985 1-Yr 961 3-Yr 937 5-Yr 877 10-Yr 817 15-Yr 757 20-Yr
Monthly Rolling Time Periods
LC U.S. Large Cap Index vs
SC U.S. Small Cap Index
% of Periods Large Cap Beats Small Cap
% of Periods Small Cap Beats Large Cap
46% 45% 42% 31% 24% 18%
54% 56% 58% 69% 76% 82%
985 1-Yr 961 3-Yr 937 5-Yr 877 10-Yr 817 15-Yr 757 20-Yr
Monthly Rolling Time Periods
Sources, Updates, and Disclosures: ifabt.com, Appx A

Figure 9-7

Value, Blend and Growth Indexes Around the World

Annualized Returns and Standard Deviation Over Various Periods

Categories	Annualized Return	Standard Deviation
U.S. Large Capitalization Stocks - 83 Years (1/1/1928 - 12/31/2010)		
Fama/French U.S. Large Value Index	10.45%	26.29%
Fama/French U.S. Large Blend Index	9.85%	19.26%
Fama/French U.S. Large Growth Index	9.05%	18.91%
U.S. Small Capitalization Stocks - 83 Years (1/1/1928 - 12/31/2010)		
Fama/French U.S. Small Value Index	13.82%	30.23%
Fama/French U.S. Small Blend Index	11.95%	26.66%
Fama/French U.S. Small Growth Index	8.97%	28.50%
Non-U.S. Developed Markets Stocks - 36 Years (1/1/1975 - 12/31/2010)		
Fama/French International Value Index	15.73%	18.69%
Dimensional International Small Index	15.72%	18.26%
MSCI EAFE Index	10.76%	17.49%
Emerging Markets Stocks - 22 Years (1/1/1989 - 12/31/2010)		
Fama/French Emerging Markets Value Index	18.17%	25.68%
Fama/French Emerging Markets Blend Index	13.68%	23.84%
Fama/French Emerging Markets Growth Index	11.43%	23.73%

Sources: CRSP, Fama/French Data, ifabt.com

The Importance Of History

Although all disclosure statements from investment advisory firms are required to state that "past performance does not guarantee future results," studying the past can empower individuals to make better choices for the future. Market history demonstrates the enduring nature of capitalism and exposes the benefits of investing based on long-term risk and return data. The historical data enables investors to build an asset allocation that meets their own particular risk capacity and equips them with the knowledge to withstand short-term volatility. History is also a record of how well investors price assets on a daily basis.

Step 10: Risk Capacity

"Investment Policy [asset allocation] is the foundation upon which portfolios should be constructed and managed."

– Charles D. Ellis, Ph.D., *Investment Policy*, 1985

"Rip Van Winkle would be the ideal stock market investor: Rip could invest in the market before his nap and when he woke up 20 years later, he'd be happy. He would have been asleep through all the ups and downs in between. But few investors resemble Mr. Van Winkle. The more often an investor counts his money—or looks at the value of his mutual funds in the newspaper—the lower his risk tolerance."

– Richard Thaler, Ph.D., Economist,
University of Chicago Booth School of Business

"What if your advisor talks only about returns, not risk?... It's his job to take risk into account by telling you the range of possible outcomes you face. If he won't, go to a new planner, someone who will get real."

– William Sharpe, Ph.D., Nobel Laureate, *Money* Magazine, 2008

Design a portfolio you are not likely to trade... akin to premarital counseling advice; try to build a portfolio that you can live with for a long, long time."

– Robert D. Arnott, "Is Your Alpha Big Enough to Cover Your Taxes?," 1999

A risk taker gots'ta know his risk capacity,
then hang on for his payout with true tenacity.
– The Speculation Blues

ENVISION THE MARKET AS A WILD BULL, bucking up and down, rearing and spinning. Investors are like bull riders, trying to hang on as the bull kicks and twists, making for a tumultuous ride. Matching the right portfolio to an individual's ability to handle risk is akin to finding the right bull that each investor can ride through all the ups and downs of the market.

Each investor has a unique risk capacity and can be identified by a risk capacity score, a measure of how much risk an individual can manage. This score is based on five specific risk dimensions of an investor: 1) time horizon and liquidity needs; 2) attitude toward risk; 3) net worth; 4) income and savings rate; and 5) investment knowledge.

Risk capacity can be regarded as a measurement of an investor's ability to earn stock market returns. Calculating risk capacity is the first step to deciding which portfolio will generate optimal returns for each investor. A risk capacity score determines the proper risk exposure for an investor's portfolio.

Problems

Improper Assessment Of Risk Capacity

The problem many investors face is the improper measurement of their risk capacity. Each of the five dimensions has to be carefully examined and then quantified. Some dimensions carry more weight in the determination of a final score. The survey must be carefully designed, and investors must be honest and accurate when answering the questions.

Solutions

Risk Capacity Survey

An easy and efficient way to determine an investor's risk capacity is to complete a questionnaire or a survey that evaluates and quantifies each of the five dimensions of risk capacity. One such survey can be found at ifarcs.com, which quantifies risk capacity using numerical values from 1 to 100. These values correspond to various portfolios created with the indexes referenced in Step 9.

Higher scores signify a higher capacity for risk, a longer time horizon and an ability to withstand market volatility. Investors with higher scores are generally recommended to hold portfolios with a larger allocation of global equities. In contrast, lower scores signify a lower risk capacity and a higher need for liquidity. Investors with lower scores are steered toward more conservative portfolios that hold a higher proportion of short-term investments such as fixed income.

Risk Capacity Results

The pages following the five dimensions contain portraits that represent four risk capacities by age, family composition, activities, careers, and lifestyles. These movie poster style portraits are designed to capture the characteristics of individuals who score 100, 75, 50, or 25 on a risk capacity survey.

Dimension One

Time Horizon And Liquidity Needs

Archimedes is often referenced as saying, "Give me a lever long enough and a place to stand, and I can move the earth." In the world of investing, that lever is time. The longer investors can hold onto their portfolios, the greater their risk capacity. Will an investor need 20% of the value of his investment portfolio in two years, five years, seven years, ten years, or longer? Usually, the closer a person is to retirement, the shorter his or her investment horizon becomes. Risk-calibrated index portfolios carry recommended holding periods that range from four to fifteen years. The longer an investor holds onto a risky investment, the greater the chance of obtaining its average historical return and the greater the ability to reduce the uncertainty of these returns through time diversification.

Sample Risk Capacity Survey Question:

How many years will it be before you need to withdraw a total of 20% of all your investments for living or other expenses?

A. Less than 2 years
B. From 2 to 5 years
C. From 5 to 10 years
D. From 10 to 15 years
E. More than 15 years

Dimension Two

Attitude Toward Risk

This risk dimension assesses aversion or attraction to risk, providing an estimation of an investor's willingness or ability to experience an investment loss. The last 50 years have shown that stock market investing can be a wild ride, with a lot of volatility and uncertainty. Investors who hold riskier investments can expect higher returns, but greater short-term volatility. Some people take less risk than they're actually capable of taking, preferring the tranquility of Ferdinand the Bull over the untamed violence of Hurricane the Bull to carry them on their ride through the market.

Sample Risk Capacity Survey Question:

What is the worst twelve-month percentage loss you would tolerate for your long-term investments, beyond which you would be inclined to sell some or all of your investment?

A. A loss of 50%
B. A loss of 40%
C. A loss of 30%
D. A loss of 20%
E. A loss of 10%

Dimension Three

Net Worth

What is the current value of an investor's long-term investments or golden nest egg? Net worth is the value of an investor's assets minus liabilities, or in other words, what is owned minus what is owed. Investors have a positive net worth when they own more than they owe. An individual's total net worth can provide a cushion against short-term stock market volatility and the uncertainty of future cash needs. Because life itself is a random walk, investors can never be completely certain of what their cash needs will look like tomorrow. The more assets in reserve, the greater the capacity for risk.

Sample Risk Capacity Survey Question:

What is the current value of your long-term investments? Please include your taxable accounts, retirement savings plan with your employer and your individual retirement accounts (IRAs).

A. Less than $25,000
B. $25,000 to $50,000
C. $50,000 to $100,000
D. $100,000 to $250,000
E. $250,000 or more

Dimension Four

Income And Savings Rate

The Income and Savings Rate dimension estimates excess income and ability to add to savings. A high score indicates that a large percentage of income is discretionary and is available for investing. A low score indicates that all or almost all income is being used for ordinary expenses and not being added to annual investments. A higher income also bolsters the ability to respond to emergencies without cashing out portfolio funds. Having to take money out of your portfolio after it has declined creates irreparable harm to your long-term returns. Having a solid income will minimize the chance you will need to dip into your retirement account. That is why this dimension is an important consideration when assessing risk capacity.

Sample Risk Capacity Survey Question:

What is your total annual income?

A. Less than $50,000
B. $50,000 to $100,000
C. $100,000 to $150,000
D. $150,000 to $250,000
E. $250,000 or more

Dimension Five

Investment Knowledge

An individual who understands several key concepts that impact investing, such as the failure of active management, the Random Walk Theory, the Efficient Market Hypothesis, the Five Factor Model, and Modern Portfolio Theory has a greater capacity for risk than someone without this understanding. Knowledgeable investors understand that their potential for high returns depends on their risk exposure, allowing them to ignore short-term market fluctuations and focus on long-term results.

Sample Risk Capacity Survey Question:

The performance of stock pickers must be examined on an adjusted basis. When comparing the returns of a stock picker's portfolio to an index, which factors must be considered before determining if the stock picker has beaten the index?

A. Proper accounting of returns, including cash flows in and out of the account
B. The exposure to market risk, size risk and value risk of both portfolios
C. A statistical analysis of the difference in returns with a measure of the significance of the difference such as the t-statistic
D. Standard deviations or volatility measurements
E. All of the above

Risk Capacity 100: Red

Most Aggressive:

Individuals who score 100 on a risk capacity survey (scaled from 1-100) likely possess nerves of steel with a general proclivity toward high risk activities tantamount to skydiving, NASCAR racing, surfing typhoon waves, or other extreme sports. This type of investor has a strong gut for withstanding extreme volatility in exchange for maximum portfolio growth potential, as well as a substantial amount of investable capital, a secure income stream and an in-depth knowledge about how the stock market really works. These investors may be on the younger side with the capacity to wait at least 15 years before withdrawing as much as 20% of their investments. Over the course of their investment's lifetime, these individuals are able to expose their capital to high levels of risk and commit themselves to staying the course during times of considerable market volatility, such as the 57% decline that occurred over the 1-year, 4-month period from November 2007 to February 2009. See a matching risk exposure at the end of Step 11. Along with their ability to take on high risk, they are extremely disciplined in buying and holding the appropriate asset classes without engaging in emotional trading or jumping in and out of the market. They are willing to tie themselves to the mast and ignore the media and doomsayers who sing their siren songs with intensity.

Very few investors have a risk capacity of 100. Please take the Risk Capacity Survey before investing any capital.

Risk Capacity 75: Dark Blue

Moderately Aggressive:

Younger professionals with new careers and parents who are starting families and beginning to save money for their dependent children's college would likely score somewhere in the risk capacity 75 range. These individuals generally possess a high degree of understanding about the sources of stock market returns and are willing to take substantial risks to capture the higher expected returns associated with increased volatility. These investors understand the long-term benefits of the multi-factor model of investing and are aware that they are entitled to earn returns commensurate with the risks they take. They are also prone to thrill seeking, demonstrating their penchant for risk and adventure. Although they have a higher risk capacity than others, they may require a bit of fixed income to soften their portfolio's volatility. They may need some access to a small percentage of liquid assets to accommodate the unforeseen events that unfold in life's random walk. This risk capacity is suitable for investors who have at least 13 years before needing approximately 20% of their investments and are willing to accept a higher degree of volatility in order to achieve higher portfolio growth potential. Risk exposures associated with this level of risk capacity lost about 50% of their value over a 1-year, 4-month period in 2007 to 2009. See a matching risk exposure at the end of Step 11.

Risk Capacity 50: Sea Green

Moderate:

Individuals in their late-40s to mid-50s with growing families and careers in full swing would likely score close to a 50 on a risk capacity survey. These investors may have children graduating from high school or college with younger children still at home. Some may be eyeing retirement, making plans for future activities, hobbies or travel. Such individuals would have about 8 years before they would need to withdraw approximately 20% or more of their investments and would be willing to accept a moderate degree of volatility in order to achieve moderate portfolio growth. This capacity for risk is appropriate for those who can stomach a moderate amount of risk in their portfolios and have the emotional fortitude to close their eyes to the market's highs and lows, choosing instead to focus on the long-term historical return which is the expected return. The risk exposure that would be appropriate for this capacity would have lost about 36% during the worst 1-year, 4-month period from 2007 to 2009. Such investors would need or want to invest in stock market equities with an eye toward fueling long-term growth, but would remain mindful of their need to dampen volatility given their window to retirement. See a matching risk exposure at the end of Step 11.

Risk Capacity 25: Ice Blue

Conservative:

Investors in their mid-70s who are enjoying their golden years would most likely score close to a 25 on a risk capacity survey. These investors have earned the opportunity to live off their savings and investments after years of contributing to the labor force. They may be engaged in the lives of their grandchildren and regularly participate in hobbies and leisurely activities. A risk capacity level of 25 is suitable for these investors who have at least 5 years before needing approximately 20% of their investments and are willing to accept a conservative degree of risk for incremental appreciation with emphasis on capital preservation. At this stage in their lives, these individuals are less able to take on risk. These individuals would shun stock market risk in exchange for a softer ride through the markets during their later years of retirement. A portfolio of risk that would be appropriate for this conservative investor lost about 20% of its value during the worst period of decline in 2007 to 2009. See a matching risk exposure at the end of Step 11.

An Investor's Role In Risk Capacity

When investors actively participate in the investment process by conducting the self-examination required to establish a risk capacity score, they better position themselves for investment success. This process allows them to identify how much risk they can truly take, and they develop a keen understanding of the inextricable link between risk and return.

Annual Returns
Growth of $10000
Annual Ret
Growth of

Step 11: Risk Exposure

"We can extrapolate from the study that for the long-term individual investor, who maintains a consistent asset allocation and leans toward index funds, asset allocation determines about 100% of performance."

– Roger Ibbotson, Ph.D., Ibbotson Associates, "The True Impact of Asset Allocation on Returns," 2000

"Diversification is your buddy."

– Merton Miller, Ph.D., Nobel Laureate, 1990

"A good portfolio is more than a long list of good stocks and bonds. It is a balanced whole, providing the investor with protections and opportunities with respect to a wide range of contingencies."

– Harry Markowitz, Ph.D., Nobel Laureate, 1990, Professor of Economics UCSD, "Portfolio Selection: Efficient Diversification of Investments," 1959

"Investment planning is about structuring exposure to risk factors."

– Gene Fama, Jr., "The Error Term," 2001

Traders think that money grows from speculation,
but indexers know it's just risk compensation.
– The Speculation Blues

In the early 1950s, Harry Markowitz applied his mathematical expertise to investing. Markowitz, then a Ph.D. candidate in economics at the University of Chicago, believed the investment "experts" erred by urging investors to focus solely on returns of individual stocks with no consideration of the concept of risk exposure. He set out to reveal how investors could improve their stock market performance by optimizing the trade-off between risk and return. In his 1952 Nobel Prize-winning paper, "Portfolio Selection,"[73] Markowitz established the importance of diversification. He asserted the best portfolios include non-correlated stocks that act and move independently from each other. Today trillions of dollars worldwide are invested according to his principles of risk and return, known collectively as Modern Portfolio Theory.

The blend of investments that is appropriate for a particular investor is known as asset allocation, also called risk exposure, and is based on an investor's risk capacity. Asset allocation is the most important factor in optimizing a portfolio's expected returns, thus it is essentially the most important decision an individual investor can make. This concept also extends to larger institutional investments, such as state pension funds, fire and police pension plans, church funds, college endowments, and any other funds governed by committees.

As presented in Step 8, Eugene Fama and Kenneth French identified that as much as 97% of equity returns are explained by a portfolio's exposure to market, size and value. Their research expanded upon Markowitz's and Sharpe's initial findings regarding risk and return. While Fama and French demonstrated that portfolios constructed of small and value companies have historically outperformed the total market portfolio over the long term, the risks associated with these small and value portfolios have also been higher.

Problems

Investors Frequently Take The Wrong Risks

Some investors tend to avoid risk when it comes to their investments. They want returns without any risks, but avoiding all risk is the same as avoiding potential returns. Others take on too much risk, while many take risks that just don't reward. All these "wrong risk" behaviors are the crux of the poor performance many investors experience. Risk should be embraced in appropriate doses that match an investor's risk capacity. There is a right amount and type of risk for every investor. Risk provides opportunity, and a taste for appropriate risk is a good thing.

As was shown in Step 9, certain asset classes, such as small and value, have a long history of sufficiently rewarding investors for the risks associated with them. However, there are also several asset classes that carry risk but have been inefficient in delivering returns commensurate with the risks taken. This kind of risk is not worth taking. As such, many investors struggle to develop an asset allocation that captures the right blend of the markets that have maximized returns at given levels of risk. Case in point, many investors seem comfortable investing in companies that are best described as glamour or growth stocks, presuming they perform better than small or value companies. These investors would be surprised to learn that growth companies actually have a poor history of delivering risk-commensurate returns. Commodities, private equity and technology indexes have also failed to historically maximize returns for risks taken. Failing to understand which blend of investments are worth their risk causes investors to earn lower returns than they could if they simply bought, held and rebalanced a blend of indexes that optimizes risks and returns.

Investors Get Commodity Fever

Commodities have developed a reputation for providing a hedge against inflation and an apparent negative correlation to equities. Further research into this subject reveals that no such advantage proves true. A compelling study[74] by former USC finance professor, Truman Clarke, details the lack of substantiation for the bold claims made by commodities proponents. A commodity is a hard asset, an item that is purchased on the hope that an increased demand or a decreased supply for the item will cause its value to increase. "Remember when you buy a commodity, you're not buying something that generates earnings and profit. You're buying a hard asset and hoping another buyer will be willing to pay more for that asset in the future," wrote Matt Krantz in a June 2008 *USA Today* article titled, "Read this before you jump on the commodities bandwagon."[75]

Commodity investments differ from stock investments in that companies, as a whole, have earned profits that have translated into an average return of about 9.5% per year. Under most conditions, their stock value is expected to increase in line with their growth in profits. The expectation of price appreciation for commodities is not based on profits, but rather on supply and demand. In short, commodities have not provided expected returns.

In November 2010, noted economist and professor of finance at Dartmouth, Kenneth French, conveyed his findings regarding commodities. He stated, "The high volatility of commodity prices makes it impossible to accurately estimate the expected returns, volatilities and covariances of commodity funds, but theory suggests that if commodity returns are negatively correlated with the rest of the market, the expected risk premium on commodities is small, perhaps negative. Finally, commodity funds are poor inflation hedges. Most of the variation in commodity prices is unrelated to inflation. In fact, commodity indices are typically 10 to 15 times more volatile than inflation. As a result, investors who use commodity funds to hedge inflation almost certainly increase the risk of their portfolios."[76]

The simple yet painful lesson for investors remains a cautionary tale regarding commodities speculation.

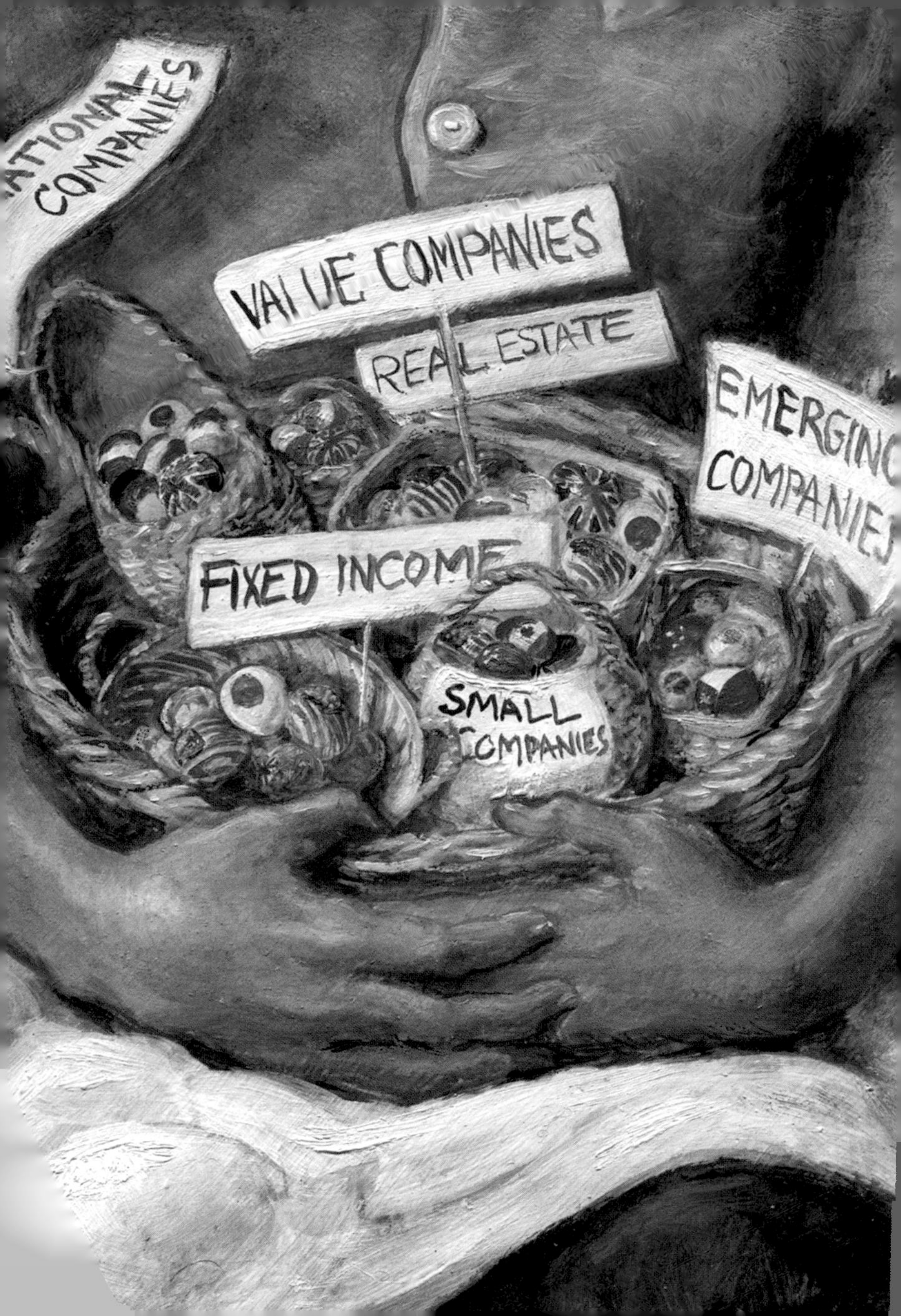

ATIONAL COMPANIES
VALUE COMPANIES
REAL ESTATE
EMERGIN COMPANIES
FIXED INCOME
SMALL COMPANIES

Solutions

Efficient Diversification: The Key To Success

A diversified portfolio which captures the right blend of market indexes reaps the benefit of carrying the systematic risk of the entire market while minimizing exposure to the unsystematic and concentrated risk associated with individual stocks and bonds, countries, industries, or sectors. The only risk that remains is the risk of the market itself, a risk that must be taken in order to capture market returns.

As capitalism has expanded throughout the world, it has become increasingly important to allocate a significant portion of one's portfolio to international securities. In the 1970's, the U.S. comprised more than 68% of global equity value, but today it comprises less than 50%. Investors achieve an enormous benefit of increasing diversification and capturing the expected returns of global capitalism by investing in index funds comprised of international developed countries and emerging markets countries in risk-appropriate doses.

An additional important aspect of diversification is diversifying across time. When investors maintain a globally diversified portfolio for long periods of time, they are able to maximize their ability to capture the complete range of returns that are offered by the global markets. Index portfolios with a high exposure to stock equities require a longer holding period than fixed income portfolios in order to efficiently maximize their ability to achieve an expected outcome.

The hypothetical stock certificate represents an investment in Capitalism, Inc., showing estimates for year-end 2010 of total market value, sales, net profits, number of CEO's, and number of employees who work for an investor who buys and holds a globally diversified index portfolio. With a total market cap of $30.5 trillion, over 12 thousand CEO's worldwide, and over 61 million employees selling products in 192 countries, it is not reasonable to ever believe that Capitalism, Inc. will go out of business. And if it did, your money would be worthless.

Risk-Calibrated Portfolios

The stacked chart of Figure 11-1 shows the general asset class allocations for 10 of 100 different risk-calibrated index

Figure 11-1

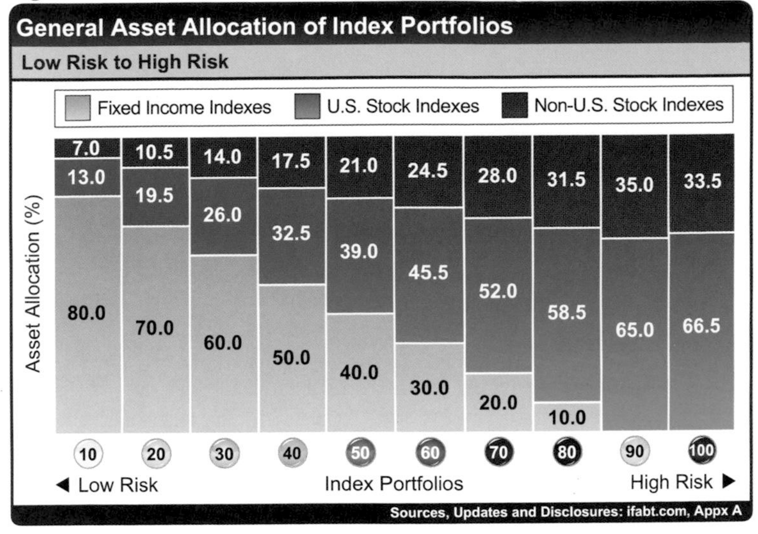

portfolios. In the chart, gold represents each portfolio's weighting in fixed income, green represents its percentage of U.S. equities, and brown represents its exposure to international and emerging markets. Almost all of the asset allocations carry the same index class components—fixed income, U.S. stocks and non-U.S. stocks—but weighs each differently. For example, the least risky index portfolio displayed, number 10, is heavily weighted in fixed income, carrying very little global equity exposure. This portfolio is well suited to an investor with a very low risk capacity—in general, someone with a short investment time horizon and current liquidity needs. An example of this type of investor would be an older retiree.

In contrast, the more risky index portfolios numbered 90 and 100 are all-equity portfolios that are heavily invested in U.S.

equity funds and carry greater concentration in international and emerging markets. The highest risk capacity Index Portfolio 100 is suitable for either a young 21-year old just starting out or someone who generally is very fluent in the language of riskese, will not need to liquidate his investments for a minimum of 15 years, has a high net worth and net income, and a strong stomach for volatility.

A general rule of thumb in calculating the percentage of equities (combined U.S. and non-U.S.) in each portfolio is to add 10 to the portfolio number. For example, the percentage of stocks in Portfolio 50 is 50 + 10 = 60%. This rule of thumb applies to Portfolios 1-90. Beyond Portfolio 90, the composition is 100% equities, just different degrees of tilt toward small cap and value.

The index portfolios shown in Figure 11-2 have diversified away uncompensated risks, so that the risk of investing in the markets is all that remains. The higher risk Index Portfolios 75 and 100 have a very high market exposure and a considerable tilt toward small and value indexes. The increased volatility of these higher risk index portfolios had higher returns over the 35-year period from January 1, 1976 to December 31, 2010, relative to the less volatile Index Portfolios 25 and 50. As the chart shows, an individual who invested $1 in a lower risk Index Portfolio 25 would have grown his investment to $21.00 in the 35-year period. However that same dollar invested in a higher risk Index Portfolio 100 would have grown to $125.00. This example provides sound proof for the importance of establishing the efficient asset allocation that is best matched to an investor's risk capacity.

Figure 11-2

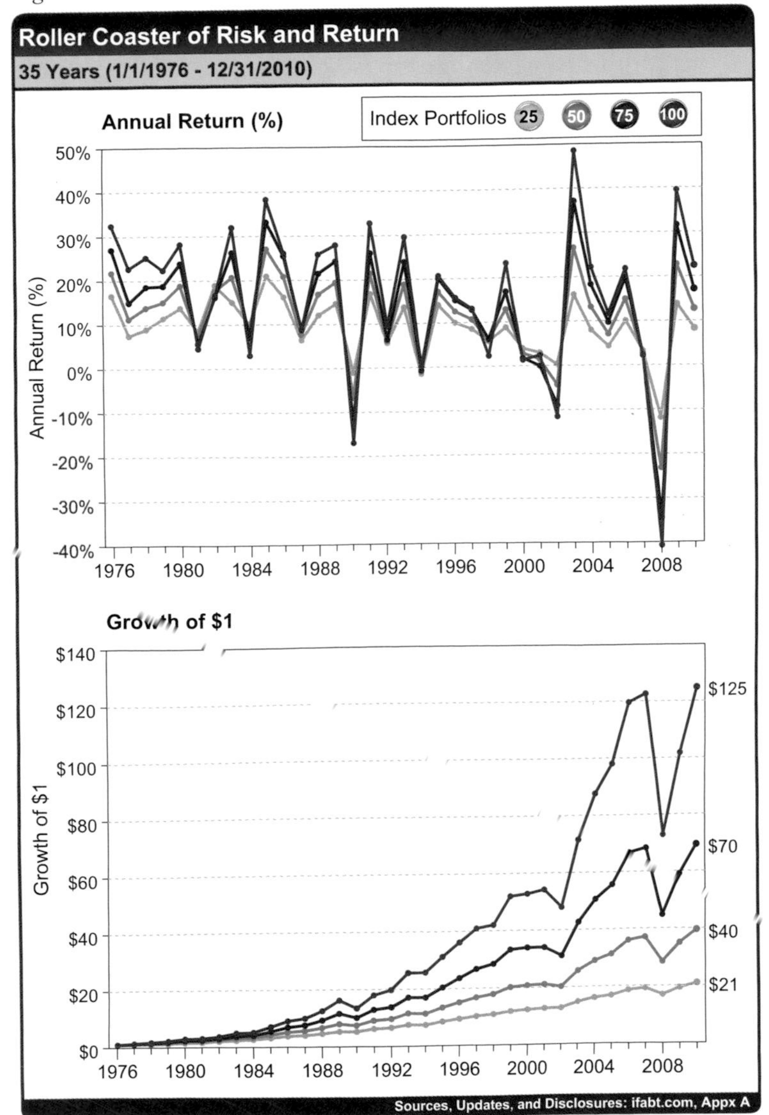
Roller Coaster of Risk and Return
35 Years (1/1/1976 - 12/31/2010)
Annual Return (%)
Index Portfolios 25 50 75 100
50%
40%
30%
20%
10%
0%
-10%
-20%
-30%
-40%
Annual Return (%)
1976 1980 1984 1988 1992 1996 2000 2004 2008
Growth of $1
$140
$120
$100
$80
$60
$40
$20
$0
Growth of $1
$125
$70
$40
$21
1976 1980 1984 1988 1992 1996 2000 2004 2008
Sources, Updates, and Disclosures: ifabt.com, Appx A

Portfolio Construction

Once investors identify the asset allocation that matches their risk capacity, they have a choice to make as to how to best implement that asset allocation. A handful of passively managed fund providers offer asset class indexes, namely Vanguard and Dimensional Fund Advisors (DFA). The index portfolios referenced in this book are implemented with funds from DFA, a highly regarded fund company which provides pure implementations of Modern Portfolio Theory and the Fama/French Five Factor Model, purposefully isolating risk factors to efficiently capture higher expected returns for the level of risk chosen. This isolation is beneficial because it allows the DFA funds to achieve a stronger tilt toward the small and value risk factors that have shown to deliver higher returns at comparable levels of risk.

Figure 11-3 illustrates a 12-year comparison between 20 index portfolios comprised of funds from DFA and 20 Vanguard portfolios which carry the same asset allocation weightings. This time period was used due to live data available. Results are net of fund fees and a 0.9% advisor fee for both strategies. The chart shows that at every level of risk, the index portfolios utilizing DFA funds had a higher annualized return than the index portfolios using Vanguard funds.

Figure 11-4 shows the constituent Vanguard Portfolios 25, 50, 75, and 100 displayed in Figure 11-3. All of the funds used in this comparison are Vanguard's index funds with the longest history of returns data.

Figure 11-3

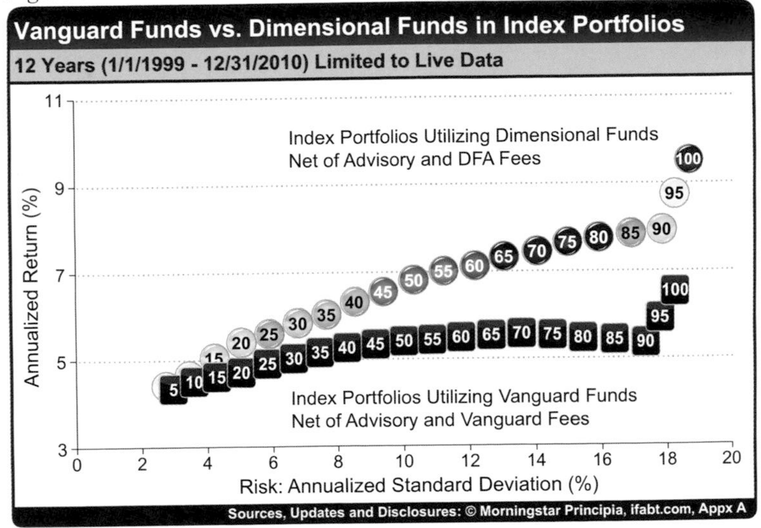

Figure 11-4

Asset Allocation of Index Portfolios Utilizing Vanguard Funds

12 Years (1/1/1999 - 12/31/2010)

Vanguard Index Funds		Allocation of Vanguard Funds			
		25	50	75	100
Vanguard 500 Index Investor	VFINX	7.00%	12.00%	17.00%	12.00%
Vanguard Value Index	VIVAX	7.00%	12.00%	17.00%	12.00%
Vanguard Small Cap Index	NAESX	3.50%	6.00%	8.50%	20.00%
Vanguard Small Cap Value Index	VISVX	3.50%	6.00%	8.50%	20.00%
Vanguard REIT Index	VGSIX	3.50%	6.00%	8.50%	5.00%
Vanguard Pacific Stock Index	VPACX	2.33%	4.00%	5.67%	6.00%
Vanguard European Stock Index	VEURX	4.67%	8.00%	11.33%	12.00%
Vanguard Emerging Mkts Stock Idx	VEIEX	3.50%	6.00%	8.50%	13.00%
Vanguard Short-Term Bond Index	VBISX	65.00%	40.00%	15.00%	0.00%

Sources, Updates, and Disclosures: © Morningstar Direct, ifabt.com

Figure 11-5 is a similar chart that replaces the Vanguard portfolios with portfolios of iShares exchange-traded funds. The beginning date is two years later (due to the limited availability of live ETF data), but the results are similar. The size of the DFA advantage is directly proportional to the risk level of the portfolio. Although several brokerage firms offer a "free-trades" promotion with select ETFs, investors should proceed cautiously with their trades, staying cognizant of the bid/ask spread, the depth of the order book, and the possible divergence between market price and net asset value. Investors who don't know what any of that means probably should refrain from trading ETFs. Finally, investors must avoid the temptation to use ETFs as market-timing tools.

Figure 11-6 shows the constituent iShares exchange-traded funds used in the iShares Portfolios 25, 50, 75, and 100 displayed in Figure 11-5. Although iShares offers more than one ETF in each asset class, these funds were chosen to obtain the longest possible history of returns data.

DFA funds are available through a select group of registered investment advisors to whom the company provides comprehensive data from CRSP on numerous indexes dating all the way back to 1928. This allows for analysis of data that is usually only available to academic researchers.

DFA's emphasis on training advisors to educate investors has contributed immensely to the ability of investors to capture the returns offered by the compensated risk factors of the market.

Figure 11-5

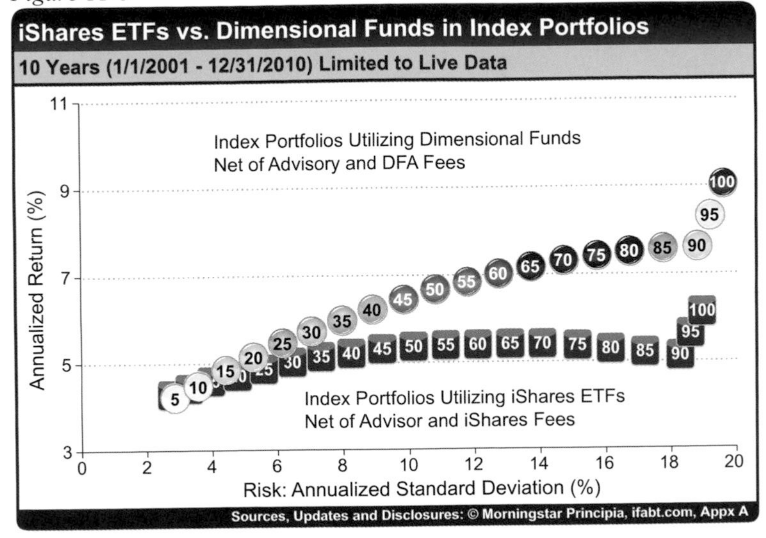

Figure 11-6

Asset Allocation of Index Portfolios Utilizing iShares ETFs

10 Years (1/1/2001 - 12/31/2010)

iShares Index Funds		Allocation of iShares ETFs			
		25	50	75	100
iShares S&P 500	IVV	7.00%	12.00%	17.00%	12.00%
iShares Russell 1000 Value	IWD	7.00%	12.00%	17.00%	12.00%
iShares Russell 2000	IWM	3.50%	6.00%	8.50%	20.00%
iShares Russell 2000 Value	IWN	3.50%	6.00%	8.50%	20.00%
iShares Cohen & Steers Realty	ICF	3.50%	6.00%	8.50%	5.00%
iShares MSCI EAFE Value	EFV	7.00%	12.00%	17.00%	18.00%
iShares MSCI Emerging Markets	EEM	3.50%	6.00%	8.50%	13.00%
iShares Barclays 1-3 Year Treasury	SHY	32.50%	20.00%	7.50%	0.00%
iShares Barclays 3-7 Year Treasury	IEI	32.50%	20.00%	7.50%	0.00%

Sources, Updates, and Disclosures: © Morningstar Direct, ifabt.com

Dalbar surveyed investment advisors four times between 1997 and 2004. The study was titled, "The Professionals' Pick." Dalbar rated DFA the best overall no-load mutual fund company in 1997, 2000, 2002, and number two in 2004. DFA was also rated #1 in 2010 and 2011 by Cogent Research and #1 by *Barron's* in 2010. See Figure 11-7.

It's All In The Mix

A globally diversified portfolio has historically delivered the most efficient returns for the risk that is built into each individual portfolio. Figure 11-8 plots the risk and reward optimizations for 20 index portfolios and various indexes, alongside an S&P 500 Index over the 50-year period from January 1, 1961 to December 31, 2010. Note the higher annualized returns of the index portfolios that have the same risk (annualized standard deviation) as the S&P 500 Index. Also note the returns of the emerging market asset classes when isolated on their own (high risk with compensated returns). The index portfolios shown are all comprised of an efficient blend of indexes. For a sample of specific portfolio allocations, see the end of this step.

The chart shows the S&P 500 had essentially the same risk (15.10%) as Portfolio 90 (15.30%) but delivered a lower return: 9.75% vs. 12.34%. The S&P 500 actually delivered a return closer to the return of Portfolio 45, which shows the risk of the S&P 500 was not compensated the same. A higher annualized return could have been delivered by taking less risk. This chart shows the value of diversifying beyond large cap companies in the U.S., as reflected in the S&P 500. Portfolios 45-90 all

Figure 11-7

Fund Company Ratings

15 Years (1997 - 2011)

Company	Rating
Dalbar 1997 Rankings	
Dimensional Fund Advisors	3.86
Vanguard Group	3.82
Oakmark Funds	3.79
T. Rowe Price	3.79
American Funds	3.79
Janus Funds	3.72
MFS Funds	3.62
SEI Financial	3.61
PIMCO Advisors	3.60
Franklin Templeton Funds	3.58
Dalbar 2000 Rankings	
Dimensional Fund Advisors	3.81
Janus Funds	3.76
PIMCO	3.71
American Skandia	3.70
INVESCO	3.67
Oppenheimer Funds	3.66
Vanguard	3.66
American Funds	3.65
AIM	3.63
MFS Funds	3.62
Dalbar 2002 Rankings	
Dimensional Fund Advisors	3.93
American Funds	3.84
Artisan Funds	3.82
Oakmark Funds	3.73
State Street Research	3.71
PIMCO Advisors	3.64
SEI Financials	3.64
Smith Barney Mutual Funds	3.64
WM Group	3.64
Calvert	3.58

Company	Rating
Dalbar 2004 Rankings	
General Opinion Top 4	
Dodge and Cox Funds	3.96
Dimensional Fund Advisors	3.93
American Funds	3.84
Pacific Funds	3.82
Investment Management Top 4	
Dimensional Fund Advisors	3.96
First Eagle Funds	3.91
Dodge and Cox Funds	3.90
Calamos	3.89
Cogent Research Rankings	
Advisor Commitment Ranking 2010	
Dimensional Fund Advisors	1
BlackRock	2
PIMCO	3
American Funds	4
Advisor Commitment Ranking 2011	
Dimensional Fund Advisors	1
J.P. Morgan Funds	2
PIMCO	3
Vanguard	4
Barron's 2010 Ratings	
Dimensional Fund Advisors	67.98
Nuveen Fund Advisors	66.79
Principal Management	64.57
Oppenheimer Funds	64.04
Waddell & Reed	63.04
Aberdeen Asset Management	62.63
Lord Abbett	62.28
Legg Mason	61.28
Ivy Investment Management	60.09
Russell Investment	59.50

Sources: Dalbar, "Changing of the Guard" by David Drucker Research, 11/2004, Cogent Research, Barron's, "That's Better Now", by Michael Shari, 2/2011

Figure 11-8

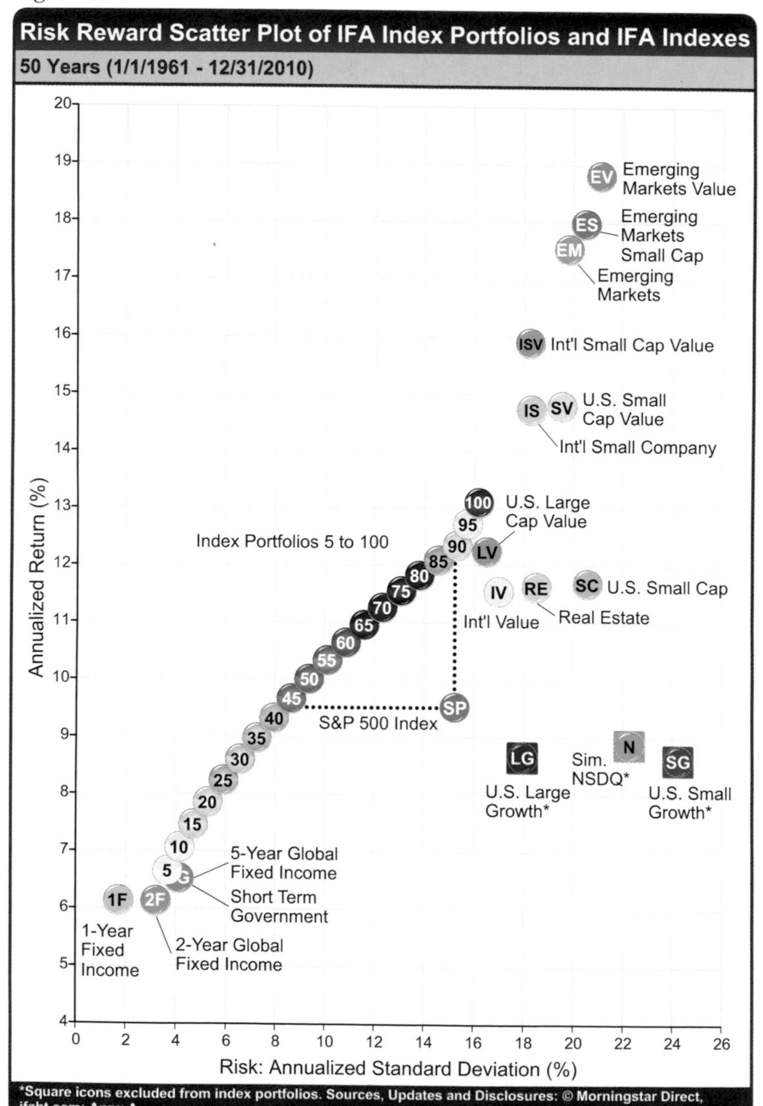
Risk Reward Scatter Plot of IFA Index Portfolios and IFA Indexes
50 Years (1/1/1961 - 12/31/2010)
Annualized Return (%)
Risk: Annualized Standard Deviation (%)
Index Portfolios 5 to 100
EV Emerging Markets Value
ES Emerging Markets Small Cap
EM Emerging Markets
ISV Int'l Small Cap Value
SV U.S. Small Cap Value
IS Int'l Small Company
100 U.S. Large Cap Value
LV
IV Int'l Value
RE Real Estate
SC U.S. Small Cap
SP S&P 500 Index
LG U.S. Large Growth*
N Sim. NSDQ*
SG U.S. Small Growth*
5-Year Global Fixed Income
Short Term Government
1F 1-Year Fixed Income
2F 2-Year Global Fixed Income
*Square icons excluded from index portfolios. Sources, Updates and Disclosures: © Morningstar Direct, ifabt.com; Appx A

delivered higher annualized returns with the same or less risk than the S&P 500.

Figure 11-9 shows 50 years of monthly return distributions for four index portfolios. These histograms represent 600 months of risk and return data from January 1, 1961 to December 31, 2010. Note the wider bell curve distributions in the higher risk Portfolios 100 and 75 as compared to the lower risk Portfolios 50 and 25. This indicates that the riskier portfolios had a larger range of outcomes over time.

This wider range or increased volatility has also carried a higher degree of return. Of the four portfolios shown, the least risky Portfolio 25 had the narrowest range of monthly return outcomes over the 50-year period. This narrower range or decreased volatility is the trade-off for lower returns, relative to Portfolios 100, 75 and 50 that had higher risk and higher returns. The charts also reflect the growth of a $1 investment in each portfolio over the 50-year period. Remember that an investor's actual returns will vary from these asset class allocations due to the timing of withdrawals and contributions, rebalancing strategies and costs, fees, and other factors.

As was shown in the previous charts and discussions, efficient diversification among low-cost index funds is a very effective means for investing one's assets. Further, index portfolios that carry risk-appropriate blends of the indexes that have historically rewarded investors is a highly prudent strategy. Indeed, while one cannot obtain any guarantee of future success based on the past, the 83 years of data associated with the style-pure index portfolio allocations is arguably as

Figure 11-9

Distribution of Monthly Returns of Index Portfolios

50 Years (1/1/1961 - 12/31/2010)

Index Portfolio 100: Bright Red

Average Monthly Return: 1.14%
Monthly Standard Deviation: 4.67%
Growth of $1: $468.12

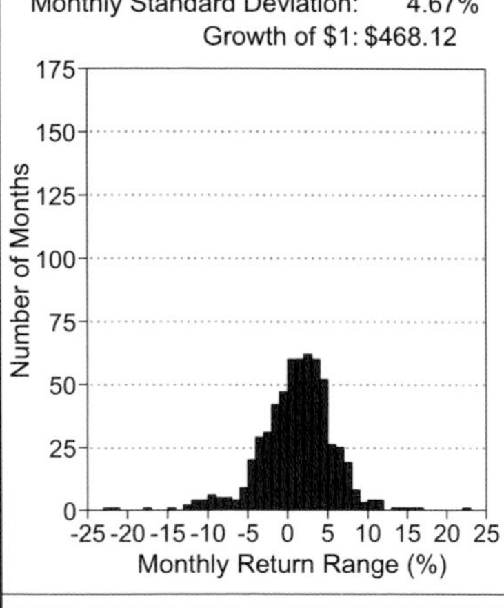

Index Portfolio 75: Dark Blue

Average Monthly Return: 0.99%
Monthly Standard Deviation: 3.76%
Growth of $1: $234.77

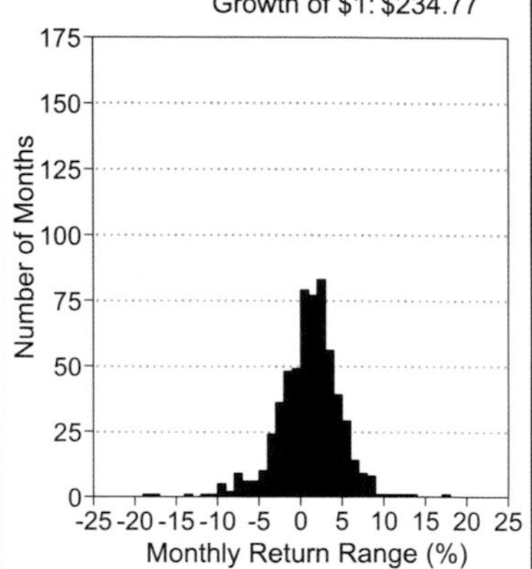

Index Portfolio 50: Sea Green

Average Monthly Return: 0.83%
Monthly Standard Deviation: 2.71%
Growth of $1: $117.38

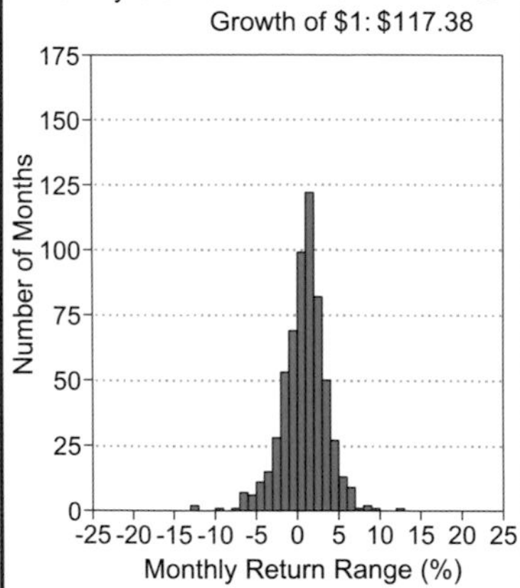

Index Portfolio 25: Ice Blue

Average Monthly Return: 0.68%
Monthly Standard Deviation: 1.71%
Growth of $1: $52.16

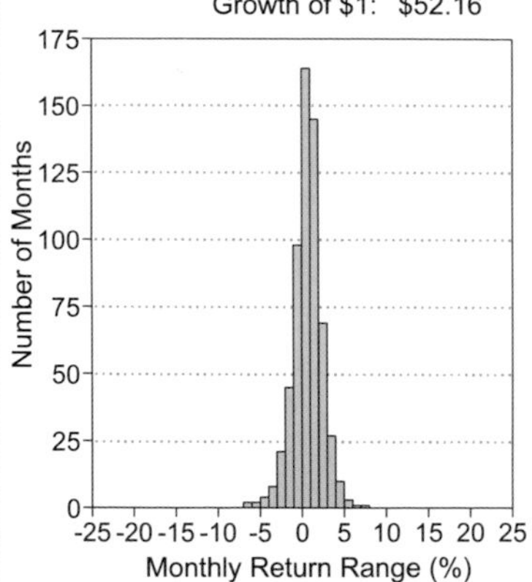

Sources, Updates and Disclosures: ifabt.com, Appx A

good as it gets for any investor, individual or institutional.

The data table in Figure 11-10 represents the short-term and long-term risk and return data for the S&P 500 and 10 index portfolios with varying degrees of exposure to fixed income and stock market equities. Growth of $1 is also shown for each portfolio. When seeking to construct a portfolio with a high degree of probability of success, it is advisable for investors to pay very careful attention to the 20, 50 and 83-year data columns on the right hand side. The 50-year return is largely considered the historic return and a good estimate of the future or expected return. The left columns which show the year-to-date, 1, 3 and 5-year returns are shown in order to make investors aware of the short-term volatility of the various investments and should not be considered useful for determining which portfolio is right for an investor.

Notice in the 50-year column the correlation between the higher risk numbers and the impact on returns as measured in percentages and dollars over time. Also notice the benefits of diversification that efficiently implemented risk and captured higher returns compared to the S&P 500. Index Portfolios 60-80 outstripped returns at a lower level of risk, and Index Portfolios 90-100 substantially improved returns relative to the S&P 500 at similar levels of risk. As you can see from the abundance of data shown, a knowledge of the long-term risk and return characteristics of the index portfolios enables an investor to make a sound investment choice that is based on history and probabilities, thus avoiding the hazards of speculation.

Figure 11-10

Index Portfolios and S&P 500 Over Various Periods

83 Years, 10 Months (1/1/1928 - 10/31/2011)

Portfolio		YTD ending 10/31/11	1 Yr ending 2010	1 Yr ending 2009	1 Yr ending 2008	3 Yrs 2008-2010	5 Yrs 2006-2010	20 Yrs 1991-2010	50 Yrs 1961-2010	83 Yrs 1928-2010
SP	Growth $1	$1.01	$1.15	$1.26	$0.63	$0.92	$1.12	$5.75	$104	$1,941
	Return %	1.30%	15.06%	26.46%	-37.00%	-2.86%	2.29%	9.14%	9.75%	9.55%
	Risk %	N/A	19.26%	22.28%	21.02%	22.16%	17.82%	15.06%	15.10%	19.32%
100	Growth $1	$0.93	$1.23	$1.40	$0.59	$1.02	$1.27	$9.14	$468	$6,675
	Return %	-6.98%	22.66%	39.63%	-40.55%	0.61%	4.96%	11.70%	13.09%	11.19%
	Risk %	N/A	22.72%	29.94%	28.06%	28.44%	22.99%	16.56%	16.19%	22.76%
90	Growth $1	$0.94	$1.20	$1.37	$0.59	$0.97	$1.21	$7.61	$335	$4,323
	Return %	-5.64%	19.98%	37.13%	-41.17%	-1.08%	3.94%	10.68%	12.34%	10.61%
	Risk %	N/A	21.95%	29.44%	27.73%	27.92%	22.51%	15.76%	15.30%	21.81%
80	Growth $1	$0.95	$1.18	$1.34	$0.63	$1.00	$1.24	$7.02	$265	$3,185
	Return %	-4.91%	18.21%	33.57%	-36.63%	0.02%	4.34%	10.23%	11.81%	10.21%
	Risk %	N/A	19.73%	26.37%	24.25%	24.80%	20.02%	14.11%	13.79%	19.53%
70	Growth $1	$0.96	$1.16	$1.30	$0.68	$1.03	$1.25	$6.41	$206	$2,226
	Return %	-4.18%	16.43%	30.00%	-32.10%	0.92%	4.61%	9.74%	11.25%	9.73%
	Risk %	N/A	17.50%	23.36%	20.96%	21.77%	17.61%	12.48%	12.30%	17.32%
60	Growth $1	$0.97	$1.15	$1.26	$0.72	$1.05	$1.26	$5.81	$157	$1,479
	Return %	-3.45%	14.66%	26.44%	-27.56%	1.64%	4.76%	9.20%	10.64%	9.19%
	Risk %	N/A	15.27%	20.40%	17.86%	18.83%	15.25%	10.88%	10.84%	15.15%
50	Growth $1	$0.97	$1.13	$1.23	$0.77	$1.07	$1.26	$5.22	$117	$935
	Return %	-2.72%	12.89%	22.88%	-23.03%	2.21%	4.80%	8.62%	10.00%	8.59%
	Risk %	N/A	13.04%	17.48%	14.92%	15.97%	12.95%	9.30%	9.39%	13.03%
40	Growth $1	$0.98	$1.11	$1.19	$0.82	$1.08	$1.26	$4.66	$86.06	$563
	Return %	-1.99%	11.11%	19.31%	-18.49%	2.62%	4.74%	8.00%	9.32%	7.93%
	Risk %	N/A	10.81%	14.60%	12.13%	13.17%	10.70%	7.75%	7.98%	10.95%
30	Growth $1	$0.99	$1.09	$1.16	$0.86	$1.09	$1.25	$4.12	$61.93	$323
	Return %	-1.25%	9.34%	15.75%	-13.96%	2.88%	4.59%	7.34%	8.60%	7.21%
	Risk %	N/A	8.58%	11.76%	9.48%	10.45%	8.50%	6.23%	6.60%	8.90%
20	Growth $1	$0.99	$1.08	$1.12	$0.91	$1.09	$1.24	$3.62	$43.73	$177
	Return %	-0.52%	7.56%	12.19%	-9.43%	3.01%	4.34%	6.65%	7.85%	6.44%
	Risk %	N/A	6.37%	8.96%	6.97%	7.79%	6.35%	4.76%	5.30%	6.91%
10	Growth $1	$1.00	$1.06	$1.09	$0.95	$1.09	$1.22	$3.16	$30.30	$92.13
	Return %	0.21%	5.79%	8.62%	-4.89%	3.01%	4.01%	5.92%	7.06%	5.60%
	Risk %	N/A	4.18%	6.21%	4.65%	5.22%	4.26%	3.38%	4.15%	5.02%

Annualized return net of advisory and fund fees, see ifafee.com. Risk measured in annualized standard deviation. Sources, Updates and Disclosures: © Morningstar Direct, ifabt.com, ifacalc.com, Appx A

Matching Risk Exposure To Risk Capacity

Unlike horseshoes, close enough isn't good enough for investors who want to maximize their ability to capitalize on the exchange between risk and return. For this reason, when selecting a diversified portfolio, the primary consideration should be identifying and investing in a blend of indexes that best matches risk capacity.

Many investors choose a common 60/40 asset allocation, regardless of their risk capacity. As you now know, a superior strategy is to invest in a portfolio that directly corresponds to a particular risk capacity. This sophisticated approach enables investors to take on just the right amount of risk—not too much or not too little—allowing them to maximize their expected outcome.

The significant benefits associated with capturing just the right amount of risk are elegantly displayed in Figure 11-11, which shows the growth of $1,000 in 100 different index portfolios over the 50 years from 1961 to 2010. Each of these engineered portfolios is designed with different blends of equities and fixed income. This continuum of risk and return provides investors the opportunity to invest in a targeted asset allocation that matches their risk capacity score between 1 and 100. The chart further validates the value of carefully matching an investor's risk capacity to a corresponding risk exposure, avoiding the rounding up or down of the analysis. As you can see, a small change in risk made a substantial difference in the growth of $1,000 over this 50-year period.

Figure 11-11

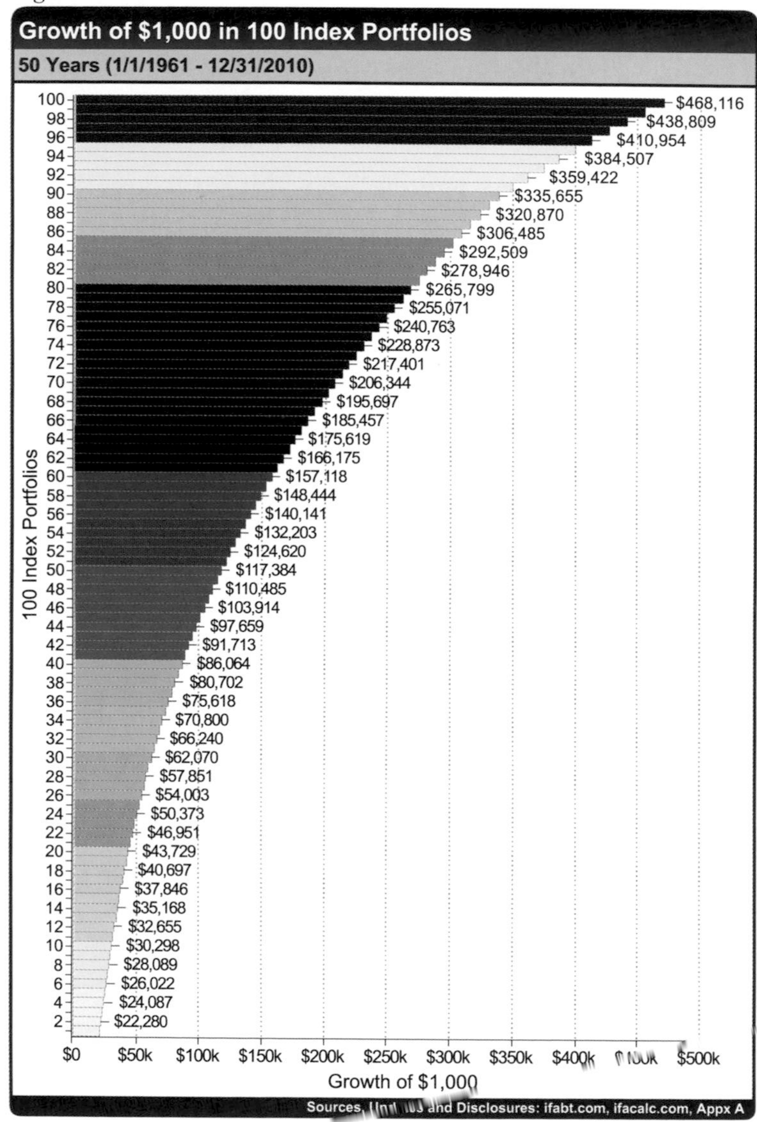
Growth of $1,000 in 100 Index Portfolios
50 Years (1/1/1961 - 12/31/2010)
100 Index Portfolios
100
98
96
94
92
90
88
86
84
82
80
78
76
74
72
70
68
66
64
62
60
58
56
54
52
50
48
46
44
42
40
38
36
34
32
30
28
26
24
22
20
18
16
14
12
10
8
6
4
2
$468,116
$438,809
$410,954
$384,507
$359,422
$335,655
$320,870
$306,485
$292,509
$278,946
$265,799
$255,071
$240,763
$228,873
$217,401
$206,344
$195,697
$185,457
$175,619
$166,175
$157,118
$148,444
$140,141
$132,203
$124,620
$117,384
$110,485
$103,914
$97,659
$91,713
$86,064
$80,702
$75,618
$70,800
$66,240
$62,070
$57,851
$54,003
$50,373
$46,951
$43,729
$40,697
$37,846
$35,168
$32,655
$30,298
$28,089
$26,022
$24,087
$22,280
$0
$50k
$100k
$150k
$200k
$250k
$300k
$350k
$400k
$500k
Growth of $1,000
ifabt.com, ifacalc.com, Appx A

Prudent Investing

The process of prudent long-term investing requires thorough and thoughtful discernment. The best way to earn optimal returns is by buying and holding a passively managed and globally diversified index portfolio, matching an investor's risk exposure to his or her risk capacity and relying on 83 years of historical risk and returns data. In Step 10, an explanation of four unique risk capacities was provided for risk capacity scores 100, 75, 50, and 25. Fact sheets for the four index portfolios that match those risk capacity scores are provided on the following pages. These portfolio fact sheets consist of a list of the indexes contained in each portfolio, simulated returns and volatility data, charts that represent annual returns and growth of $1, a 50-year monthly rolling period analysis, and a histogram of monthly rolling periods for the time intervals matched to the average holding period for each level of risk capacity. To reiterate, the most important question an investor can ask is, "What mix of indexes is best for me?"

Index Portfolio 100: Bright Red

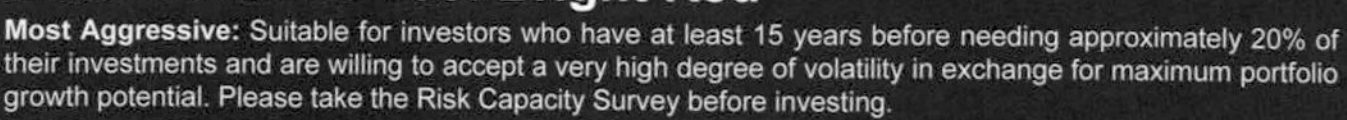

Most Aggressive: Suitable for investors who have at least 15 years before needing approximately 20% of their investments and are willing to accept a very high degree of volatility in exchange for maximum portfolio growth potential. Please take the Risk Capacity Survey before investing.

Index Portfolio Allocation

General Asset Class		Specific Index	
24.0%	US Large	12.00%	U.S. Large Company Index (LC)
		12.00%	U.S. Large Cap Value Index (LV)
40.0%	US Small	20.00%	U.S. Small Cap Index (SC)
		20.00%	U.S. Small Cap Value Index (SV)
5.0%	Real Estate	5.00%	Real Estate Index (RE)
18.0%	International	6.00%	International Value Index (IV)
		6.00%	International Small Company Index (IS)
		6.00%	International Small Cap Value Index (ISV)
13.0%	Emerging Markets	4.00%	Emerging Markets Index (EM)
		4.00%	Emerging Markets Value Index (EV)
		5.00%	Emerging Markets Small Cap Index (ES)
0.0%	Fixed Income	0.00%	One-Year Fixed Income Index (1F)
		0.00%	Two-Year Global Fixed Income Index (2F)
		0.00%	Short Term Government Index (3G)
		0.00%	Five-Year Global Fixed Income Index (5F)

Simulated Returns and Volatility Data

	1 yr ending 2010	1 yr ending 2009	1 yr ending 2008	1 yr ending 2007	1 yr ending 2006	3 yrs 2008-2010	5 yrs 2006-2010	10 yrs 2001-2010	20 yrs 1991-2010	30 yrs 1981-2010	50 yrs 1961-2010	83 yrs 1928-2010
Growth of $1 ($)	1.23	1.40	0.59	1.03	1.22	1.02	1.27	2.36	9.14	38.98	468.12	6,675
Annualized Return (%)	22.66	39.63	-40.55	2.51	22.02	0.61	4.96	8.96	11.70	12.99	13.09	11.19
Standard Deviation (%) (Annualized Volatility)	22.72	29.94	28.06	11.29	10.73	28.44	22.99	19.60	16.56	15.99	16.19	22.76

Annual Returns: 50 Years (1/1/1961 - 12/31/2010)

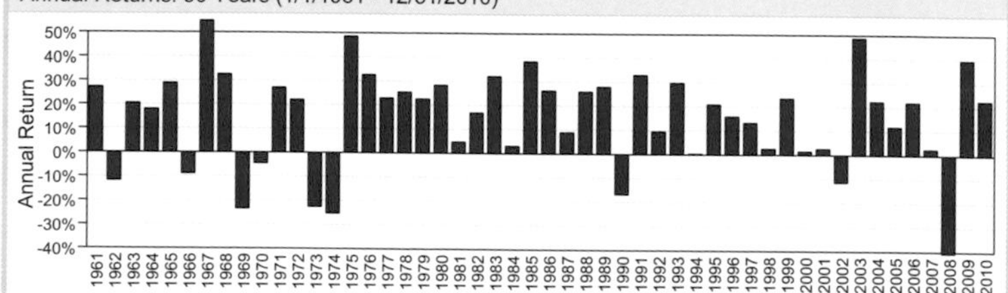

Growth of $1: 50 Years (1/1/1961 - 12/31/2010) - Log Scale

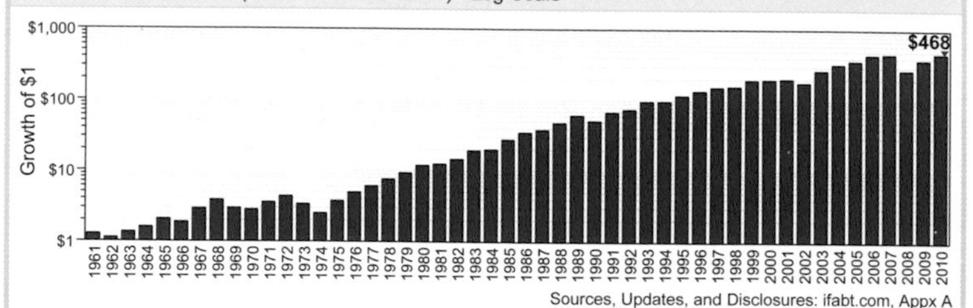

Sources, Updates, and Disclosures: ifabt.com, Appx A

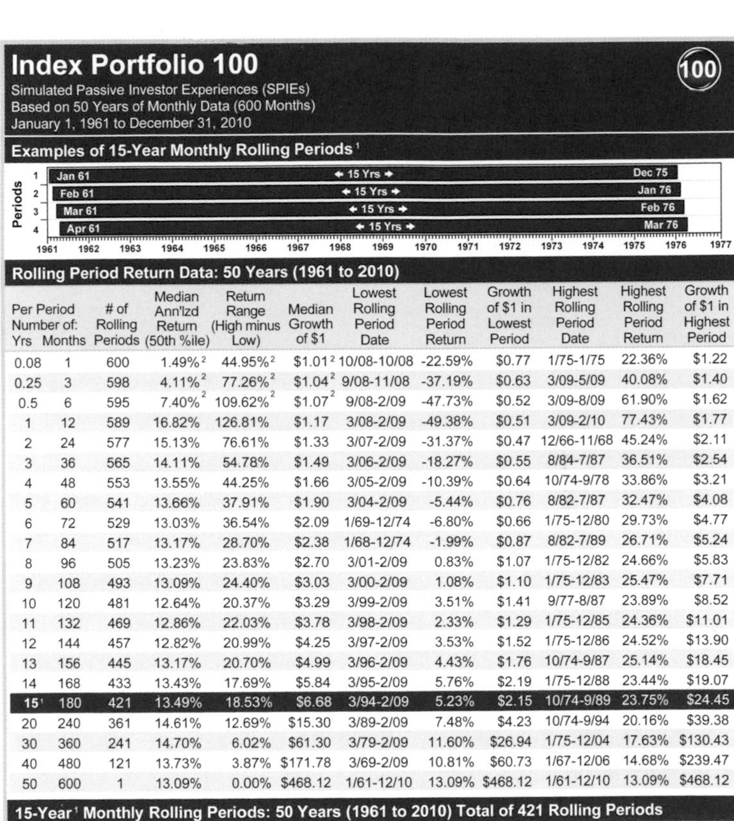

Index Portfolio 100

Simulated Passive Investor Experiences (SPIEs)
Based on 50 Years of Monthly Data (600 Months)
January 1, 1961 to December 31, 2010

Examples of 15-Year Monthly Rolling Periods[1]

Rolling Period Return Data: 50 Years (1961 to 2010)

Per Period Number of: Yrs	Months	# of Rolling Periods	Median Ann'lzd Return (50th %ile)	Return Range (High minus Low)	Median Growth of $1	Lowest Rolling Period Date	Lowest Rolling Period Return	Growth of $1 in Lowest Period	Highest Rolling Period Date	Highest Rolling Period Return	Growth of $1 in Highest Period
0.08	1	600	1.49%[2]	44.95%[2]	$1.01[2]	10/08-10/08	-22.59%	$0.77	1/75-1/75	22.36%	$1.22
0.25	3	598	4.11%[2]	77.26%[2]	$1.04[2]	9/08-11/08	-37.19%	$0.63	3/09-5/09	40.08%	$1.40
0.5	6	595	7.40%[2]	109.62%[2]	$1.07[2]	9/08-2/09	-47.73%	$0.52	3/09-8/09	61.90%	$1.62
1	12	589	16.82%	126.81%	$1.17	3/08-2/09	-49.38%	$0.51	3/09-2/10	77.43%	$1.77
2	24	577	15.13%	76.61%	$1.33	3/07-2/09	-31.37%	$0.47	12/66-11/68	45.24%	$2.11
3	36	565	14.11%	54.78%	$1.49	3/06-2/09	-18.27%	$0.55	8/84-7/87	36.51%	$2.54
4	48	553	13.55%	44.25%	$1.66	3/05-2/09	-10.39%	$0.64	10/74-9/78	33.86%	$3.21
5	60	541	13.66%	37.91%	$1.90	3/04-2/09	-5.44%	$0.76	8/82-7/87	32.47%	$4.08
6	72	529	13.03%	36.54%	$2.09	1/69-12/74	-6.80%	$0.66	1/75-12/80	29.73%	$4.77
7	84	517	13.17%	28.70%	$2.38	1/68-12/74	-1.99%	$0.87	8/82-7/89	26.71%	$5.24
8	96	505	13.23%	23.83%	$2.70	3/01-2/09	0.83%	$1.07	1/75-12/82	24.66%	$5.83
9	108	493	13.09%	24.40%	$3.03	3/00-2/09	1.08%	$1.10	1/75-12/83	25.47%	$7.71
10	120	481	12.64%	20.37%	$3.29	3/99-2/09	3.51%	$1.41	9/77-8/87	23.89%	$8.52
11	132	469	12.86%	22.03%	$3.78	3/98-2/09	2.33%	$1.29	1/75-12/85	24.36%	$11.01
12	144	457	12.82%	20.99%	$4.25	3/97-2/09	3.53%	$1.52	1/75-12/86	24.52%	$13.90
13	156	445	13.17%	20.70%	$4.99	3/96-2/09	4.43%	$1.76	10/74-9/87	25.14%	$18.45
14	168	433	13.43%	17.69%	$5.84	3/95-2/09	5.76%	$2.19	1/75-12/88	23.44%	$19.07
15[1]	180	421	13.49%	18.53%	$6.68	3/94-2/09	5.23%	$2.15	10/74-9/89	23.75%	$24.45
20	240	361	14.61%	12.69%	$15.30	3/89-2/09	7.48%	$4.23	10/74-9/94	20.16%	$39.38
30	360	241	14.70%	6.02%	$61.30	3/79-2/09	11.60%	$26.94	1/75-12/04	17.63%	$130.43
40	480	121	13.73%	3.87%	$171.78	3/69-2/09	10.81%	$60.73	1/67-12/06	14.68%	$239.47
50	600	1	13.09%	0.00%	$468.12	1/61-12/10	13.09%	$468.12	1/61-12/10	13.09%	$468.12

15-Year[1] Monthly Rolling Periods: 50 Years (1961 to 2010) Total of 421 Rolling Periods

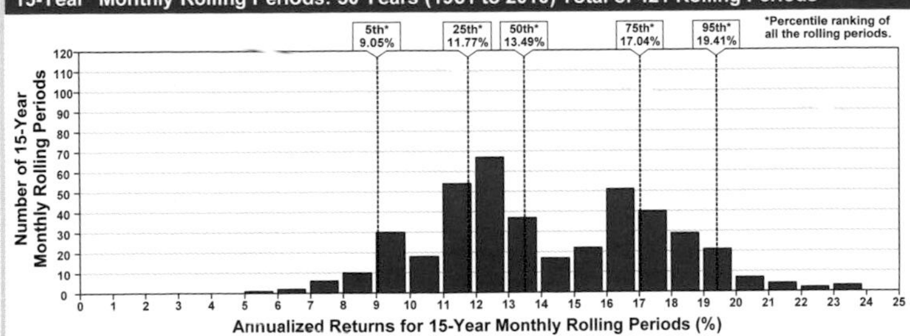

[1] 15-years represents the estimated average holding period for investors who score 100 on the Risk Capacity Survey at ifa.com.
[2] The Median Annualized Returns, Return Range, and Median Growth of $1 shown for 1, 3, and 6 month periods are not annualized.

Sources, Updates, and Disclosures: ifabt.com, Appx A

Index Portfolio 75: Dark Blue

Moderately Aggressive: Suitable for investors who have at least 13 years before needing approximately 20% of their investments and are willing to accept a higher degree of volatility in order to achieve higher portfolio growth potential. Please take the Risk Capacity Survey before investing.

Index Portfolio Allocation

General Asset Class		Specific Index	
34.0%	US Large	17.00%	U.S. Large Company Index (LC)
		17.00%	U.S. Large Cap Value Index (LV)
17.0%	US Small	8.50%	U.S. Small Cap Index (SC)
		8.50%	U.S. Small Cap Value Index (SV)
8.5%	Real Estate	8.50%	Real Estate Index (RE)
17.0%	International	8.50%	International Value Index (IV)
		4.25%	International Small Company Index (IS)
		4.25%	International Small Cap Value Index (ISV)
8.5%	Emerging Markets	2.55%	Emerging Markets Index (EM)
		2.55%	Emerging Markets Value Index (EV)
		3.40%	Emerging Markets Small Cap Index (ES)
15.0%	Fixed Income	3.75%	One-Year Fixed Income Index (1F)
		3.75%	Two-Year Global Fixed Income Index (2F)
		3.75%	Short Term Government Index (3G)
		3.75%	Five-Year Global Fixed Income Index (5F)

Simulated Returns and Volatility Data

	1 yr ending 2010	1 yr ending 2009	1 yr ending 2008	1 yr ending 2007	1 yr ending 2006	3 yrs 2008-2010	5 yrs 2006-2010	10 yrs 2001-2010	20 yrs 1991-2010	30 yrs 1981-2010	50 yrs 1961-2010	83 yrs 1928-2010
Growth of $1 ($)	1.17	1.32	0.66	1.02	1.20	1.01	1.25	2.03	6.72	27.15	234.77	2,680
Annualized Return (%)	17.32	31.78	-34.36	2.37	19.91	0.49	4.49	7.36	9.99	11.63	11.54	9.98
Standard Deviation (%) (Annualized Volatility)	18.61	24.86	22.58	9.67	7.94	23.27	18.81	15.72	13.29	12.95	13.04	18.42

Annual Returns: 50 Years (1/1/1961 - 12/31/2010)

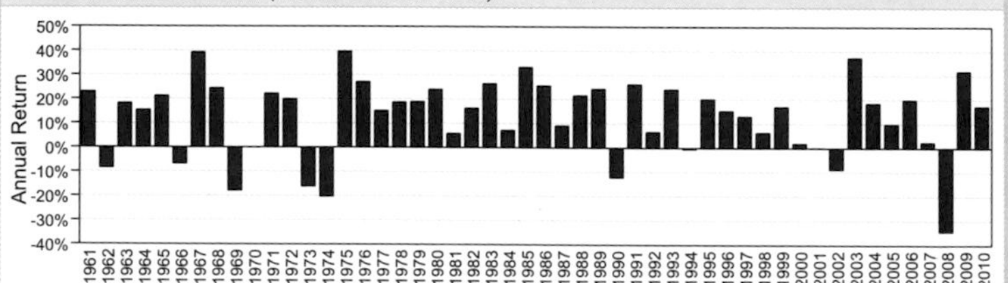

Growth of $1: 50 Years (1/1/1961 - 12/31/2010) - Log Scale

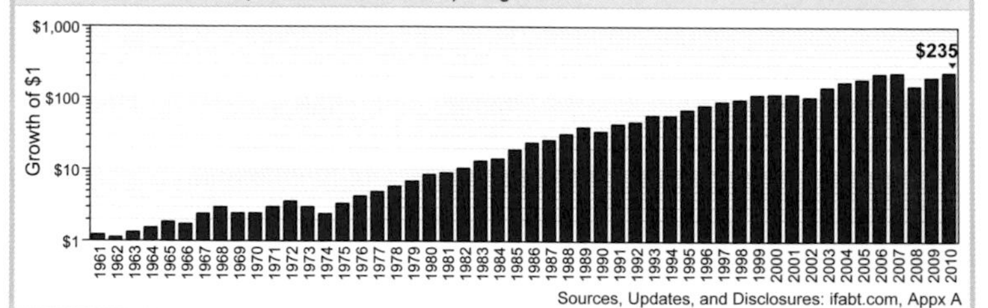

Sources, Updates, and Disclosures: ifabt.com, Appx A

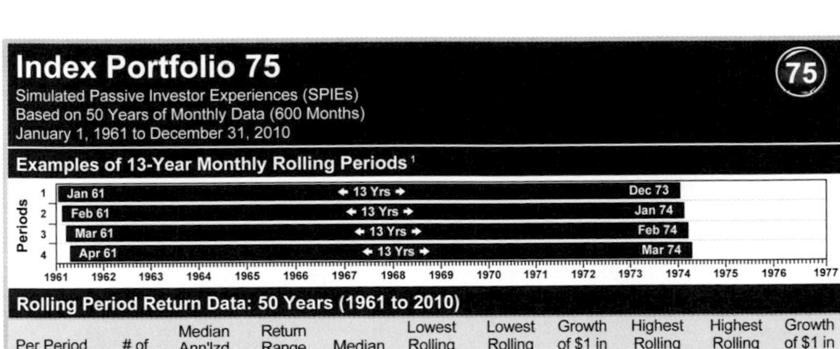

Rolling Period Return Data: 50 Years (1961 to 2010)

Per Period Number of: Yrs	Months	# of Rolling Periods	Median Ann'lzd Return (50th %ile)	Return Range (High minus Low)	Median Growth of $1	Lowest Rolling Period Date	Lowest Rolling Period Return	Growth of $1 in Lowest Period	Highest Rolling Period Date	Highest Rolling Period Return	Growth of $1 in Highest Period
0.08	1	600	1.30%[2]	36.04%[2]	$1.01[2]	10/08-10/08	-18.56%	$0.81	1/75-1/75	17.48%	$1.17
0.25	3	598	3.53%[2]	62.35%[2]	$1.04[2]	9/08-11/08	-30.44%	$0.70	3/09-5/09	31.91%	$1.32
0.5	6	595	6.63%[2]	90.34%[2]	$1.07[2]	9/08-2/09	-40.83%	$0.59	3/09-8/09	49.51%	$1.50
1	12	589	14.47%	104.14%	$1.14	3/08-2/09	-42.98%	$0.57	3/09-2/10	61.16%	$1.61
2	24	577	13.27%	62.20%	$1.28	3/07-2/09	-26.61%	$0.54	9/85-8/87	35.59%	$1.84
3	36	565	12.31%	47.63%	$1.42	3/06-2/09	-14.64%	$0.62	8/84-7/87	32.99%	$2.35
4	48	553	11.89%	37.35%	$1.57	3/05-2/09	-8.05%	$0.71	7/82-6/86	29.30%	$2.80
5	60	541	11.93%	33.29%	$1.76	3/04-2/09	-4.00%	$0.82	8/82-7/87	29.29%	$3.61
6	72	529	11.46%	27.91%	$1.92	1/69-12/74	-3.56%	$0.80	10/81-9/87	24.35%	$3.70
7	84	517	11.21%	24.17%	$2.10	1/68-12/74	0.01%	$1.00	8/82-7/89	24.18%	$4.55
8	96	505	11.43%	20.76%	$2.38	3/01-2/09	0.82%	$1.07	8/82-7/90	21.58%	$4.77
9	108	493	11.41%	19.64%	$2.64	3/00-2/09	1.38%	$1.13	1/75-12/83	21.02%	$5.57
10	120	481	11.23%	18.36%	$2.90	3/99-2/09	2.71%	$1.31	9/77-8/87	21.07%	$6.77
11	132	469	11.32%	18.55%	$3.25	3/98-2/09	2.19%	$1.27	1/75-12/85	20.75%	$7.96
12	144	457	11.39%	17.81%	$3.65	3/97-2/09	3.34%	$1.48	1/75-12/86	21.15%	$10.00
13[1]	156	445	11.37%	17.60%	$4.06	3/96-2/09	4.23%	$1.71	10/74-9/87	21.84%	$13.03
14	168	433	11.85%	14.85%	$4.79	3/95-2/09	5.43%	$2.10	1/75-12/88	20.28%	$13.26
15	180	421	11.73%	15.69%	$5.28	3/94-2/09	4.99%	$2.08	10/74-9/89	20.68%	$16.77
20	240	361	13.18%	10.70%	$11.89	3/89-2/09	6.75%	$3.69	10/74-9/94	17.44%	$24.93
30	360	241	13.13%	4.69%	$40.49	3/79-2/09	10.57%	$20.39	1/75-12/04	15.27%	$70.97
40	480	121	12.19%	3.04%	$99.50	3/69-2/09	9.91%	$43.80	1/67-12/06	12.95%	$130.29
50	600	1	11.54%	0.00%	$234.77	1/61-12/10	11.54%	$234.77	1/61-12/10	11.54%	$234.77

13-Year[1] Monthly Rolling Periods: 50 Years (1961 to 2010) Total of 445 Rolling Periods

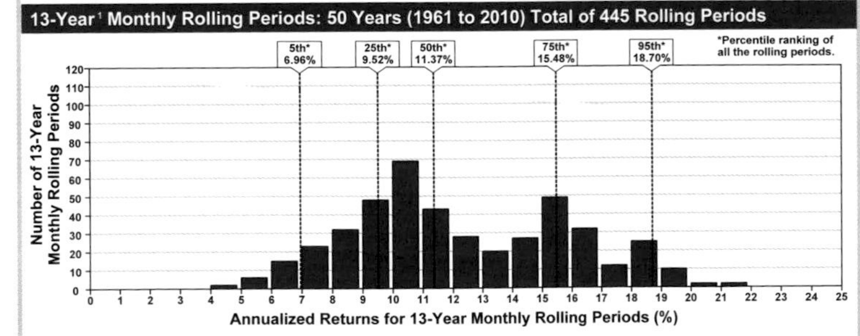

[1] 13-years represents the estimated average holding period for investors who score 75 on the Risk Capacity Survey at ifa.com.

[2] The Median Annualized Returns, Return Range, and Median Growth of $1 shown for 1, 3, and 6 month periods are not annualized

Sources, Updates, and Disclosures: ifabt.com, Appx A

Index Portfolio 50: Sea Green

Moderate: Suitable for investors who have 8 years before needing approximately 20% of their investments and are willing to accept a moderate degree of volatility in order to achieve moderate portfolio growth. Please take the Risk Capacity Survey before investing.

Index Portfolio Allocation

General Asset Class		Specific Index	
24.0%	US Large	12.00%	U.S. Large Company Index (LC)
		12.00%	U.S. Large Cap Value Index (LV)
12.0%	US Small	6.00%	U.S. Small Cap Index (SC)
		6.00%	U.S. Small Cap Value Index (SV)
6.0%	Real Estate	6.00%	Real Estate Index (RE)
12.0%	International	6.00%	International Value Index (IV)
		3.00%	International Small Company Index (IS)
		3.00%	International Small Cap Value Index (ISV)
6.0%	Emerging Markets	1.80%	Emerging Markets Index (EM)
		1.80%	Emerging Markets Value Index (EV)
		2.40%	Emerging Markets Small Cap Index (ES)
40.0%	Fixed Income	10.00%	One-Year Fixed Income Index (1F)
		10.00%	Two-Year Global Fixed Income Index (2F)
		10.00%	Short Term Government Index (3G)
		10.00%	Five-Year Global Fixed Income Index (5F)

Simulated Returns and Volatility Data

	1 yr ending 2010	1 yr ending 2009	1 yr ending 2008	1 yr ending 2007	1 yr ending 2006	3 yrs 2008-2010	5 yrs 2006-2010	10 yrs 2001-2010	20 yrs 1991-2010	30 yrs 1981-2010	50 yrs 1961-2010	83 yrs 1928-2010
Growth of $1 ($)	1.13	1.23	0.77	1.03	1.15	1.07	1.26	1.90	5.22	18.75	117.38	935.67
Annualized Return (%)	12.89	22.88	-23.03	2.91	15.08	2.21	4.80	6.61	8.62	10.26	10.00	8.59
Standard Deviation (%) (Annualized Volatility)	13.04	17.48	14.92	6.92	5.67	15.97	12.95	10.81	9.30	9.27	9.39	13.03

Annual Returns: 50 Years (1/1/1961 - 12/31/2010)

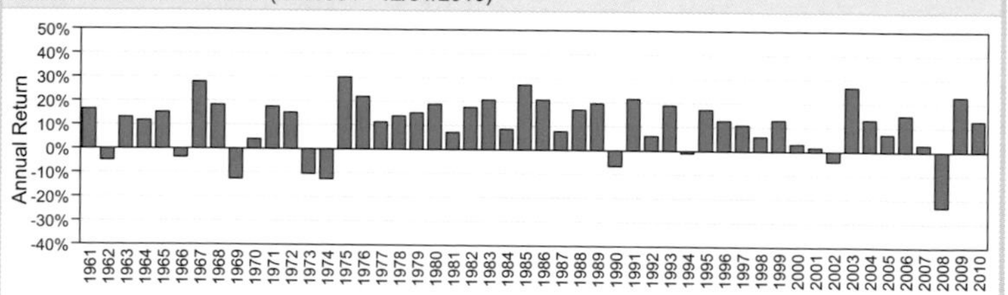

Growth of $1: 50 Years (1/1/1961 - 12/31/2010) - Log Scale

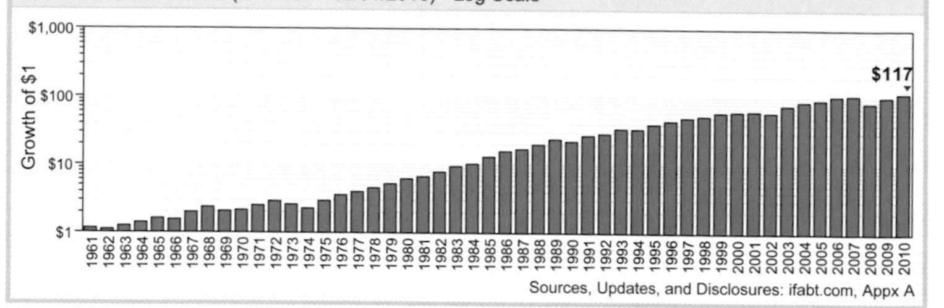

Sources, Updates, and Disclosures: ifabt.com, Appx A

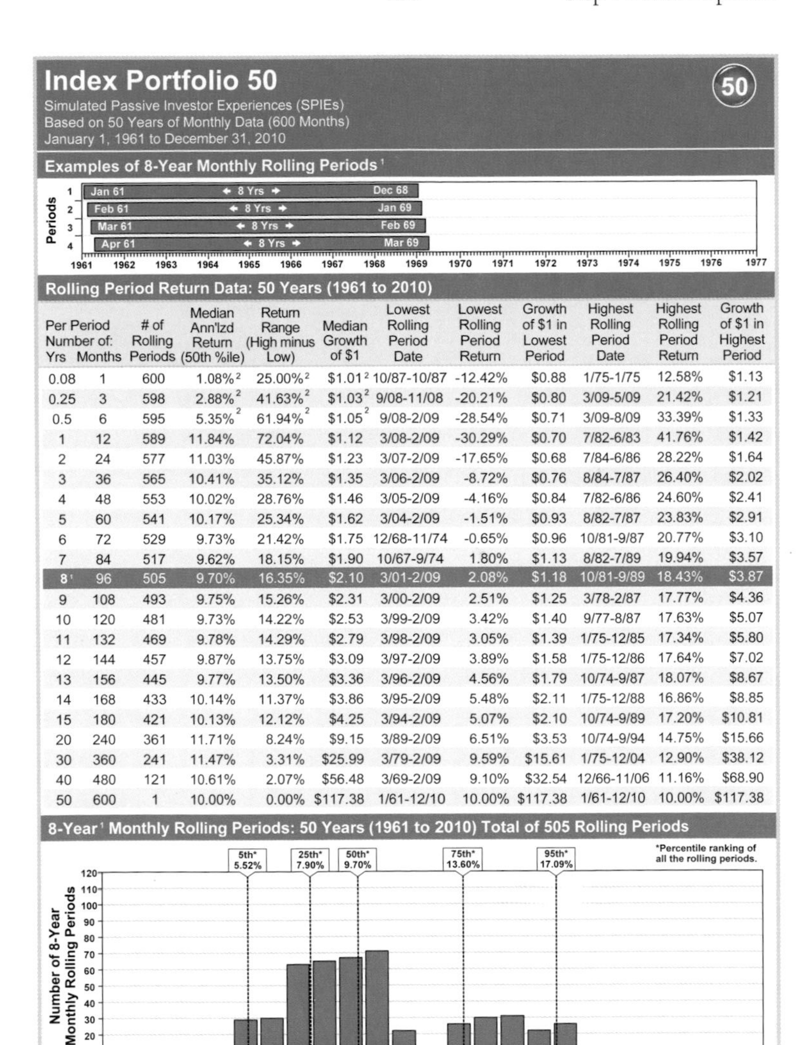

Index Portfolio 50

Simulated Passive Investor Experiences (SPIEs)
Based on 50 Years of Monthly Data (600 Months)
January 1, 1961 to December 31, 2010

Examples of 8-Year Monthly Rolling Periods[1]

Rolling Period Return Data: 50 Years (1961 to 2010)

Per Period Number of: Yrs	Months	# of Rolling Periods	Median Ann'lzd Return (50th %ile)	Return Range (High minus Low)	Median Growth of $1	Lowest Rolling Period Date	Lowest Rolling Period Return	Growth of $1 in Lowest Period	Highest Rolling Period Date	Highest Rolling Period Return	Growth of $1 in Highest Period
0.08	1	600	1.08%[2]	25.00%[2]	$1.01[2]	10/87-10/87	-12.42%	$0.88	1/75-1/75	12.58%	$1.13
0.25	3	598	2.88%[2]	41.63%[2]	$1.03[2]	9/08-11/08	-20.21%	$0.80	3/09-5/09	21.42%	$1.21
0.5	6	595	5.35%[2]	61.94%[2]	$1.05[2]	9/08-2/09	-28.54%	$0.71	3/09-8/09	33.39%	$1.33
1	12	589	11.84%	72.04%	$1.12	3/08-2/09	-30.29%	$0.70	7/82-6/83	41.76%	$1.42
2	24	577	11.03%	45.87%	$1.23	3/07-2/09	-17.65%	$0.68	7/84-6/86	28.22%	$1.64
3	36	565	10.41%	35.12%	$1.35	3/06-2/09	-8.72%	$0.76	8/84-7/87	26.40%	$2.02
4	48	553	10.02%	28.76%	$1.46	3/05-2/09	-4.16%	$0.84	7/82-6/86	24.60%	$2.41
5	60	541	10.17%	25.34%	$1.62	3/04-2/09	-1.51%	$0.93	8/82-7/87	23.83%	$2.91
6	72	529	9.73%	21.42%	$1.75	12/68-11/74	-0.65%	$0.96	10/81-9/87	20.77%	$3.10
7	84	517	9.62%	18.15%	$1.90	10/67-9/74	1.80%	$1.13	8/82-7/89	19.94%	$3.57
8[1]	96	505	9.70%	16.35%	$2.10	3/01-2/09	2.08%	$1.18	10/81-9/89	18.43%	$3.87
9	108	493	9.75%	15.26%	$2.31	3/00-2/09	2.51%	$1.25	3/78-2/87	17.77%	$4.36
10	120	481	9.73%	14.22%	$2.53	3/99-2/09	3.42%	$1.40	9/77-8/87	17.63%	$5.07
11	132	469	9.78%	14.29%	$2.79	3/98-2/09	3.05%	$1.39	1/75-12/85	17.34%	$5.80
12	144	457	9.87%	13.75%	$3.09	3/97-2/09	3.89%	$1.58	1/75-12/86	17.64%	$7.02
13	156	445	9.77%	13.50%	$3.36	3/96-2/09	4.56%	$1.79	10/74-9/87	18.07%	$8.67
14	168	433	10.14%	11.37%	$3.86	3/95-2/09	5.48%	$2.11	1/75-12/88	16.86%	$8.85
15	180	421	10.13%	12.12%	$4.25	3/94-2/09	5.07%	$2.10	10/74-9/89	17.20%	$10.81
20	240	361	11.71%	8.24%	$9.15	3/89-2/09	6.51%	$3.53	10/74-9/94	14.75%	$15.66
30	360	241	11.47%	3.31%	$25.99	3/79-2/09	9.59%	$15.61	1/75-12/04	12.90%	$38.12
40	480	121	10.61%	2.07%	$56.48	3/69-2/09	9.10%	$32.54	12/66-11/06	11.16%	$68.90
50	600	1	10.00%	0.00%	$117.38	1/61-12/10	10.00%	$117.38	1/61-12/10	10.00%	$117.38

8-Year[1] Monthly Rolling Periods: 50 Years (1961 to 2010) Total of 505 Rolling Periods

[1] 8-years represents the estimated average holding period for investors who score 50 on the Risk Capacity Survey at ifa.com.
[2] The Median Annualized Returns, Return Range, and Median Growth of $1 shown for 1, 3, and 6 month periods are not annualized.

Sources, Updates, and Disclosures: ifabt.com, Appx A

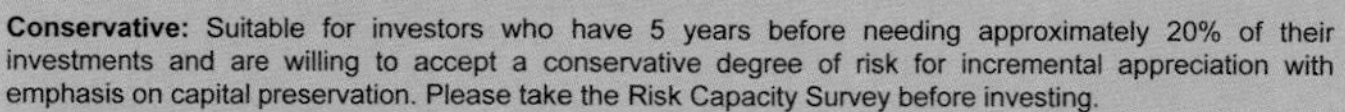

Index Portfolio 25: Ice Blue

Conservative: Suitable for investors who have 5 years before needing approximately 20% of their investments and are willing to accept a conservative degree of risk for incremental appreciation with emphasis on capital preservation. Please take the Risk Capacity Survey before investing.

Index Portfolio Allocation

General Asset Class		Specific Index	
14.0%	US Large	7.00%	U.S. Large Company Index (LC)
		7.00%	U.S. Large Cap Value Index (LV)
7.0%	US Small	3.50%	U.S. Small Cap Index (SC)
		3.50%	U.S. Small Cap Value Index (SV)
3.5%	Real Estate	3.50%	Real Estate Index (RE)
7.0%	International	3.50%	International Value Index (IV)
		1.75%	International Small Company Index (IS)
		1.75%	International Small Cap Value Index (ISV)
3.5%	Emerging Markets	1.05%	Emerging Markets Index (EM)
		1.05%	Emerging Markets Value Index (EV)
		1.40%	Emerging Markets Small Cap Index (ES)
65.0%	Fixed Income	16.25%	One-Year Fixed Income Index (1F)
		16.25%	Two-Year Global Fixed Income Index (2F)
		16.25%	Short Term Government Index (3G)
		16.25%	Five-Year Global Fixed Income Index (5F)

Simulated Returns and Volatility Data

	1 yr ending 2010	1 yr ending 2009	1 yr ending 2008	1 yr ending 2007	1 yr ending 2006	3 yrs 2008-2010	5 yrs 2006-2010	10 yrs 2001-2010	20 yrs 1991-2010	30 yrs 1981-2010	50 yrs 1961-2010	83 yrs 1928-2010
Growth of $1 ($)	1.08	1.14	0.88	1.03	1.10	1.09	1.24	1.69	3.87	12.16	52.16	240.90
Annualized Return (%)	8.45	13.97	-11.69	3.46	10.24	2.96	4.48	5.41	7.00	8.68	8.23	6.83
Standard Deviation (%) (Annualized Volatility)	7.47	10.36	8.20	4.11	3.33	9.11	7.42	6.16	5.48	5.75	5.94	7.90

Annual Returns: 50 Years (1/1/1961 - 12/31/2010)

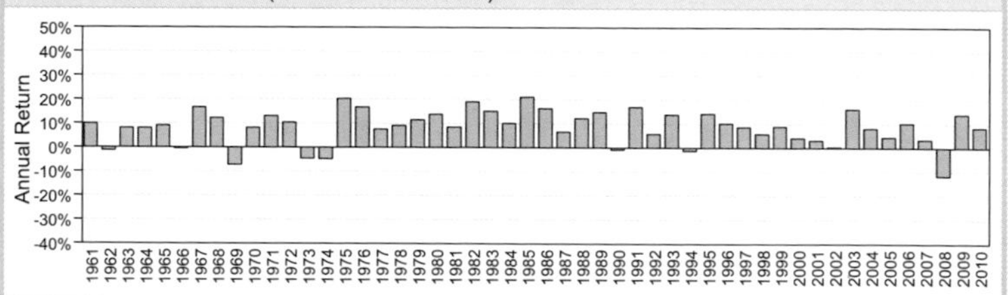

Growth of $1: 50 Years (1/1/1961 - 12/31/2010) - Log Scale

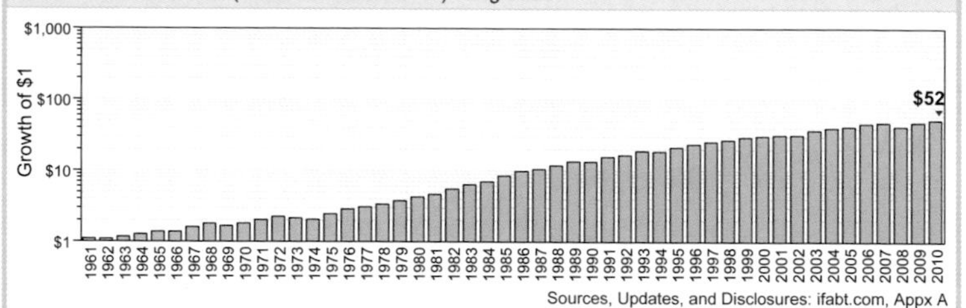

Sources, Updates, and Disclosures: ifabt.com, Appx A

Index Portfolio 25

Simulated Passive Investor Experiences (SPIEs)
Based on 50 Years of Monthly Data (600 Months)
January 1, 1961 to December 31, 2010

Examples of 5-Year Monthly Rolling Periods[1]

Periods
1 Jan 61 ← 5 Yrs → Dec 65
2 Feb 61 ← 5 Yrs → Jan 66
3 Mar 61 ← 5 Yrs → Feb 66
4 Apr 61 ← 5 Yrs → Mar 66
1961 1962 1963 1964 1965 1966 1967 1968 1969 1970 1971 1972 1973 1974 1975 1976 1977

Rolling Period Return Data: 50 Years (1961 to 2010)

Per Period Number of: Yrs	Months	# of Rolling Periods	Median Ann'lzd Return (50th %ile)	Return Range (High minus Low)	Median Growth of $1	Lowest Rolling Period Date	Lowest Rolling Period Return	Growth of $1 in Lowest Period	Highest Rolling Period Date	Highest Rolling Period Return	Growth of $1 in Highest Period
0.08	1	600	0.79%[2]	14.59%[2]	$1.01[2]	10/87-10/87	-6.91%	$0.93	1/75-1/75	7.67%	$1.08
0.25	3	598	2.16%[2]	24.48%[2]	$1.02[2]	9/08-11/08	-10.63%	$0.89	4/80-6/80	13.85%	$1.14
0.5	6	595	4.08%[2]	34.95%[2]	$1.04[2]	9/08-2/09	-15.81%	$0.84	3/09-8/09	19.14%	$1.19
1	12	500	8.81%	48.63%	$1.09	3/08-2/09	-16.90%	$0.83	7/82-6/83	31.73%	$1.32
2	24	577	8.41%	31.50%	$1.18	3/07-2/09	-8.77%	$0.83	7/84-6/86	22.73%	$1.51
3	36	565	8.18%	23.14%	$1.27	3/06-2/09	-3.27%	$0.91	8/84-7/87	19.87%	$1.72
4	48	553	7.98%	20.72%	$1.36	3/05-2/09	-0.80%	$0.97	7/82-6/86	19.91%	$2.07
5[1]	60	541	8.12%	18.07%	$1.48	3/04-2/09	0.43%	$1.02	7/82-6/87	18.51%	$2.34
6	72	529	8.02%	15.24%	$1.59	10/68-9/74	1.87%	$1.12	4/80-3/86	17.11%	$2.58
7	84	517	7.84%	13.92%	$1.70	3/02-2/09	2.81%	$1.21	4/80-3/87	16.73%	$2.95
8	96	505	8.03%	12.42%	$1.86	3/01-2/09	2.85%	$1.25	10/81-9/89	15.27%	$3.12
9	108	493	8.13%	11.37%	$2.02	3/00-2/09	3.20%	$1.33	4/80-3/89	14.56%	$3.40
10	120	481	8.14%	10.41%	$2.19	3/99-2/09	3.70%	$1.44	9/77-8/87	14.11%	$3.74
11	132	469	8.18%	10.41%	$2.37	3/98-2/09	3.52%	$1.46	9/75-8/86	13.94%	$4.20
12	144	457	8.26%	10.19%	$2.59	3/97-2/09	4.07%	$1.61	9/74-8/86	14.26%	$4.95
13	156	445	8.20%	9.63%	$2.78	3/96-2/09	4.56%	$1.79	10/74-9/87	14.19%	$5.61
14	168	433	8.46%	8.23%	$3.12	3/95-2/09	5.21%	$2.04	10/74-9/88	13.44%	$5.84
15	180	421	8.81%	8.77%	$3.55	3/94-2/09	4.86%	$2.04	10/74-9/89	13.62%	$6.79
20	240	361	10.01%	5.93%	$6.74	3/89-2/09	6.00%	$3.21	9/74-8/94	11.93%	$9.53
30	360	241	9.61%	2.03%	$15.69	3/79-2/09	8.40%	$11.23	1/75-12/04	10.42%	$19.58
40	480	121	8.87%	1.16%	$29.95	3/69-2/09	8.04%	$22.04	12/66-11/06	9.20%	$33.82
50	600	1	8.23%	0.00%	$52.16	1/61-12/10	8.23%	$52.16	1/61-12/10	8.23%	$52.16

5-Year[1] Monthly Rolling Periods: 50 Years (1961 to 2010) Total of 541 Rolling Periods

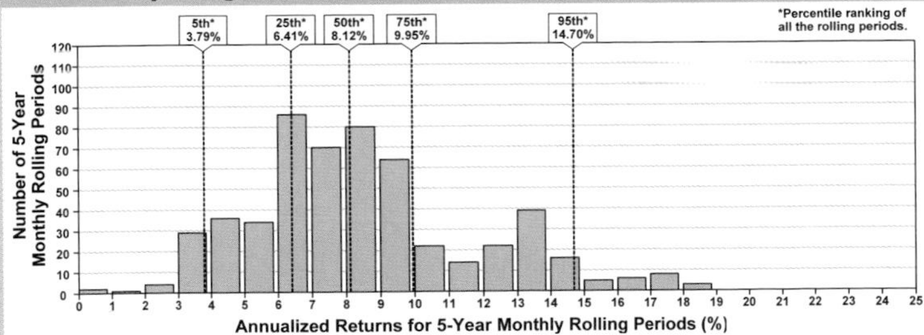

[1] 5-years represents the estimated average holding period for investors who score 25 on the Risk Capacity Survey at ifa.com.
[2] The Median Annualized Returns, Return Range, and Median Growth of $1 shown for 1, 3, and 6 month periods are not annualized.

Sources, Updates, and Disclosures: ifabt.com, Appx A

STEP 12: INVEST AND RELAX

"A decade ago, I really did believe that the average investor could do it himself. I was wrong. I've come to the sad conclusion that only a tiny minority, at most one percent, are capable of pulling it off. Heck, if Helen Young Hayes, Robert Sanborn, Julian Robertson, and the nation's largest pension funds can't get it right, what chance does John Q. Investor have?"

– William Bernstein, Ph.D., M.D., "*The Probability of Success,*" 2003

"Index funds are the only rational alternative for almost all mutual fund investors."

– Mark Hulbert, "The Prescient Are Few," *NY Times*, July 13, 2008

"Investors who had an appropriate asset allocation and who invested in a globally diversified portfolio of low-cost index funds have prospered."

– Daniel R. Solin, "Smart Advice for the HuffPost Investor," July 22, 2008

"Most institutional and individual investors will find the best way to own common stock is through an index fund that charges minimal fees. Those following this path are sure to beat the net results [after fees and expenses] delivered by the great majority of investment professionals."

– Warren Buffett, 1996 Shareholder Letter

While the passive relax on a tropical cruise,
the active are singin' the Speculation Blues.
– The Speculation Blues

As we have wound our way through the first 11 steps, I have explained the pitfalls of the active investor. I have warned against the dangers of stock picking and time picking (market timing). I have spelled out the problems with manager picking. I have pointed a flashlight at the silent partners lurking in the shadows. I've done all of it to get you to the point where you can tie yourself to the mast and resist the siren songs of active management.

As you've learned, the stock market has delivered healthy returns to those who invest for the long term. However, staying the course is difficult due to the bombardment of bad news that causes us concern about our financial certainty. For example, confidence was high on October 9, 2007, when the Dow Jones Industrial Average (DJIA) reached its peak of 14,164. The DJIA then steadily declined for over a year, followed by a sharp drop of 22% in the 8 trading days from October 1 to 10, 2008. The market then continued its decline over the next five months and bottomed out at 6,547 on March 6, 2009. Many investors pulled out of the market during this prolonged and painful time period. Those who threw in the towel because they did not trust the market to rebound have irrevocably hampered their ability to capture their share of the market recovery.

Passive investors intellectually understand the merits of indexing. But unfortunately, even passive investors are prone to emotional decision making. For this reason, the right passive advisor fulfills a critically important role in your investment success.

Problems

Investors "Go It Alone"

Even many passive investors get in their own way of success. As the legendary investor Benjamin Graham stated, "The investor's chief problem, and even his worst enemy, is likely to be himself." An investor may want to consider the low fees paid to a passive index funds advisor as a casualty insurance premium, insuring the investor against himself.

Commissions = Conflict

An advisor who receives a commission with every trade is acting in conflict with a client's best interest. In fact, in April 2005, the SEC set forth regulations that require commissioned financial professionals to include the following language on their advertising materials:

"Your account is a brokerage account and not an advisory account. Our interests may not always be the same as yours. Please ask us questions to make sure you understand your rights and our obligations to you, including the extent of our obligations to disclose conflicts of interest and to act in your best interests. We are paid both by you and, sometimes, by people who compensate us based on what you buy. Therefore, our profits, and our salespersons' compensation, may vary by product and over time." This language reveals the all-too-common discrepancies that arise between a broker's goals and a client's needs.

Solutions

Fee-Only Fiduciaries

When choosing a financial advisor, an investor is best served by working with a fiduciary. Commission-based financial professionals are not fiduciaries. By law, a fiduciary is obligated to act solely in the best interest of the client, putting the client's needs above his own at all times.

A registered investment advisor (RIA) is a fiduciary and is paid solely for advice, accepting no form of compensation for any investment products recommended to clients. An RIA helps investors:

- Invest according to their risk capacity
- Properly allocate assets across a blend of globally diversified, passively managed index funds
- Maintain a portfolio with appropriate and consistent risk exposure
- Avoid the impulse to react to market volatility that results in lower long-term returns
- Minimize investment costs and taxes

The following descriptions detail additional valuable wealth management strategies that an RIA can help implement.

Asset Location

Just as important as asset allocation is asset location. For a client who has a mixture of accounts including taxable, traditional IRAs and Roth IRAs, it is helpful to construct one portfolio that includes multiple asset classes that are divided among different accounts. The ultimate purpose of this approach is to optimize after-tax returns. A good passive advisor will evaluate the purpose of each account to determine if it should be stand-alone or part of a hybrid structure.

When choosing which asset classes to place in different account types, a good passive advisor would consider the following:

1. For Roth IRAs where all investment growth is tax-free, the best strategy is to include the asset classes with the highest expected returns. Examples include emerging markets and international small value.
2. For traditional IRAs where withdrawals are taxed as ordinary income, the best strategy is to include the asset classes that are least tax-efficient. Examples include real estate investment trusts (REITs) and fixed income.
3. For taxable accounts, the best strategy utilizes tax-managed funds whenever possible. Examples include tax-managed funds for U.S. large company, U.S. large cap value, U.S. small blend, U.S. small cap value, and international value.

A good advisor will carefully trade all accounts in unison, along with an eye toward tax-efficiency, minimization of transaction costs and maintenance of the client's designated risk level.

Rebalancing

Periodic portfolio rebalancing is an important strategy for achieving investing goals. Rebalancing involves selling shares of assets that have appreciated significantly and buying more of those that have underperformed, ensuring a consistent level of risk exposure in a portfolio. See ifa.com/rb.

Figure 12-1 depicts the benefits of maintaining the discipline of rebalancing. It seems counterintuitive to sell off a portion of an investment that has outperformed others in order to buy one that has underperformed. However, imbalanced portfolios with asset classes that have grown beyond their target allocations take on inappropriate risk exposures. History shows that passive rebalancers are rewarded for their discipline in the end. At times, circumstances may necessitate a shift in a portfolio's target asset allocation because of a change in an investor's capacity for risk.

Figure 12-1

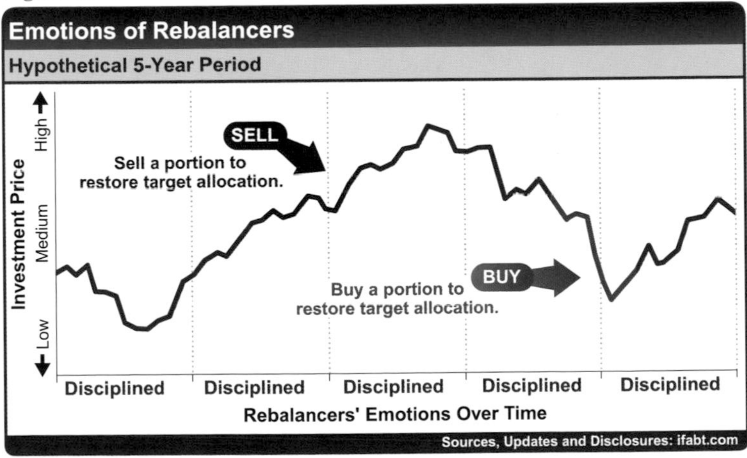

The Glide Path

An investor is well served by incrementally reducing risk with age—a glide path strategy—which amounts to a 1% reduction in the equity allocation of a portfolio per year over a lifetime.[77]

When young investors embark on their careers and start to save money, they are long on human capital and short on financial capital. As investors age and save for their retirement, there is a natural exchange of human and financial capital. Figure 12-2 is a hypothetical illustration of an individual's financial glide path through life. It illustrates an investor's transition from living off of his or her labor (human capital) to living off his or her savings (financial capital). See ifa.com/gp.

Figure 12-2

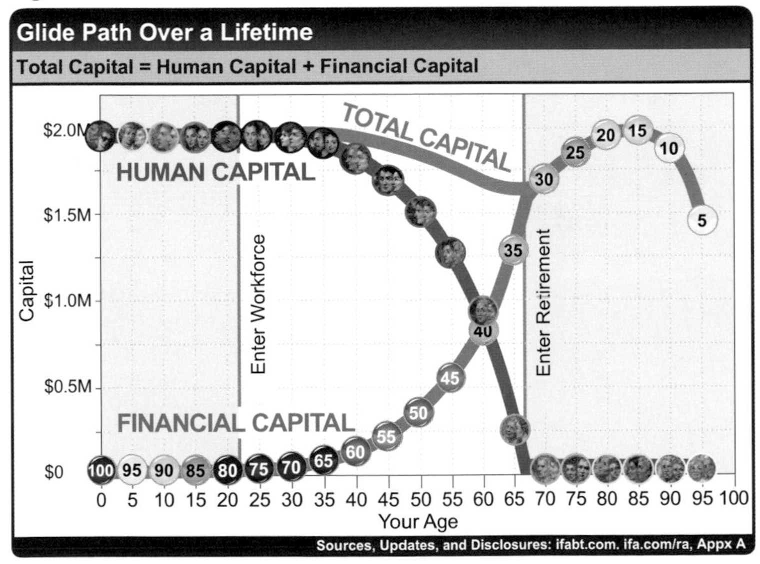

Tax Loss Harvesting

A market downturn provides a silver lining in the dark skies. Tax loss harvesting is a way to reduce tax liability either due to rebalancing or capital gains distributions. To save on future capital gains taxes, investors might consider this strategy: 1) Sell the mutual funds in your taxable accounts that have declined more than 10% and $10,000; 2) Immediately invest the assets in a substantially different index fund, realizing a capital loss; 3) Purchase the original funds back after 31 days from the sale; 4) Report the realized capital losses to your accountant to offset future capital gains and a portion of your income. Losses can be carried forward until they've been offset by future capital gains or income. There are some risks associated with tax loss harvesting, so an investor should consult with their accountant prior to making a decision to tax loss harvest. To learn more, visit ifa.com/tlh.

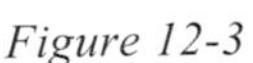

Figure 12-3

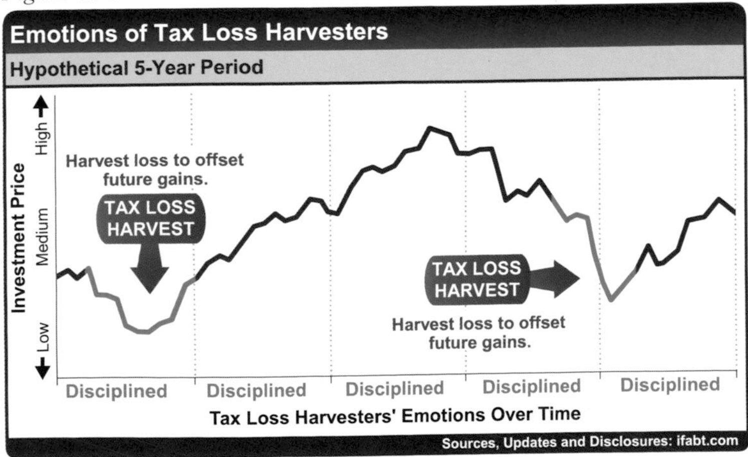

Retirement Analyzer

A retirement analyzer is a valuable retirement planning tool that enables investors to assess their financial health, specifically their probability of running out of money during retirement. It is best used as a guide in making decisions on saving, spending, and investing and should be revisited annually. The retirement analyzer at ifa.com/ra provides the tools to assess an investor's probability of portfolio survival.

The results of a Monte Carlo simulation are heavily dependent on the following specific inputs:

1. Beginning portfolio value
2. The number of years for the projection
3. Future cash flows (both deposits and withdrawals)
4. Inflation rate to be applied to the cash flows
5. The distribution of returns
6. Investment strategy

The retirement analyzer performs a Monte Carlo simulation which generates 10,000 individual scenarios. Each scenario is calculated using randomly selected annual returns from distributions based on the performance of historical data. Quite often, the results of an initial analysis will appear unsatisfactory. Several changes in assumptions can be made to improve the results:

1. Save a larger percentage of salary
2. Spend less in retirement
3. Retire later
4. Shorten life expectancy

5. Take more risk during the working years
6. Take less risk during the drawdown phase
7. Use glide path (steadily decreases risk over time)

Figure 12-4 depicts the results of a portfolio simulation for an individual with a retirement age starting at 67. The green bars ranging from dark to light represent the probability of the portfolio surviving through that age. A portfolio survival simulation is an excellent tool for investors to establish a degree of confidence about the sustainability of their portfolio through their lifetime. Revisiting the Monte Carlo Simulation each year allows investors to make sure they are on course—much like an onboard navigation system for a car. The closer one gets to their destination, the more finely tuned the directions become.

Figure 12-4

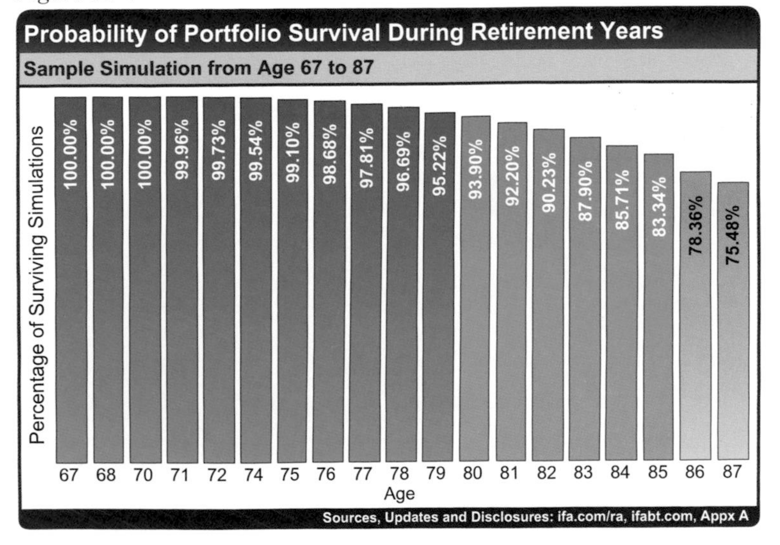

Your Next Step

We now arrive at the conclusion of our 12-Step Journey. Along our path, we have brought to light the detrimental impact our own emotions and behaviors can wreak on our investments.

We have taken a brief walk through the milestones of financial science and been enlightened by a group of academic legends who paved the way by contributing research that facilitates our ability to better understand risk, return, and the collective wisdom of people and markets.

We have crossed the path of some fallen stars who provide a cautionary lesson on why we should primarily respect the market's uncanny ability to spontaneously price all known information and to willingly accept that the current price is the best estimate of a fair price.

Our random walk has led us to better understand the futility of blindly chasing after winning fund managers, knowing their recent hot performance is a function of luck, not repeatable skill.

We have learned the deleterious results that come from attempting to predict the future performance of markets, sectors, or styles and the erosive costs associated with this speculation.

We have explored the probability of outcomes and have been guided to an understanding of how and why risk and return walk hand-in-hand.

We have traveled backward in time to learn that the travails of today are not so dissimilar from those of history. Global capitalism has continued its onward march, having led its shareholders to the prosperity of the markets.

We have evaluated how much risk we can stomach and have

been encouraged to be willing participants in market volatility.

We have been shown a rainbow of potential investment portfolios that cuts across a wide spectrum of risk and return.

And finally, we have learned the value of walking with a trusted passive advisor who will guide us through the peaks and valleys of the market, away from the temptations of speculation and toward a more rewarding and tranquil way of investing.

Each step of this book has been opened with a stanza from "*The Speculation Blues,*" a song I wrote that summarizes the many emotions and struggles of active investors—the lyrics of which can be found on the following pages. This song details how those who go it alone, speculating instead of investing, unnecessarily struggle on their investment journey.

I wrote this book to lead investors to a more peaceful and profitable investment strategy. We have climbed the 12 Steps together. I sincerely hope this journey has brought you to a deeper understanding of investing and strengthened your ability to achieve a brighter financial future.

The Speculation Blues

Lyrics by Mark Hebner

- The lure of fast money makes you think active,
  but the record proves you're better off passive.
- Professors came to a shocking conclusion,
  the active advantage was just an illusion.
- The stock market gamble can be an addiction,
  you'll search, but won't find that winnin' prediction.
- Traders devour the news like a school of piranha,
  while the passive find peace in a tradeless nirvana.
- The bets laid down on predictin' that news,
  will surely bring on the Speculation Blues.
- All them scholars toilin' at the universities,
  uncovered the fact that risk was just probabilities.
- They said that investors should diversify,
  and tell their stock brokers "good luck and goodbye."
- The traders oughta learn from Nobel Laureates,
  but they keep on makin' them long and short bets.
- Once you get the efficient market hypothesis,
  you'll no longer be fooled by market randomness.
- Stockaholics search for the best stock to choose,
  but end up cryin' the Speculation Blues.
- Instead of Morgan or Cramer, or Barney or Lynch,
  you're better off with Bogle, Fama or French.
- The wisdom of crowds throughout the land,
  will act like the force of the invisible hand.

- Everyone knows there ain't no free lunch,
  but the pickers keep thinkin' they can win from a hunch.
- Your broker's out buyin' himself a fine yacht,
  and you're gettin' nothin' from the stocks that he bought.
- Stock gamblin' can be like drinkin' that booze,
  leavin' you singin' the Speculation Blues.
- Market timers dream of makin' a killin' on a trend,
  but buyin' and holdin' wins out in the end.
- Fund managers trade as though taxes don't matter,
  but tradin' too much just makes Uncle Sam fatter.
- Silent partners have a feast on most investors,
  but you know that they suck the least from savvy indexers.
- Traders think that money grows from speculation,
  but indexers know it's just risk compensation.
- Trades placed online just guessin' tomorrow's news,
  leads those gamblers into the Speculation Blues.
- So before investing your hard earned green,
  catch a good vibe for the variance and the mean.
- The smart money man is best served,
  by checkin' out how the bell is curved.
- For when it's skinny and the average is high,
  the traders can't beat it no matter how hard he try.
- A risk taker gots'ta know his risk capacity,
  then hang on for his payout with true tenacity.
- While the passive relax on a tropical cruise,
  the active are singin' the Speculation Blues.

Watch the music video at: speculationblues.com

About the Artist

Lala Ragimov

I would like to extend a special thank you to master artist, Lala Ragimov, who painted 62 original and beautiful oil paintings that are located throughout the book. The originals of these paintings are proudly displayed at the headquarters of Index Funds Advisors in Irvine, California. Lala was born in Moscow and draws her artistic inspiration from the painters of the Venetian Renaissance and Flemish Baroque periods.

Lala earned a Bachelor of Fine Arts from the world-renowned California Institute of the Arts in 2003 and a Master of Fine Arts degree from California State University, Long Beach in 2009. Today Lala is a Fine Art Instructor and creates art and illustrations for Index Funds Advisors, biomedical manuals, magazines, art exhibitions, and many private collectors.

Appendix A

The following descriptions of IFA Indexes indicate how indexes are strung together to simulate similar risk and return characteristics back to 1928. This reduces the standard error of the mean which is unacceptably high for periods less than 20 or 30 years. When IFA Indexes are shown in Index Portfolios, all return data reflects a deduction of 0.9% annual investment advisory fee, which is the maximum advisory fee charged by IFA. Unless indicated otherwise, data shown for each individual IFA Index is shown without a deduction of the IFA advisory fee. This method is used because the creation, choice, monitoring and rebalancing of diversified index portfolios are the services of the independent investment advisor. Therefore, fees are deducted from the whole portfolio data but not the index data. Live Dimensional Fund Advisors' (DFA) fund data reflects the deduction of mutual fund advisory fees, brokerage fees, other expenses incurred by the mutual funds and incorporates actual trading results. Simulated index data also reflects DFA's current mutual fund expense ratios for the entire period. Both simulated and live data reflect total returns, including dividends, except for IFA/NSDQ Index. For updates on sources and descriptions of data see www.ifaindexes.com.

LC IFA U.S. Large Company Index (LC)

Time-Series Construction

January 1928 – December 1990: S&P 500 Ibbotson Associates SBBI data courtesy of Morningstar Direct minus 0.0125%/mo (mutual fund exp ratio)
January 1991 – April 2010: DFA US Large Company Symbol: DFLCX
May 2010 – Present : DFA US Large Company Portfolio Symbol: DFUSX

Investment Objective of DFA US Large Company Portfolio (DFUSX) The US Large Company Portfolio is a no-load mutual fund designed to approximate the investment performance of the S&P 500 Index. The Portfolio intends to invest in all the stocks that comprise the S&P 500 Index in approximately the same proportions as they are represented in the Index. The S&P 500 Index is comprised of a broad and diverse group of stocks. Generally, these are the US stocks with the largest market capitalizations and, as a group, they represent approximately 75% of the total market capitalization of all publicly traded US stocks.

Average Annual Total Return	One Year	Three Years	Five Years	Ten Years
US Large Company Portfolio	1.07%	1.31%	-1.10%	2.81%
S&P 500 Index	1.14%	1.23%	-1.18%	2.82%

Price/Earning (exclude negatives)	11.94	Number of Holdings	501
Dividend Yield	2.38%	Weighted Average Market Cap	$86,936M
Expense Ratio (as of 10/31/10)	0.10%	Weighted Average Book-to-Market	0.61

All Data as of Sept 30, 2011. For updates see www.ifaindexes.com.

LV IFA U.S. Large Cap Value Index (LV)

Time-Series Construction

January 1928 – February 1993: Dimensional US Large Cap Value Index minus 0.0225%/mo (mutual fund exp ratio)
March 1993 – Present: DFA US Large Cap Value Portfolio Symbol: DFLVX

Investment Objective of DFA US Large Cap Value Portfolio I (DFLVX) The US Large Cap Value Portfolio is a no-load mutual fund designed to capture the returns and diversification benefits of a broad cross-section of US value companies, on a market-cap weighted basis. The Portfolio invests in securities of US companies with market capitalizations within the largest 90% of the market universe or larger than the 1,000th largest US company, whichever results in a higher market capitalization break. The market universe is comprised primarily of companies listed on the New York Stock Exchange, American Stock Exchange, and Nasdaq Global Market. After identifying the aggregate market capitalization break, a value screen is applied to the universe. Securities are considered value stocks primarily because a company's shares have a high book value in relation to their market value (BtM). This BtM sort excludes firms with negative or zero book values. In assessing value, additional factors such as price-to-cash flow or price-to-earnings ratios may be considered. The criteria for assessing value are subject to change from time to time.

Average Annual Total Return	One Year	Three Years	Five Years	Ten Years
US Large Cap Value Portfolio (I)	-3.86%	-1.31%	-3.69%	4.40%
Russell 1000 Value Index	-1.89%	-1.52%	-3.53%	3.35%

Price/Earning (exclude negatives)	10.19	Number of Holdings	222
Dividend Yield	2.34%	Weighted Average Market Cap	$45,521M
Expense Ratio (as of 10/31/10)	0.28%	Weighted Average Book-to-Market	1.18

All Data as of Sept 30, 2011. For updates see www.ifaindexes.com.

SC IFA U.S. Small Cap Index (SC)

Time-Series Construction

January 1928 – March 1992: Dimensional US Small Cap Index minus 0.0317%/mo (mutual fund exp ratio)

April 1992 – Present : DFA US Small Cap Portfolio Symbol: DFSTX

Investment Objective of DFA US Small Cap Portfolio I (DFSTX) The US Small Cap Portfolio is a no-load mutual fund designed to capture the returns and diversification benefits of a broad cross-section of US small companies, on a market-cap weighted basis. The Portfolio invests in securities of US companies with market capitalizations within the smallest 10% of the market universe or smaller than the 1,000th largest US company, whichever results in a higher market capitalization break. The market universe is comprised primarily of companies listed on the New York Stock Exchange, American Stock Exchange, and Nasdaq Global Market.

Average Annual Total Return	One Year	Three Years	Five Years	Ten Years
US Small Cap Portfolio (I)	-1.83%	2.99%	0.21%	7.33%
Russell 2000 Index	-3.53%	-0.37%	-1.02%	6.12%

Price/Earning (exclude negatives)	13.02	Number of Holdings	2,519
Dividend Yield	1.10%	Weighted Average Market Cap	$1,046M
Expense Ratio (as of 10/31/10)	0.37%	Weighted Average Book-to-Market	0.78

All Data as of Sept 30, 2011. For updates see www.ifaindexes.com.

RE IFA Real Estate Index (RE)

Time-Series Construction

January 1928 – December 1977: 50% IFA US Small Cap Index and 50% IFA Small Cap Value Index

January 1978 – December 1992: Dow Jones US Select REIT Index minus 0.0275%/mo (mutual fund exp ratio)

January 1993 – June 2008: DFA US Real Estate Securities Symbol: DFREX

July 2008 – Present: DFA Global Real Estate Securities Portfolio Symbol: DFGEX

Investment Objective of DFA Global Real Estate Securities Portfolio (DFGEX) The Global Real Estate Securities Portfolio is a no-load mutual fund designed to achieve long-term capital appreciation. The Portfolio invests in a broad range of securities of US and non-US companies in the real estate industry, including companies in developed and emerging markets, with a focus on real estate investment trusts or companies that Dimensional considers to be REIT-like entities. The Portfolio primarily purchases shares of Dimensional's Real Estate Securities Portfolio and International Real Estate Securities Portfolio. In addition to investing in these underlying funds, the Portfolio also may invest directly in securities of companies in the real estate industry. The Portfolio currently invests in a diverse group of developed and emerging markets that have been authorized for investment by the Advisor's Investment Committee.

Average Annual Total Return	One Year	Three Years	Five Years	Inception*
Global Real Estate Sec. Portfolio	-0.76%	-0.49%	NA	-4.49%
S&P Global REIT Index**	-1.67%	-1.82%	NA	-6.17%

Price/Earning (exclude negatives)	19.41	Number of Holdings	311
Dividend Yield	4.80%	Weighted Average Market Cap	$8,552M
Expense Ratio (as of 10/31/10)	0.41%	Weighted Average Book-to-Market	0.77

*Inception Date 6/4/08 **Gross Dividends All Data as of Sept 30, 2011. For updates see www.ifaindexes.com.

SV IFA U.S. Small Cap Value Index (SV)

Time-Series Construction

January 1928 – February 2000: Dimensional US Targeted Value Index minus 0.0342%/mo (mutual fund exp ratio)

March 2000 – Present: DFA US Targeted Value Portfolio Symbol: DFFVX

Investment Objective of DFA Targeted Value Portfolio I (DFFVX) The US Targeted Value Portfolio is designed to capture the returns and diversification benefits of a broad cross-section of US small and mid cap value companies, on a market-cap weighted basis. The Portfolio generally invests in securities of US companies smaller than the 500th largest company in the market universe. The market universe is comprised primarily of companies listed on the New York Stock Exchange, American Stock Exchange, and Nasdaq Global Market. After identifying the aggregate market capitalization break, a value screen is applied to the universe. Securities are considered value stocks primarily because a company's shares have a high book value in relation to their market value (BtM). This BtM sort excludes firms with negative or zero book values. In assessing value, additional factors such as price-to-cash flow or price-to-earnings ratios may be considered. The criteria for assessing value are subject to change from time to time.

Average Annual Total Return	One Year	Three Years	Five Years	Ten Years
US Targeted Value Portfolio (I)	-6.09%	-0.47%	-2.03%	8.44%
Russell 2000 Value Index	-5.99%	-2.78%	-3.08%	6.47%

Price/Earning (exclude negatives)	11.30	Number of Holdings	1,586
Dividend Yield	1.20%	Weighted Average Market Cap	$1,488M
Expense Ratio (as of 10/31/10)	0.38%	Weighted Average Book-to-Market	1.20

All Data as of Sept 30, 2011. For updates see www.ifaindexes.com.

IV IFA International Value Index (IV)

Time-Series Construction

January 1928 – December 1969: IFA US Large Value Index

January 1970 – December 1974: MSCI EAFE Gross Dividends minus 0.0367%/mo (mutual fund exp ratio)

January 1975 – June 1993: MSCI EAFE Value Gross minus 0.0367%/mo (mutual fund exp ratio)

July 1993 – February 1994: LWAS/DFA International High BtM Portfolio

March 1994 – Present: DFA International Value Portfolio Symbol: DFIVX

Investment Objective of DFA International Value Portfolio I (DFIVX) The International Value Portfolio is a no-load mutual fund designed to achieve long-term capital appreciation. The Portfolio pursues its objective by investing in the stocks of large non-US companies that Dimensional believes to be value stocks at the time of purchase. Securities are considered value stocks primarily because a company's shares have a high book value in relation to its market value (BtM). This BtM sort excludes firms with negative or zero book values. In assessing value, additional factors such as price-to-cash flow or price-to-earnings ratios may be considered. The criteria for assessing value are subject to change from time to time. The Portfolio currently invests in a diverse group of developed market countries that have been authorized for investment by the Advisor's Investment Committee.

Average Annual Total Return	One Year	Three Years	Five Years	Ten Years
Intl. Value Index Portfolio	-13.35%	-2.06%	-3.79%	7.72%
MSCI EAFE Index*	-9.11%	-0.88%	-2.90%	5.50%

Price/Earning (exclude negatives)	8.94	Number of Holdings	528
Dividend Yield	3.75%	Weighted Average Market Cap	$35,380M
Expense Ratio (as of 10/31/10)	0.45%	Weighted Average Book-to-Market	1.21

*Net Dividends All Data as of Sept 30, 2011. For updates see www.ifaindexes.com.

 IFA International Small Company Index (IS)

Time-Series Construction

January 1928 – December 1969: IFA US Small Cap Index
January 1970 – September 1996: Dimensional International Small Cap Index minus 0.0458%/mo (mutual fund exp ratio)
October 1996 – Present: DFA International Small Company Portfolio Symbol: DFISX

Investment Objective of DFA International Small Company Portfolio I (DFISX) The International Small Company Portfolio is a no-load mutual fund designed to achieve long-term capital appreciation. The Portfolio pursues its objective by investing in the small companies of Canada (0-15%), Europe (25-50%), Japan (15-40%), the United Kingdom (15-35%), and the Asia-Pacific region (0-25%). The Portfolio currently invests in a diverse group of developed market countries that have been authorized for investment by the Advisor's Investment Committee.

Average Annual Total Return	One Year	Three Years	Five Years	Ten Years
Intl. Small Cap Index	-6.27%	4.95%	-0.35%	11.13%
MSCI EAFE Small Cap Index*	-7.77%	3.84%	-3.36%	7.88%

Price/Earning (exclude negatives)	10.79	Number of Holdings	4,799
Dividend Yield	3.02%	Weighted Average Market Cap	$1,336M
Expense Ratio (as of 10/31/10)	0.56%	Weighted Average Book-to-Market	0.95

*Price-Only All Data as of Sept 30, 2011. For updates see www.ifaindexes.com.

EV IFA Emerging Market Value Index (EV)

Time-Series Construction

January 1928 – December 1969: IFA US Small Cap Value Index
January 1970 – December 1988: IFA Emerging Markets Index
January 1989 – March 1998: Fama/French Emerging Markets Value Index minus 0.05%/mo (mutual fund exp ratio)
April 1998 – Present: DFA Emerging Markets Value Portfolio Symbol DFEVX

Investment Objective of DFA Emerging Markets Value Portfolio I (DFEVX) The Emerging Markets Value Portfolio is a no-load mutual fund designed to achieve long-term capital appreciation. The Portfolio pursues its objective by investing in emerging markets equity securities that Dimensional deems to be value stocks at the time of purchase. Dimensional will consider, among other things, information disseminated by the International Finance Corporation in determining and approving countries that have emerging markets. Securities are considered value stocks primarily because a company's shares have a high book value in relation to their market value (BtM). This BtM sort excludes firms with negative or zero book values. In assessing value, additional factors such as price-to-cash flow or price-to-earnings ratios may be considered. The criteria for assessing value are subject to change from time to time. The Portfolio currently invests in a diverse group of emerging market countries that have been authorized for investment by the Advisor's Investment Committee.

Average Annual Total Return	One Year	Three Years	Five Years	Ten Years
Emerging Markets Value Portfolio I	-22.16%	6.42%	6.08%	19.91%
MSCI Emerging Markets Index*	-15.89%	6.59%	5.17%	16.41%

Price/Earning (exclude negatives)	8.90	Number of Holdings	2,209
Dividend Yield	2.73%	Weighted Average Market Cap	$24,702M
Expense Ratio (as of 10/31/10)	0.60%	Weighted Average Book-to-Market	1.05

*Gross Dividend All Data as of Sept 30, 2011. For updates see www.ifaindexes.com.

EM IFA Emerging Market Index (EM)

Time-Series Construction

January 1928 – December 1969: 50% IFA US Large Value Index and 50% IFA US Small Cap Index
January 1970 – December 1987: 50% IFA Int'l Value and 50% IFA Int'l Small Cap
January 1988 – April 1994: DFA Equally Weighted Emerging Markets Index minus 0.05%/mo (mutual fund exp ratio)
May 1994 – Present: DFA Emerging Markets Portfolio Symbol: DFEMX

Investment Objective of DFA Emerging Markets Portfolio I (DFEMX) The Emerging Markets Portfolio is a no-load mutual fund designed to achieve long-term capital appreciation. The Portfolio pursues its objective by investing in emerging markets equity securities that Dimensional deems to be large company stocks at the time of purchase. Dimensional will consider, among other things, information disseminated by the International Finance Corporation in determining and approving countries that have emerging markets. The Portfolio currently invests in a diverse group of emerging market countries that have been authorized for investment by the Advisor's Investment Committee.

Average Annual Total Return	One Year	Three Years	Five Years	Ten Years
Emerging Markets Portfolio I	-14.67%	5.80%	5.86%	16.00%
MSCI Emerging Markets Index*	-15.89%	6.59%	5.17%	16.41%

Price/Earning (exclude negatives)	10.94	Number of Holdings	861
Dividend Yield	2.76%	Weighted Average Market Cap	$37,851M
Expense Ratio (as of 10/31/10)	0.60%	Weighted Average Book-to-Market	0.62

*Gross Dividend All Data as of Sept 30, 2011. For updates see www.ifaindexes.com.

ISV IFA International Small Cap Value Index (ISV)

Time-Series Construction

January 1928 – December 1969: IFA Small Cap Value Index
January 1970 – June 1981: IFA International Small Company Index
July 1981 – December 1994: Dimensional International Small Cap Value Index minus 0.0575%/mo (mutual fund exp ratio)
January 1995 – Present: DFA International Small Cap Value Portfolio Symbol: DISVX

Investment Objective of DFA International Small Cap Value Portfolio I (DISVX) The International Small Cap Value Portfolio is a no-load mutual fund designed to achieve long-term capital appreciation. The Portfolio pursues its objective by investing in the stocks of small non-US companies that Dimensional believes to be value stocks at the time of purchase. Securities are considered value stocks primarily because a company's shares have a high book value in relation to their market value (BtM). This BtM sort excludes firms with negative or zero book values. In assessing value, additional factors such as price-to-cash flow or price-to-earnings ratios may be considered. The criteria for assessing value are subject to change from time to time. The Portfolio currently invests in a diverse group of developed market countries that have been authorized for investment by the Advisor's Investment Committee.

Average Annual Total Return	One Year	Three Years	Five Years	Ten Years
Intl. Small Cap Value	-8.37%	2.65%	-1.77%	11.91%
MSCI EAFE Small Cap Index*	-7.76%	3.14%	-4.09%	7.46%

Price/Earning (exclude negatives)	9.00	Number of Holdings	2,266
Dividend Yield	2.95%	Weighted Average Market Cap	$1,202M
Expense Ratio (as of 10/31/10)	0.70%	Weighted Average Book-to-Market	1.59

*Price-Only All Data as of Sept 30, 2011. For updates see www.ifaindexes.com.

 IFA Emerging Market Small Cap Index (ES)

Time-Series Construction

January 1928 – December 1969: IFA US Small Cap Index
January 1970 – December 1988: IFA Emerging Markets Index
January 1989 – February 1998: Fama/French Emerging Markets Small minus 0.065%/mo (mutual fund exp ratio)
March 1998 – Present: DFA Emerging Markets Small Cap Portfolio Symbol: DEMSX

Investment Objective of DFA Emerging Markets Small Cap Portfolio I (DEMSX) The Emerging Markets Small Cap Portfolio is a no-load mutual fund designed to achieve long-term capital appreciation. The Portfolio pursues its objective by investing in emerging markets equity securities that Dimensional deems to be small company stocks at the time of purchase. Dimensional will consider, among other things, information disseminated by the International Finance Corporation in determining and approving countries that have emerging markets. The Portfolio currently invests in a diverse group of developed market countries that have been authorized for investment by the Advisor's Investment Committee.

Average Annual Total Return	One Year	Three Years	Five Years	Ten Years
Emg. Markets Small Cap Portfolio I	-19.47%	13.45%	8.24%	19.41%
MSCI Emerging Markets Index*	-15.89%	6.59%	5.17%	16.41%

Price/Earning (exclude negatives)	10.27	Number of Holdings	2,738
Dividend Yield	2.84%	Weighted Average Market Cap	$1,204M
Expense Ratio (as of 10/31/10)	0.78%	Weighted Average Book-to-Market	0.85

*Gross Dividend All Data as of Sept 30, 2011. For updates see www.ifaindexes.com.

 IFA One-Year Fixed Income Index (1F)

Time-Series Construction

January 1928 – June 1963: One-Month T-Bills minus 0.015%/mo (mutual fund exp ratio)
July 1963 – July 1983: One-Year T-Note Index minus 0.015%/mo (mutual fund exp ratio)
August 1983 – Present: DFA One-Year Fixed Income Portfolio Symbol DFIHX

Investment Objective of Investment Objective of DFA One-Year Fixed Income Portfolio (DFIHX) The investment objective of the DFA One-Year Fixed Income Portfolio is to achieve stable real returns in excess of the rate of inflation with a minimum of risk. Generally, the Portfolio will acquire high-quality obligations that mature within one year from the date of settlement. However, when greater yields are available, substantial investments may be made in securities maturing within two years from the date of settlement as well. In addition, the Portfolio intends to concentrate investments in the banking industry under certain circumstances.

Average Annual Total Return	One Year	Three Years	Five Years	Ten Years
One-Year Fixed Income Index Portfolio	0.68%	2.06%	2.83%	2.71%
One-Year US Treasury Note*	0.55%	1.26%	2.76%	2.61%

Duration	0.90 Years
Average Portfolio Maturity Range	0.92 Years
Expense Ratio (as of 10/31/10)	0.17%

*BofA Merrill Lynch Index All Data as of Sept 30, 2011. For updates see ifaindexes.com.

2F IFA Two-Year Global Fixed Income Index (2F)

Time-Series Construction

January 1928 – June 1977: Five-Year T-Notes minus 0.015%/mo (mutual fund exp ratio)
July 1977 – December 1989: ML US Treasury Index 1-3 Years minus 0.015%/mo (mutual fund exp ratio)
January 1990 – February 1996: Citi World Gov't Bond 1-3 Years Hedged minus 0.015%/mo (mutual fund exp ratio)
March 1996 – December 2007: DFA Two-Year Global Fixed Income Portfolio Symbol: DFGFX

Investment Objective of DFA Two-Year Global Fixed Income Portfolio (DFGFX) The investment objective of the Two-Year Global Fixed Income Portfolio is to maximize total returns consistent with preservation of capital. Generally, the Portfolio will acquire high-quality obligations that mature within two years from the date of settlement. The Portfolio expects to invest in obligations issued or guaranteed by countries that are members of the Organization of Economic Cooperation and Development, but may invest in other countries as well. Investments in corporate debt obligations, bank obligations, commercial paper, repurchase agreements, and obligations of other US and international issuers with high quality ratings may also be included. The Portfolio will also enter into forward foreign currency contracts solely for the purpose of hedging against fluctuations in currency exchange rates.

Average Annual Total Return	**One Year**	**Three Years**	**Five Years**	**Ten Years**
Two-Year Global Fixed Income Portfolio	0.93%	2.35%	3.02%	2.90%
World Gov't Bond Index 1-3 Years*	0.99%	2.40%	3.40%	3.18%

Duration 1.29 Years
Average Portfolio Maturity Range 1.32 Years
Expense Ratio (as of 10/31/10) 0.18%

*Citigroup Index, Hedged All Data as of Sept 30, 2011. For updates see ifaindexes.com.

IFA Short Term Government Index (3G)

Time-Series Construction

January 1928 – December 1972: Five-Year T-Notes minus 0.0192%/mo (mutual fund exp ratio)
January 1973 – May 1987: Barclays Intermediate Government Bond Index minus 0.0192%/mo (mutual fund exp ratio)
June 1987 – Present: DFA Short-Term Govt. Portfolio (Five-Year Gov't Income) Symbol: DFFGX

Investment Objective of DFA Short-Term Government Portfolio (DFFGX) The investment objective of the Short-Term Government Portfolio (formerly the Five-Year Government Portfolio) is to maximize total returns available from the universe of debt obligations of the US government and US government agencies. Ordinarily, the Portfolio will invest at least 80% of its assets in US government obligations and US government agency obligations that mature within five years from the date of settlement. The Portfolio may also acquire repurchase agreements backed by US government securities.

Average Annual Total Return	**One Year**	**Three Years**	**Five Years**	**Ten Years**
DFA Short-Term Gov't Portfolio	2.42%	5.14%	4.67%	4.37%
Capital US Gov't Bond Index Int.*	2.18%	3.83%	4.84%	4.01%

Duration 2.76 Years
Average Portfolio Maturity Range 2.90 Years
Expense Ratio (as of 10/31/10) 0.23%

*Barclays Index All Data as of Sept 30, 2011. For updates see ifaindexes.com.

 IFA Five-Year Global Fixed Income Index (5F)

Time-Series Construction

January 1928 – December 1984: IFA Five-Year Government Fixed Income Index

January 1985 – November 1990: Citi Global Government Bond Hedged minus 0.0233%/mo (mutual fund exp ratio)

December 1990 – Present: DFA Five-Year Global Fixed Income Portfolio Symbol: DFGBX

Investment Objective of DFA Five-Year Global Fixed Income Portfolio (DFGBX) The investment objective of the Five-Year Global Fixed Income Portfolio is to provide a market rate of return for a fixed income portfolio with low relative volatility of returns. Generally, the Portfolio will invest in high-quality obligations that mature within five years from the date of settlement. The Portfolio expects to invest in obligations issued or guaranteed by countries that are members of the Organization of Economic Cooperation and Development, but may invest in other countries as well. Investments in obligations of other foreign issuers rated AA or better, corporate debt obligations, bank obligations, and commercial paper may also be included. The Portfolio will also enter into forward foreign currency contracts solely for the purpose of hedging against fluctuations in currency exchange rates.

Average Annual Total Return	One Year	Three Years	Five Years	Ten Years
Five-Year Global Fixed Portfolio	3.17%	6.08%	4.95%	4.55%
World Gov't Bond 1-5 Years*	1.37%	3.25%	3.98%	3.62%

Duration	3.82 Years
Average Portfolio Maturity Range	4.10 Years
Expense Ratio (as of 10/31/10)	0.28%

*Citigroup Index, Hedged All Data as of Sept 30, 2011. For updates see ifaindexes.com.

 IFA NSDQ Index (N)

Time-Series Construction

January 1928 - February 1971: Fama/French US Small Growth Simulated Portfolio (ex Utilities)

Mar 1971 - Present: NASDAQ % Change; Excluding Dividends (Source: Yahoo! Finance)

Investment Objective of IFA NSDQ Index To capture the return of the NASDAQ-100 Index, excluding the impact of dividends. The NASDAQ-100 Index includes 100 of the largest domestic and international non-financial securities listed on The Nasdaq Stock Market based on market capitalization. The Index reflects companies across major industry groups including computer hardware and software, telecommunications, retail/wholesale trade and biotechnology. It does not contain securities of financial companies including investment companies.

All Data as of Sept 30, 2011. For updates see ifaindexes.com.

LG IFA U.S. Large Growth Index (LG)

Time-Series Construction

Jan 1928 - Nov 1992: Dimensional US Large Cap Growth minus 0.01%/mo (mutual fund exp ratio)
Dec 1992 - Present: Vanguard Growth Index Inst'l: VIGIX

Investment Objective of Vanguard Growth Index (VIGIX) The investment seeks to track the performance of a benchmark index that measures the investment return of large-capitalization growth stocks. The fund employs a passive management investment approach designed to track the performance of the MSCI US Prime Market Growth index, a broadly diversified index of growth stocks of large U.S. companies. It attempts to replicate the target index by investing all, or substantially all, of assets in the stocks that make up the index, holding each stock in approximately the same proportion as its weighting in the index.

Average Annual Total Return	One Year	Three Years	Five Years	Ten Years
Vanguard Growth Index	2.94%	3.82%	1.61%	3.23%

Price/Earning (exclude negatives)	16.60	Number of Holdings	430
Dividend Yield	1.40%	Weighted Average Market Cap	$34.3B
Expense Ratio (as of 12/31/10)	0.08%	Weighted Average Book-to-Market	0.30

All Data as of Aug 31, 2011. Avg. Ann. Total Return as of Sept 30, 2011. For updates see www.ifaindexes.com.

MC IFA U.S. Micro Cap Index (MC)

Time-Series Construction

Jan 1928 - Dec 1981: Dimensional US Micro Cap Index minus 0.045%/mo (mutual fund exp ratio)
Jan 1982 - Present: DFA US Micro Cap Portfolio: DFSCX

Investment Objective of DFA US Micro Cap Portfolio I (DFSCX) The US Micro Cap Portfolio is a no-load mutual fund designed to capture the returns and diversification benefits of a broad cross-section of US small companies, on a market-cap weighted basis. The Portfolio invests in securities of US companies with market capitalizations within the smallest 5% of the market universe or smaller than the 1,500th largest US company, whichever results in a higher market capitalization break. The market universe is comprised primarily of companies listed on the New York Stock Exchange, American Stock Exchange, and Nasdaq Global Market.

Average Annual Total Return	**One Year**	**Three Years**	**Five Years**	**Ten Years**
US Micro Cap Portfolio	-1.61%	0.87%	-1.58%	7.55%
Russell 2000 Index	-3.53%	-0.37%	-1.02%	6.12%

Price/Earning (exclude negatives)	13.34	Number of Holdings	2,172
Dividend Yield	1.06%	Weighted Average Market Cap	$538M
Expense Ratio (as of 10/31/10)	0.52%	Weighted Average Book-to-Market	0.88

All Data as of Sept 30, 2011. For updates see www.ifaindexes.com.

TM IFA U.S. Total Market Index (TM)

Time-Series Construction

Jan 1928 - May 1998: Dimensional US Marketwide minus 0.01%/mo (mutual fund exp ratio)
May 1992 - Present: Vanguard US Total Market Index Inst'l :VITSX

Investment Objective of Vanguard US Total Market Index (VITSX) The investment seeks to track the performance of a benchmark index that measures the investment return of the overall stock market. The fund employs a passive management strategy designed to track the performance of the MSCI US Broad Market index, which consists of all the U.S. common stocks traded regularly on the New York Stock Exchange and the Nasdaq over-the-counter market. It typically holds 1,200-1,300 of the stocks in its target index.

Average Annual Total Return	One Year	Three Years	Five Years	Ten Years
Vanguard US Total Market Index	0.72%	1.73%	-0.59%	3.90%

Price/Earning (exclude negatives)	14.6	Number of Holdings	3,324
Dividend Yield	2.21%	Weighted Average Market Cap	$29.9B
Expense Ratio (as of 12/31/10)	0.06%	Weighted Average Book-to-Market	0.50

All Data as of Aug 31, 2011. Avg. Ann. Total Return as of Sept 30, 2011. For updates see www.ifaindexes.com.

S&P 500 Index (SP)

Time-Series Construction

January 1928 - December 1989: S&P 500 Ibbotson Associates SBBI data courtesy of Morningstar Direct
January 1990 - Present: S&P 500 Index data courtesy of Morningstar Direct

Investment Objective of S&P 500 Index Widely regarded as the best single gauge of the U.S. equities market, this world-renowned index includes 500 leading companies in leading industries of the U.S. economy. Although the S&P 500 focuses on the large cap segment of the market, with approximately 75% coverage of U.S. equities, it is also a proxy for the total market. S&P 500 is part of a series of S&P U.S. indices that can be used as building blocks for portfolio construction.

Average Annual Total Return	**One Year**	**Three Years**	**Five Years**	**Ten Years**
S&P 500 Index	1.14%	1.23%	-1.18%	2.82%

Price/Earning (exclude negatives)	14.62	Number of Holdings	500
Dividend Yield	2.07%	Average Market Cap	$22,147M

All Data as of Sept 30, 2011. For updates see www.ifaindexes.com.

SG IFA U.S. Small Growth Index (SG)

Time-Series Construction

Jan 1928 - May 1998: Dimensional US Large Cap Growth minus 0.01%/mo (mutual fund exp ratio)
Jun 1998 - Present: Vanguard Small-Cap Growth Index Inst'l :VSGIX

Investment Objective of Vanguard Small-Cap Growth Index (VSGIX) The investment seeks to track the performance of a benchmark index that measures the investment return of small capitalization growth stocks. The fund employs a passive management investment approach designed to track the performance of the MSCI US Small Cap Growth index, a broadly diversified index of growth stocks of smaller U.S. companies. It attempts to replicate the target index by investing all, or substantially all, of assets in the stocks that make up the index, holding each stock in approximately the same proportion as its weighting in the index.

Average Annual Total Return	One Year	Three Years	Five Years	Ten Years
Vanguard Small-Cap Growth Index	0.55%	4.81%	2.71%	8.10%

Price/Earning (exclude negatives)	24.6	Number of Holdings	949
Dividend Yield	0.36%	Weighted Average Market Cap	$1.6B
Expense Ratio (as of 12/31/10)	0.08%	Weighted Average Book-to-Market	0.36

All Data as of Aug 31, 2011. Avg. Ann. Total Return as of Sept 30, 2011. For updates see www.ifaindexes.com.

M Fama/French Total US Market Research Factor

Time-Series Construction

July 1926 – Present: Fama/French Total US Market Research Factor minus T-Bill

Composition of Fama/French Total US Market Research Factor: The Value-Weighted US Market Index is constructed every month, using all issues listed on the NYSE, AMEX or Nasdaq with available outstanding shares and valid prices for that month and the month before.

Exclusions: American Depositary Receipts.

Rebalancing: Monthly 1926-2005
Does not include hold range and does not incur transaction costs.

Currency: USD

Sources: Dimensional Returns Version 2.2. Fama/French multifactor data provided by Fama/French.

Dividends: Reinvested in the paying company until the portfolio is rebalanced.

Fama/French US Value Research Factor

Time-Series Construction

July 1926 – Present: Fama/French US HmL Research Factor minus Growth Companies

Composition of Fama/French US HmL (High minus Low) Research Factor: The Fama/French value factor, HmL, is constructed from four size/book-to-market research portfolios that do not include hold ranges and do not incur transaction costs. HmL for July of year t to June t+1 includes all NYSE, AMEX, and NASDAQ stocks for which we have market equity for December t-1 and June of t, and (positive) book-to-market equity data for fiscal year ending in t-1.HmL is the average return on two value research portfolios minus the average return on two growth research portfolios: 1/2 (Small High + Big High) - 1/2 (Small Low + Big Low).

Sources: Dimensional Returns Version 2.2. Fama/French and multifactor data provided by Fama/French.

Exclusions: ADRs, Investment Companies, Tracking Stocks, non-US incorporated companies, Closed-end funds, Certificates, Shares of Beneficial Interests, and negative book values.

Currency: USD

S Fama/French US Small Research Factor

Time-Series Construction

July 1926 – Present: Fama/French US SmB Research Factor minus Large Companies

Composition of Fama/French US SmB (Small minus Big) Research Factor: The Fama/French small factor, SmB, is constructed from six size/book-to-market research portfolios that do not include hold ranges and do not incur transaction costs. SmB for July of year t to June t+1 includes all NYSE, AMEX, and NASDAQ stocks for which we have market equity for December t-1 and June of t, and (positive) book-to-market equity data for fiscal year ending in t-1. SmB is the average return on three small research portfolios minusthe average return on three big research portfolios: 1/3 (Small High + Small Medium + Small Low) - 1/3 (Big High + Big Medium + Big Low).

Sources: Dimensional Returns Version 2.2. Fama/French and multifactor data provided by Fama/French.

Exclusions: ADRs, Investment Companies, Tracking Stocks, non-US incorporated companies, Closed-end funds, Certificates, Shares of Beneficial Interests, and negative book values.

Currency: USD

 US Term Factor Premium

Time-Series Construction

Jan 1926 – Present: Fama/French Long Term Government Factor minus 30 Day T-Bill

Sources: Dimensional Returns Version 2.2. Fama/French multifactor data provided by Fama/French.

Currency: USD

 US Default Factor Premium

Time-Series Construction

Jan 1926 – Present: Fama/French Long Term Corp Factor minus Fama/French Long Term Gov't

Sources: Dimensional Returns Version 2.2. Fama/French multifactor data provided by Fama/French.

Currency: USD

Disclosure for Backtested Performance Information, the IFA Indexes, and IFA Index Portfolios (updates can be found at www.ifabt.com):

1. Index Funds Advisors, Inc. (IFA) is an SEC registered Investment Adviser. Information pertaining to IFA's advisory operations, services, and fees is set forth in IFAs' current Form ADV Part 2 (Brochure), a copy of which is available upon request and at www.adviserinfo.sec.gov. The performance information presented in certain charts or tables represent backtested performance based on combined simulated index data and live (or actual) mutual fund results from January 1, 1928 to the period ending date shown, using the strategy of buy and hold and on the first of each year annually rebalancing the globally diversified portfolios of index funds. Backtested performance is hypothetical (it does not reflect trading in actual accounts) and is provided for informational purposes only to indicate historical performance had the index portfolios been available over the relevant time period. IFA refers to this hypothetical data as a Simulated Passive Investor Experience (SPIE). IFA did not offer the index portfolios until November 1999. Prior to 1999, IFA did not manage client assets. The IFA indexing investment strategy is based on the principles of Modern Portfolio Theory and the Fama and French Three Factor Model for Equities and Two Factor Model for Fixed Income. Index portfolios are designed to provide substantial global diversification in order to reduce investment concentration and the resulting potential increased risk caused by the volatility of individual companies, indexes, or asset classes.

2. A review of the IFA Index Data Sources (ifaindexes.com), IFA Indexes Time Series Construction (ifa.com/pdf/tsc.pdf) and several of the Dimensional Indexes (ifa.com/pdf/DFAIndexes.pdf) is an integral part of this disclosure and should be read in conjunction with this explanation of backtested performance information presented. IFA defines index funds as mutual funds that follow a set of rules of ownership that are held constant regardless of market conditions. An important characteristic of an index fund is that its rules of ownership are not based on a forecast of short-term events. Therefore, an investment strategy that is limited to the buying and rebalancing of a portfolio of index funds is often referred to as passive investing, as opposed to active investing. Simulated index data is based on the performance of indexes and live mutual funds as described in the IFA Indexes Data Sources page. The index mutual funds used in IFA's Index Portfolios are IFA's best estimate of a mutual fund that will come closest to the index data provided in the simulated indexes. Simulated index data is used for the period prior to the inception of the relevant live mutual fund data and an

equivalent mutual fund expense ratio is deducted from simulated index data. Live (or actual) mutual fund performance is used after the inception date of each mutual fund. The IFA Indexes Times Series Construction goes back to January 1928 and consistently reflects a tilt towards small cap and value equities over time, with an increasing diversification to international markets, emerging markets and real estate investment trusts as data became available. As of January 1928, there are 4 equity indexes and 2 bond indexes; in January 1970 there are a total of 8 indexes, and there are 15 indexes in March 1998 to present. See (http://www.ifa.com/pdf/The_Evolution_of_IFA_Portfolio.pdf) to see the analysis of the evolution of these portfolios. This PDF names the indexes used in the IFA Portfolios for each period, and page 4 of the PDF shows the Time Series Construction of the IFA indexes. If the original 4 equity indexes from 1928 (IFA US Large Company Index; IFA US Large Cap Value Index; IFA US Small Cap Index; IFA US Small Cap Value Index) are held constant until December 2010, the annualized rate of return of this simplified version of IFA Index Portfolio 90 is 10.44%, after the deduction of a 0.9% IFA advisory fee and a standard deviation of 22.79%. The evolving IFA Indexes over the same period have a 10.68% annualized return for IFA Index Portfolio 90 after the same IFA advisory fees and a standard deviation of 21.99%. The stitching together of index and live fund data and adding international markets, emerging markets and REITs only had a slight impact on risk and return over this 83 year period. Instead, it demonstrates the value of a small cap and value tilt in global equity markets, since over the same period a Simulated S&P 500 Index only had a return of 9.39% (with no fees deducted), at a standard deviation of 19.31%. Backtested performance is calculated by using a computer program and monthly returns data set that start with the first day of the given time period and evaluates the returns of simulated indexes and DFA index mutual funds. In 1999, tax-managed funds became available for many different DFA index funds.

3. Backtested performance does not represent actual performance and should not be interpreted as an indication of such performance. Actual performance for client accounts may be materially lower than that of the index portfolios. Backtested performance results have certain inherent limitations. Such results do not represent the impact that material economic and market factors might have on an investment adviser's decision-making process if the adviser were actually managing client money. Backtested performance also differs from actual performance because it is achieved through the retroactive application of model portfolios (in this case, IFA's Index Portfolios) designed with the benefit of hindsight. As a result, the models theoretically may be changed from time to time and the effect on performance results could be either favorable or unfavorable.

4. History of Changes to the IFA Indexes: 1991-2000: IFA Index Portfolios 10, 30, 50, 70 and 90 were originally suggested by Dimensional Fund Advisors (ifa.com/pdf/balancedstrategies.pdf), merely as an example of globally diversified investments using their custom index mutual funds, back in 1991 with moderate modifications in 1996 to reflect the availability of index funds that tracked the emerging markets asset class. Index Portfolios between each of the above listed portfolios were created by IFA in 2000 by interpolating between the above portfolios. Portfolios 5, 95 and 100 were created by Index Funds Advisors in 2000, as a lower and higher extension of the DFA 1991 risk and return line. As of March 1, 2010, 100 IFA Index Portfolios are available to IFA clients, with IFA Index Portfolios between the shown allocations being interpolations of the 20 allocations shown. In January 2008, IFA introduced three new indexes and twenty socially responsible portfolios constructed from these three indexes and five pre-existing IFA indexes. The new indexes introduced were: IFA US Social Core Equity, IFA Emerging Markets Social Core, and IFA International Real Estate. All three use live DFA fund data as long as it has been available. Prior to live fund data, they use index data supplied by DFA modified for fund management fees. In November 2011, IFA made a change to the index data used in its large growth and small growth indexes. Fama/French data was replaced with data supplied by Dimensional Fund Advisors via its Returns 2.2 program. For large growth, the difference in annualized return was about 1% (a decrease). For small growth, the difference was about 0.2%. Go to www.ifa.com/btp/historyofchange.html to see a summary of changes made to the IFA Indexes and Index Portfolios.

5. Backtested performance results assume the reinvestment of dividends and capital gains and annual rebalancing at the beginning of each year. It is important to understand that the assumption of annual rebalancing has an impact on the monthly returns reported for the IFA Index Portfolio in both in the Risk and Reward Table (www.ifabigtable.com) and in the Index Calculator (www.ifacalc.com). For monthly rebalancing, the monthly return is calculated with the assumption that the portfolio is perfectly in balance at the beginning of each month. For annual rebalancing, the year-to-date return is calculated with the assumption that the portfolio is perfectly in balance at the beginning of the year. The latter assumption underlies the returns shown for the IFA Index Portfolios. In actual portfolios, however, rebalancing occurs at no set time, and such actions are dependent on both market conditions and individual client liquidity inflows and outflows, along with the cost impact of such transactions on the overall portfolio. Therefore actual monthly and year-to-date returns will differ from the IFA Returns Calculator. The reason for this difference is that with annual rebalancing, the monthly returns are

calculated from the ratio of the year-to-date growth of $1.00 at the end of the month to the year-to-date growth of $1.00 at the beginning of the month. For monthly rebalancing, the monthly return is calculated with the assumption that the portfolio is perfectly in balance at the beginning of the month. The performance of the IFA Index Portfolios reflects and is net of the effect of IFA's annual investment management fee of 0.9%, billed monthly, unless stated otherwise. Monthly fee deduction is a requirement of our software used for backtesting. Actual IFA advisory fees are deducted quarterly, in advance. This fee is the highest fee IFA charges. Depending on the amount of your assets under management, your investment management fee may be less. Backtested risk and return data is a combination of live (or actual) mutual fund results and simulated index data, and mutual fund fees and expenses have been deducted from both the live (or actual) results and the simulated index data. When IFA Indexes are shown in IFA Index Portfolios, all returns data reflects a deduction of 0.9% annual investment advisory fee, which is the maximum IFA fee. Unless indicated otherwise, data shown for each individual IFA Index is shown without a deduction of the IFA advisory fee. We choose this method because the creation, choice, monitoring and rebalancing of diversified index portfolios are the services of the independent investment advisor and at that point the fees are appropriate to deduct from the whole portfolio returns. Since we accept no fees from investment product firms, IFA compares index funds based on net asset value returns, which are net of the mutual fund company expense ratios only. Although index mutual funds minimize tax liabilities from short and long-term capital gains, any resulting tax liability is not deducted from performance results. Performance results also do not reflect transaction fees (as seen at www.ifafee.com) and other expenses, which reduce returns.

6. For all data periods, annualized standard deviation is presented as an approximation by multiplying the monthly standard deviation number by the square root of 12. Please note that the number computed from annual data may differ materially from this estimate. We have chosen this methodology because Morningstar uses the same method. Go to www.ifabt.com for details. In those charts and tables where the standard deviation of daily returns is shown, it is estimated as the standard deviation of monthly returns divided by the square root of 22.

7. The tax-managed index funds are not used in calculating the backtested performance of the index portfolios, unless specified in the table or chart.

8. Performance results for clients that invested in accordance with the IFA Index Portfolios will vary from the backtested performance due to market conditions and other factors, including investments cash flows, mutual

fund allocations, frequency and precision of rebalancing, tax-management strategies, cash balances, lower than 0.9% advisory fees, varying custodian fees, and/or the timing of fee deductions. As the result of these and potentially other variances, actual performance for client accounts may differ materially from (and may be lower than) that of the index portfolios. Clients should consult their account statements for information about how their actual performance compares to that of the index portfolios.

9. As with any investment strategy, there is potential for profit as well as the possibility of loss. IFA does not guarantee any minimum level of investment performance or the success of any index portfolio or investment strategy. All investments involve risk and investment recommendations will not always be profitable.

10. Past performance does not guarantee future results.

11. IFA Index Portfolio Value Data is based on a starting value of one, as of January 1, 1928.

12. DISCLAIMER: THERE ARE NO WARRANTIES, EXPRESSED OR IMPLIED, AS TO ACCURACY, COMPLETENESS, OR RESULTS OBTAINED FROM ANY INFORMATION PROVIDED HEREIN OR ON THE MATERIAL PROVIDED. This document does not constitute a complete description of our investment services and is for informational purposes only. It is in no way a solicitation or an offer to sell securities or investment advisory services. Any statements regarding market or other financial information, is obtained from sources which we, and our suppliers believe reliable, but we do not warrant or guarantee the timeliness or accuracy of this information. Neither our information providers nor we shall be liable for any errors or inaccuracies, regardless of cause, or the lack of timeliness of, or for any delay or interruption in the transmission thereof to the user. All investments involve risk, including foreign currency exchange rates, political risks, market risk, different methods of accounting and financial reporting, and foreign taxes. Your use of these materials, including www.ifa.com website is your acknowledgement that you have read and understood the full disclaimer as stated above. IFA Index Portfolios, times series, standard deviations, and returns calculations are determined in the DFA FA Returns 2.0 program. © Copyright 1999-2011, DFA, Inc.

13. IFA licenses the use of data, in part, from Morningstar Direct, a third-party provider of stock market data. Where data is cited from Morningstar Direct, the following disclosures apply: ©2011 Morningstar, Inc. All rights reserved. The information provided by Morningstar Direct and contained herein: (1) is proprietary to Morningstar and/or its content providers; (2) may not be

copied or distributed; and (3) is not warranted to be accurate, complete or timely. Neither Morningstar nor its content providers are responsible for any damages or losses arising from any use of this information.

Updated 11-3-2011. For additional updates see www.ifabt.com.

Other Information IFA Considers to Be Helpful

It is IFA's advice that the value of having a longer time series exceeds the concerns of index substitutions over the 1928 to present period. Due to the very high standard deviations of returns (21.99%) a 40 year or more sample size of data is recommended to obtain a T-statistic of 2, that allows a conclusion at a 95% or higher level of certainty. In other words, in IFA's opinion, smaller sample sizes introduce larger errors than the errors introduced by stitching together indexes and live data over time. This is the advice IFA provides to its clients.

Client portfolios are monitored and rebalanced, taking into consideration risk exposure consistency, transaction costs, and tax ramifications to maintain target asset allocations as shown in the Index Portfolios.

IFA uses tax-managed funds in taxable accounts. The tax-managed funds are consistent with the indexing strategy, however, they should not be expected to track the performance of corresponding non-tax-managed funds in the same or similar indexes. As such, the performance of portfolios using tax-managed funds will vary from portfolios that do not utilize these funds.

Clients' accounts will be rebalanced depending on the fluctuation of the asset classes and the cash flow activity of the client. It is IFA's opinion that the assumption of first of the year annual rebalancing is a reasonable approximation to reality.

IFA is not paid any brokerage commissions, sales loads, 12b1 fees, or any form of compensation from any mutual fund company or broker dealer. The only source of compensation from client investments is obtained from asset based advisory fees paid by the client. More information about advisory fees, expenses, no-load mutual fund fees, prospectuses for no-load index mutual funds, brokerage and custodian fees can be found at www.ifa.com/admin/fees.asp. Not all IFA clients follow our recommendations and depending on unique and changing client and market situations we may customize the construction and implementation of the index portfolios for particular clients, including the use of tax-managed mutual funds, tax-loss-harvesting techniques and rebalancing frequency and precision. In taxable accounts, IFA uses tax-managed index funds to manage client assets.

Some clients substitute the mutual funds recommended by IFA with investment options available through their 401k or other accounts, thereby creating a custom asset allocation. The performance of custom asset allocations may differ materially from (and may be lower than) that of the index portfolios.

APPENDIX B

Dalbar, Inc. is an independent third party not associated with Index Funds Advisors, Inc. The studies referred to in this book by DALBAR were performed by and obtained from DALBAR, Inc. The information is believed to be reliable but accuracy and completeness cannot be guaranteed. It is for informational purposes only and is not a solicitation to buy or sell securities. Use of information from DALBAR does not necessarily constitute agreement by DALBAR, Inc., of any investment philosophy or strategy presented in this book.

Morningstar, Inc. is an independent investment research firm not associated with Index Funds Advisors, Inc. When Morningstar, Inc. is sourced in this book the information: (1) is proprietary to Morningstar and/or its content providers; (2) may not be copied or distributed; (3) does not constitute investment advice offered by Morningstar; (4) is not warranted to be accurate, complete or timely; and (5) is copyrighted as follows: **©2011 Morningstar, Inc.** All rights reserved. Neither Morningstar nor its content providers are responsible for any damages or losses arising from any of this information. Past performance is no guarantee of future results. Use of information from Morningstar does not constitute agreement by Morningstar, Inc. of any investment philosophy or strategy presented in this publication.

All Standard & Poor's 500 Index Data © Copyright 2011. The McGraw-Hill Companies, Inc. Standard & Poor's including its subsidiary corporations ("S&P") is a division of The McGraw-Hill Companies, Inc. Reproduction in any form is prohibited without S&P's prior written permission. Neither S&P, its affiliates nor any of their third-party licensors: (a) guarantee the accuracy, completeness or availability of the S&P Data, or (b) make any warranty, express or implied, as to the results to be obtained by the Publisher or any other person from the use of the S&P Data or any other data or information included therein or derived therefrom, or (c) make any express or implied warranties, including any warranty of merchantability or fitness for the particular purpose or use, or (d) shall in any way be liable to the Publisher or any recipient of the Materials for any inaccuracies, errors, or omissions, regardless of cause, in the S&P Data or for any damages, whether direct or indirect or consequential, punitive or exemplary resulting therefrom.

Quotations and Portraits contained in this book are for illustrative purposes only, and in no way imply any endorsements of the goods and services of Mr. Hebner, Index Funds Advisors, Inc. or any affiliates thereof.

For book corrections and updates, go to:
www.ifapublishing.com/bookcorrections

REFERENCES

1. Quoted by Benjamin Graham in *The Intelligent Investor* (Collins Business, revised 2003), p. 54; which gives as source: Jean Strouse, *Morgan: American Financier* (Random House, 1999), pg. 11.

2. David Swensen, *Pioneering Portfolio Management: An Unconventional Approach to Institutional Investment* (New York: The Free Press, 2000).

3. Ibid., pg. 3.

4. Robert Fernholz and Brian Shay, "Toward a Dynamic Theory of Portfolio Behavior and Stock Market Equilibrium," Department of Statistics, Princeton University, Technical Report No. 163. Series 2 (1979).

5. Mark Hebner, *The Speculation Blues, Index Funds: The 12-Step Recovery Program for Active Investors*, pgs. 273-274.

6. James Montier, *The Little Book of Behavioral Investing: How not to Be Your Own Worst Enemy* (Hoboken: John Wiley & Sons, Inc., 2010).

7. Jason Zweig, *Your Money and Your Brain* (NY: Simon & Schuster, 2007).

8. Dr. Ian Ayres, Dr. Peter Ayton, Dr. Greg B. Davies, Dr. Barbara Fasolo, Professor Thorsten Hens, Sheena Iyenger, Dr. Annie Koh, Dr. Neil Stewart, Rory Sutherland, and Dr. Chun Xia, "Risk and Rules: The Role of Control in Financial Decision Making," Barclays Wealth Insights, vol. 13 (2011).

9. Dalbar, Inc., "2011 Quantitative Analysis of Investor Behavior," (2011).

10. Ibid.

11. Jason Zweig, "What Fund Investors Really Need to Know," *Money* Magazine, June 2002.

12. Sanjay Arya, John Coumarianos, Pat Dorsey, Russel Kinnel, Don Phillips, Tricia Rothschild, "Morningstar Indexes Yearbook," Morningstar, Inc., vol. 2 (2005).

13. Carol J. Loomis, "Buffet's Big Bet," *Fortune*, June 23, 2008.

14. Charles Schwab, *Charles Schwab's Guide to Financial Independence: Simple Solutions for Busy People* (New York: Three Rivers Press, 1998).

15. Hartman L. Butler Jr., "An Hour with Mr. Graham," March 1976.

16. David Swensen, *Unconventional Success: A Fundamental Approach to Personal Investment* (New York: Free Press, 2005).

17. Swensen, *Pioneering Portfolio Management: An Unconventional Approach to Institutional Investment.*

18. David Swensen, "The Mutual Fund Merry-go-Round," *New York Times* (New York, NY), Aug. 13, 2011.

19. Timothy M. Hatton, *The New Fiduciary Standard: The 27 Prudent Investment Practices for Financial Advisers, Trustees and Plan Sponsors,* (Bloomberg, 2005) pg. 33.

20. Adam Smith, *Wealth of Nations* (Oxford: Oxford University Press, 1993)

21. James Surowiecki, *The Wisdom of Crowds: Why the Many Are Smarter Than the Few and How Collective Wisdom Shapes Business, Economies, Societies and Nations* (New York: Double Day, 2004).

22. Paul Samuelson, "Proof That Properly Anticipated Prices Fluctuate Randomly," Industrial Management Review 6 (1965): 41.

23. Eugene F. Fama, "The Behavior of Stock Market Prices," The Journal of Business, vol. 38, no. 1. (1965): 34-105.

24. Eugene F. Fama, "Efficient Capital Markets: A Review of Theory and Empirical Work," The Journal of Finance, vol. 25, no. 2 (1970).

25. Eugene F. Fama and Kenneth R. French, "The Cross-Section of Expected Stock Returns," The Journal of Finance, vol. 47, no. 2 (1992).

26. Burton Malkiel, *A Random Walk Down Wall Street* (New York: W. W. Norton & Company, Inc., 1973).

27. John C. Bogle, Founder and Senior Chairman, The Vanguard Group, Keynote Speech, The Fourth Annual Superbowl of Indexing, Dec. 5, 1999.

28. Friedrich von Hayek, *The Road to Serfdom* (Chicago: University of Chicago Press, 1994).

29. Harry Markowitz, "Portfolio Selection," The Journal of Finance, vol. 7, no. 1 (1952).

30. William Sharpe, "A Simplified Model for Portfolio Analysis," Management Science, vol. 9, no. 2 (1963).

31. William Sharpe, "Capital Asset Prices: A Theory of Market Equilibrium under Conditions of Risk," The Journal of Finance, vol. 19, no. 3 (1964).

32. Nova, *The Trillion Dollar Bet*, Documentary, Lauren Aguirre (2000; Arlington: Public Broadcasting Service.), Television.

33. 20/20, *Who needs the Experts?*, Documentary, John Stossel (1992; New York: ABC News.), Television.

34. Terrance Odean, "Are Investors Reluctant to Realize Their Losses?," The Journal of Finance, vol. 53, no. 5 (1998).

35. Brad M. Barber and Terrance Odean, "Trading is Hazardous to Your Wealth: The Common Investment Performance of Individual Investors," The Journal of Finance, vol. 55, no. 2 (2000).

36. Diana Cawfield, "Manager Monitor: Bill Miller," Morningstar, Nov. 2, 2002, http://www.morningstar.ca/globalhome/industry/managermonitor.asp?reportid=187.

37. Ian McDonald, "Bill Miller Dishes On His Streak and His Strategy," *Wall Street Journal*, Jan. 6, 2005.

38. Tom Lauricella, "The Stock Picker's Defeat," *Wall Street Journal*, Dec. 10, 2008.

39. Ibid.

40. Charles Stein, "Berkowitz Leads Top Stock Pickers Hitting Bottom as Growth Slows," *Bloomberg News*, June 12, 2011.

41. Mark Hulbert, "The Prescient are Few," *New York Times* (New York, NY), Jul. 13, 2008.

42. Laurent Barras, Olivier Scaillet and Russ Wermers, "False Discoveries in Mutual Fund Performance: Measuring Luck in Estimated Alphas," The Journal of Finance, vol. 65, no. 1 (2010).

43. Richard Foster and Sarah Kaplan, *Creative Destruction: Why Companies that are Built to Last Underperform the Market-and How to Successfully Transform Them* (New York: Doubleday, 2001).

44. Meir Statman and Deniz Anginer, "Stocks of Admired Companies and Spurned Ones," Santa Clara University Leavey School of Business, Research Paper No. 10-02 (2010).

45. Edwin Elton, Martin Gruber and Christopher Blake, "Fundamental Economic Variables, Expected Returns, and Bond Fund Performance," Journal of Finance, vol. 50, no. 4 (1995).

46. Passive Beats Active - refers to Figure 3-10, pg. 96.

"125 High Yield Funds vs BarCap High Yield, 2005-2009 (5 Years)"; Standard & Poor's Indices Versus Active Funds (SPIVA) Scorecard, Year-End 2009.

"570 Peer Bond Funds vs. Vanguard Intermediate Bond Fund, 1996-2006 (10 Years)"; "The Little Book of Common Sense Investing" page 143.

"194 Peer Bond Funds vs. Vanguard Long-Term Muni Bond Fund, 1996-2006 (10 Years)"; "The Little Book of Common Sense Investing" page 145.

"47 Government Long Funds vs BarCap Long Government, 2005-2009 (5 Years)"; Standard & Poor's Indices Versus Active Funds (SPIVA) Scorecard, Year-End 2009.

"51 Government Intermediate Funds vs BarCap Intermediate Government, 2005-2009 (5 Years)"; Standard & Poor's Indices Versus Active Funds (SPIVA) Scorecard, Year-End 2009.

"42 Government Short Funds vs BarCap 1-3 Years Government, 2005-2009 (5 Years)"; Standard & Poor's Indices Versus Active Funds (SPIVA) Scorecard, Year-End 2009.

"103 Investment Grade Long Funds vs BarCap Long Government/ Credit, 2005-2009 (5 Years)"; Standard & Poor's Indices Versus Active Funds (SPIVA) Scorecard, Year-End 2009.

"187 Investment Grade Intermediate Funds vs BarCap Intermediate Government/Credit, 2003-2008 (5 Years)"; Standard & Poor's Indices Versus Active Funds (SPIVA) Scorecard, Year-End 2009.

"63 Investment Grade Short Funds vs BarCap 1-3 Years Government, 2003-2008 (5 Years)"; Standard & Poor's Indices Versus Active Funds (SPIVA) Scorecard, Year-End 2009.

"81 General Municipal Debt Funds vs S&P National AMT-Free Municipal Bound Index, 2005-2009 (5 Years)"; Standard & Poor's Indices Versus Active Funds (SPIVA) Scorecard, Year-End 2009.

"40 CA Municipal Debt Funds vs S&P California AMT-Free Municipal Bound Index, 2005-2009 (5 Years)"; Standard & Poor's Indices Versus Active Funds (SPIVA) Scorecard, Year-End 2009.

"125 Funds vs Vanguard Intermediate Bond Index, 1996-2010 (15 Years)"; Morningstar Direct 12/2010.

47. Eugene Fama, Dimensional Financial Advisor Conference, Santa Monica, CA, July 22, 2011.

48. William Sharpe, "Likely Gains from Market Timing," Financial Analysts Journal, vol. 31, no. 2 (1975).

49. "Technical Note: Calculation of Forecasting Accuracy", SEI Corporation position paper, April 1992.

50. Forecast Accuracy Chart (see following page).

51. Michael Edesess, *The Big Investment Lie: What Your Financial Advisor Doesn't Want You to Know* (San Francisco: Berrett-Koehler Publishers, Inc., 2007).

52. John Graham and Campbell Harvey, "Market Timing Ability and Volatility Implied in Investment Newsletters' Asset Allocation Recommendations," *Journal of Financial Economics*, vol. 42, no. 3 (1996).

53. "Calming Words for Troubled Times," money.cnn.com, last modified April 28, 2008, http://money.cnn.com/galleries/2008/pf/0804/gallery.expert_opinions.moneymag/12.html.

54. Robert C. Higgins, *Analysis for Financial Management* (New York: McGraw-Hill/Irwin, 2004).

55. Eugene F. Fama, Lawrence Fisher, Michael Jensen, and Richard Roll, "The Adjustment of Stock Prices to New Information," *International Economic Review*, vol. 10, no. 1 (1969).

56. Swensen, *Pioneering Portfolio Management: An Unconventional Approach to Institutional Investment* (New York: The Free Press, 2000).

57. Bob Dylan, *The Times They Are a-Changin'*, song, Columbia Studios, 1964.

58. Amit Goyal and Sunil Wahal, "The Selection and Termination of Investment Management Firms by Plan Sponsors," *The Journal of Finance*, vol. 63, no. 4 (2008).

59. Swensen, *Pioneering Portfolio Management: An Unconventional Approach to Institutional Investment* (New York: The Free Press, 2000).

60. Upton Sinclair, *I, Candidate for Governor: And How I Got Licked* (1935), ISBN 0-520-08198-6; repr. University of California Press, 1994, pg. 109.

61. Sydney P. Freedberg and Connie Humburg, "Easy Investments Beat State's Expert Pension Planners," *St. Petersburg Times* (St. Petersbug, FL), Jul. 31, 2011.

62. State Retirement Systems Data from public information, includes states that provided 10 and 23 yrs of returns for fiscal years ending 6/30, and are net of fees; Index Portfolios are net of fund fees and 0.05% Advisory Fee. See www.pension-gate.com/ states for additional disclosures.

63. Ibid.

Reference 50: Step 4, Page 101

Forecast Accuracy

Forecasts Range From 12/28/1998 to 8/15/2011

Market Gurus	Earliest Forecast	Last Modified	Graded Forecasts	Accuracy
Jon Markman Speculates	1/4/07	6/30/11	26	67%
Jack Schannep's Sweepstakes	7/17/02	8/1/11	58	66%
Ken Fisher Chronicles	1/10/00	8/3/11	106	64%
Cabot Market Letter Outlooks	8/1/02	8/15/11	36	62%
Louis Navellier: Calculating the Market's Moves	3/29/01	8/15/11	104	61%
The Aden Sisters on the Stock Market	6/26/06	8/4/11	20	61%
Steve Sjuggerud's Sentiment	7/24/06	8/5/11	37	60%
Jason Kelly: The Neatest Little Market Advice?	9/14/01	5/23/11	125	59%
Carl Swenlin's Technical Windsock	1/6/06	8/12/11	109	57%
Richard Moroney, Divining Dow Theory	8/2/02	3/18/11	53	54%
Gary Kaltbaum: An Edge for Investors?	5/2/05	8/8/11	131	53%
James Dines: A Living Legend?	4/15/02	5/9/11	31	50%
Bernie Schaeffer: The Schaeffer's Edge?	11/15/00	7/1/11	72	49%
Jeremy Grantham: Train Wreck Spotter	8/23/00	8/11/11	29	48%
Stephen Leeb: Wall Street Wonder?	1/27/03	8/2/11	25	48%
Clif Droke's Contrarian Triangulation	7/2/03	8/1/11	81	48%
Gary Savage, Tracking Smart Money?	5/18/07	8/13/11	89	47%
Carl Futia Telling	4/28/05	7/29/11	79	47%
Marc Faber: Nabob of Negativism?	10/19/00	8/10/11	123	46%
Dennis Slothower's Timing	6/7/02	8/8/11	125	45%
Gary D. Halbert Forecasts and Trends	1/8/02	3/29/11	90	45%
Tim Wood: You Have Been Warned!	4/4/03	8/10/11	167	44%
Nadeem Walayat's Oraculations	7/21/06	8/7/11	57	44%
Jim Jubak on the Big Picture	1/5/01	7/22/11	129	44%
Bill Cara: Populist Market Pundit	1/7/05	8/7/11	184	43%
Comstock's Commentary	3/17/05	8/4/11	165	43%
Price Headley's Trends	5/12/00	8/8/11	332	42%
John Mauldin's Thoughts	1/5/01	7/2/11	211	40%
Linda Schurman: The Astrologer vs "Stock Star"	7/1/04	4/1/11	54	40%
Bob Hoye: Rational Fringe?	8/5/05	6/30/11	46	38%
Richard Russell: Investment Newsletter	6/13/00	8/8/11	154	37%
Bill Fleckenstein: Apocalypse Soon	8/2/02	7/22/11	139	37%
Abby Joseph Cohen, the Sunny Side	12/28/98	1/8/11	55	35%
Robert McHugh: Caution Is Warranted?	2/19/04	8/12/11	116	32%
Curt Hesler: Being Cautious	1/3/03	1/3/11	80	31%
Steven Jon Kaplan: Overly Contrarian?	5/1/02	8/9/11	71	27%
Steve Saville: From the Top Down	3/5/03	1/26/11	32	26%

64. State Retirement Systems Data from public information, includes states that provided 11 and 24 yrs. of returns for fiscal years ending 12/31, and are net of fees; Index Portfolios are net of fund fees and 0.05% Advisory Fee. See www.pension-gate.com/ for additional disclosures.

65. Ibid.

66. Paul Samuelson, *The Journal of Portfolio Management,* "Challenge to Judgment," 1974, 1.1:17-19.

67. S&P Indices, Research and Design, "Standard and Poor's Indices Versus Active Funds Scorecard (SPIVA), Year-End 2010)," (2011).

68. Steve Bailey and Steven Syre, "Fidelity's bulking up on large-caps Emerging Growth fund especially relies on big stocks," *Boston Globe* (Boston, MA) Nov. 12, 1998.

69. S&P Indices, Research and Design, "Standard and Poor's Indices Versus Active Funds Scorecard (SPIVA), Year-End 2010)," (2011).

70. John Bogle, *The Little Book of Common Sense Investing: The Only Way to Guarantee Your Fair Share of Stock Market Returns* (Hoboken: John Wiley & Sons, Inc., 2007).

71. Source: J. R. Newman (ed.) *The World of Mathematics*, New York: Simon and Schuster, 1956. pg. 1482.

72. Douglas Clement, "Interview with Eugene Fama," The Region (a publication of The Federal Reserve Bank of Minneapolis), December 2007.

73. Harry Markowitz, Portfolio Selection, The Journal of Finance, Vol. 7, No. 1. (Mar., 1952), pgs. 77-91.

74. Truman Clarke, "Commodity Futures in Portfolios," Dimensional Fund Advisors (2004).

75. Matt Krantz, "Read this before you jump on the commodities bandwagon," *USA Today* (McLean, VA), Jun. 24, 2008.

76. Kenneth French, "Q&A: What Role for Commodities?," Fama/ French Forum, November 1, 2010, http://www.dimensional.com/ famafrench/2010/11/what-role-for-commodities.html.

77. People and Portfolios: Glide Path for Retirement Success Chart (see following page).

Reference 77: Step 12, Page 265

People and Portfolios: Glide Path for Retirement Success

Based on an Actual Monte Carlo Simulation (One of 10,000 Trials)

Age	Index Port-folio	83-Year Ann'lzd Return	83-Year Ann'lzd Std Dev.	Annual Contribution Amount[1,2]	Annual Withdrawal Amount[1,3]	Salary[1,4]	Human Capital[5]	Financial Capital	Total Capital[5]
0	100	11.19%	22.76%	$0	$0	$0	$1,929,195	$0	$1,929,195
5	95	10.91%	22.27%	$0	$0	$0	$1,929,195	$0	$1,929,195
10	90	10.61%	21.81%	$0	$0	$0	$1,929,195	$0	$1,929,195
15	85	10.42%	20.66%	$0	$0	$0	$1,929,195	$0	$1,929,195
20	80	10.21%	19.53%	$0	$0	$0	$1,929,195	$0	$1,929,195
25	75	9.98%	18.42%	$3,060	$0	$38,245	$1,937,454	$13,863	$1,951,317
30	70	9.73%	17.32%	$3,547	$0	$44,337	$1,921,684	$41,682	$1,963,366
35	65	9.47%	16.23%	$4,112	$0	$51,399	$1,869,643	$86,532	$1,956,175
40	60	9.19%	15.15%	$4,767	$0	$59,585	$1,772,040	$157,144	$1,929,184
45	55	8.90%	14.09%	$5,526	$0	$69,076	$1,617,740	$263,942	$1,881,682
50	50	8.59%	13.03%	$6,406	$0	$80,077	$1,393,428	$424,693	$1,818,121
55	45	8.27%	11.98%	$7,427	$0	$92,832	$1,083,224	$661,774	$1,744,998
60	40	7.93%	10.95%	$8,609	$0	$107,617	$668,227	$996,224	$1,664,451
65	35	7.58%	9.92%	$9,981	$0	$124,758	$125,981	$1,484,805	$1,610,786
70	30	7.21%	8.90%	$0	$78,880	$0	$0	$1,719,617	$1,719,617
75	25	6.83%	7.90%	$0	$91,443	$0	$0	$1,915,321	$1,915,321
80	20	6.44%	6.91%	$0	$106,008	$0	$0	$1,989,634	$1,989,634
85	15	6.03%	5.94%	$0	$122,892	$0	$0	$1,975,007	$1,975,007
90	10	5.60%	5.02%	$0	$142,465	$0	$0	$1,806,068	$1,806,068
95	5	5.16%	4.16%	$0	$165,157	$0	$0	$1,449,272	$1,449,272

[1] Annual amount is at the beginning of the 5-year period.
[2] Annual savings rate is 8% of salary.
[3] Annual withdrawals start at age 67 at 4.5% of financial capital and inflate at 3% per year.
[4] Salary Starts at $35,000 at age 22 and inflates at 3% per year.
[5] Human capital is the present value of future salary. Total capital is the sum of human and financial capital.

Sources, Updates and Disclosures: ifabt.com, ifa.com/ra, Appx A

INDEX

A

B

C

D

E

F

G

H

I

J

K

L

M

R

S

T